TOD SLOAN

BY
HIMSELF

San Diego State University Press

TOD SLOAN
BY HIMSELF

EDITED FOR ORIGINAL PUBLICATION BY
A. DICK LUCKMAN

SAN DIEGO STATE UNIVERSITY PRESS

Copyright © 1988 by San Diego State University Press

All rights reserved. No part of this publication may be reproduced or transmitted in any form or by any means, electronic or mechanical, including photocopy, recording, or any information storage and retrieval system, without permission in writing from the publisher.

Requests for permission to make copies of any part of the work should be mailed to:

    Permissions
    San Diego State University Press
    San Diego State University
    San Diego, CA 92182

Printed in the United States of America

Library of Congress Cataloging-in-Publication Data

Sloan, Tod, 1874–
    Tod Sloan, by himself / edited for original publication by A. Dick Luckman.
        p.   cm.
    Reprint. Originally published: New York : Brentano's, 1915.
    Includes index.
    ISBN 0-916304-78-7 : $8.00
    1. Sloan, Tod, 1874–   . 2. Jockeys—United States—Biography.
3. Jockeys—England—Biography. I. Luckman, A. Dick. II. Title.
SF336.S553A3   1988
798.4'3'0924—dc19
[B]   88-15818
                                                                                        CIP

First edition

A B C D E

Preface

HERE, ALMOST THREE QUARTERS of a century after he wrote them, are Tod Sloan's memoirs, within reach of most American readers for the first time. Originally published in England in 1915 and later that same year reprinted by Brentano's of New York, *Tod Sloan, By Himself* has long been out of print in both countries, a much-prized rarity sought after by collectors of sporting literature and virtually impossible for ordinary readers to get hold of. All of us interested in the history of American sport are therefore very much indebted to the Sport Literature Association for re-issuing the book now in its complete form, with its original illustrations.

What is it that justifies bringing back to life this once famous—and finally notorious—American sporting figure? The first thing is that the book presents a figure of exceptional historical importance: a young and diminutive man who did something truly revolutionary, transforming the rhythm of thoroughbred racing in America, in Great Britain, and on the Continent, by altering the style of riding. It is arguable that no single American sporting figure has had as great an impact on a major sport as did Tod Sloan on his. That is a large claim, one I'll try to support in due course. In any event, Tod Sloan's achievement gains in personal interest as one learns from these pages that it was achieved by a jockey who had, for most of his life, been terrified of horses and who had been dismissed, only a few years before, by knowledgeable judges, as a hopelessly incompetent rider. No wonder that, in Tod Sloan's matter-of-fact, often laconic, discursive re-telling of his life there is something else, something deeper, a magical quality, a hint of an Aesop fable or of a fairytale, the toad that is changed into a prince.*

In addition, these pages give us a vivid picture, from an entirely fresh and unexpected perspective, of a major theme of American culture in the 19th century—the transatlantic theme of the New World and its relation to the Old. The British had of course always been aware of American horse racing, at a distance. After all, they had founded it in the 18th century by exporting some of their thoroughbred stock to the colonies. It became much more familiar to them in 1856 when Richard Ten Broeck launched the first "American invasion" of British racing by bringing a stable of his horses over to challenge them on their own turf. But even though Ten Broeck did very well, winning important races and a lot of money, British racing had been unchanged by his challenge. It was more a reconnaissance mission than an invasion. With seemingly unshakeable complacency it seemed to the British quite fantastic to imagine that the Americans actually had anything important to teach them about *their* sport. The very same thing was happening, in these same years, in two other sports the British had invented and wholly dominated—prize fighting and yachting. In both of those the

---

* I develop this theme in more detail in "Tod Sloan: Fairy Tales and Nightmares," *Arete: The Journal of Sport Literature*, I:2, Spring, 1984, 95-112.

Americans abruptly, dramatically gained the upper hand. Horse racing, however, was a different affair, a more complex, a rich, more deeply rooted institution, which was at the center of established British culture. Therefore, Tod Sloan's "invasion," at the end of the 19th century, had a greater effect, and a different one. Sloan's impact on British racing involved more than his personality (though that too aroused comment and antagonism) or his background as compared to Ten Broeck or to James Keene, who had also led an American foray to Britain in the 1870s. It had to do with altered historical and economic conditions. In the seemingly artless words (as these were told to, and put down by, Dick Luckman, a contemporary English sporting journalist, a bit of a maverick himself and therefore a sympathetic transcriber of Tod Sloan's thoughts) we find ourselves, as readers, involved in a large historical drama—an assault by the middle class upon one of the last bastions of aristocratic privilege. Tod Sloan gives us an insider's look at what was happening to the Sport of Kings as it became increasingly dominated by businessmen and by the interests they represented.

That is one of the significances of Sloan's career, the context which establishes his historical importance. It is the bulk of his book. But there is something we learn from him, also important in American sport, and we find this in the first all-too-brief opening chapters. It has to do with the United States of his youth. He takes us back to the rural Midwest (he was born and raised in Indiana in the 1870s) in which entertainment and amusement were as yet relatively unorganized, informal. What is recreated for us is the individual entrepreneurial, risk-taking sporting culture which was being rapidly displaced by a much more complex, rationalized, and highly publicized sporting world. Tod Sloan made the transition from the one to the other, triumphing (briefly) in this newer world of multi-billionaires and of monopoly. Just as his story is about class, so too in its widest sense it is about industrialization, about the application of rationalizing capitalism to horse racing. There is less and less room in that international market for Tod Sloan's individualist hustling, his old fashioned manipulating and gambling. Not that his morals were any worse than or different from those of the robber barons for whom he rode in America or of the masterful all-powerful aristocrats who clamored for his services in Britain; but they were worldly and he was naive; they were powerful and he was not; they realized how much appearances mattered in business calculations, and Tod never grasped this point. As horse racing became a big business dependent upon public support, it had to be policed and regulated. Tod Sloan came to be seen as a threat to the system. This mixture of cynicism and hypocrisy irresistibly reminds one of the contemporary situation in American collegiate and professional sports in regard to drugs.

Finally, *Tod Sloan, By Himself* justifies its re-appearance by bringing us, on a very personal level and in a direct and disturbing way, the tragic *denouement* of this story of wizardry, magical talent, and youthful folly. The memoirs originated in Tod Sloan's desperate desire to vindicate himself. Hence the wisdom of reproducing the English volume for this was a vindication directed first to the British. It was in

Great Britain Tod Sloan's fate was decided. How amused and scornful this uneducated young man would have been to hear his story described as an *apologia pro vita sua*—but so it was, and is. No reader can escape coming to some conclusion about the issue presented—Tod Sloan's veracity and the veracity of the charges brought against him. But the trouble was, and is, that a judgement was made, conclusively and crushingly, without allowing any procedural recourse to the object of it. There are moments when Tod Sloan's story prefigures those haunting studies of nameless guilt and inescapable authority associated with Franz Kafka's central Europe. This is not far-fetched. Tod Sloan was judged guilty of a crime which was never named.

These seem to me to suggest some of the themes which, with the benefit of seventy-five years' hindsight, we can bring to our own reading of *Tod Sloan*, now that it is possible for all of us to turn its pages. Let's look more fully at each of these.

* * *

Tod Sloan became famous in his day because he introduced a new style of riding, which his initially sceptical contemporaries derisively described as the "monkey seat," "the American seat," the "monkey on a stick," the "crouch seat," and no doubt other unmentionable things. He moved up, in a semi-crouch, high on the horse's neck, driving forward, looking down over the horse's head, with very short stirrups and a short rein. For two hundred years before this jockeys had always ridden in a very different way. The rider had sat far back in the saddle, uprightly perpendicular to the horse, with long stirrups and a long rein, a point of calm stability as the horse stretched its legs out ahead and behind. This was the classic style depicted beautifully by generations of painters, from the English 18th century recorders of aristocratic sporting life to the late 19th century impressionism of Edgar Degas. It was more than the classic riding style—it was the *only* riding style. Apparently it had not consciously occurred to anyone to question this way of riding or to imagine an alternative. I say "consciously occurred" because there was a group of marginal American jockeys, exercise and stable boys who had tentatively modified the traditional style by moving a little forward and semi-crouching on the horse's neck. They may have done this because they didn't have the proper equipment or because no one had ever bothered to teach them the classic manner. Most of these riders were black, almost all achieved no name or fame in racing. And none of them carried their modest, preliminary modification to its logical outcome.

Tod Sloan did. Moving up, crouching above the neck, gave him, a very small man even for a jockey, much better control, a clearer look ahead and at where the other horses were. The initial response was not only derisive but shocked. The derision was partly esthetic—hence the variations on the "monkey" theme. The shock also had to do with the genuine fear of many trainers and jockeys that riding up high would be dangerous for the jockey and would certainly damage the horse: undue weight on its front legs would break it down. (The danger to the jockey didn't get so much attention. Jockeys were a dime-a-dozen and expendable; valuable thoroughbreds were not.) So, when Sloan introduced his new riding style, first in California and then in the major eastern racetracks, beginning in 1894 and during the next half dozen years, people jeered, mocked, raged—and watched as Tod Sloan won more and more frequently. He didn't lose control, and the horses didn't break down. Other jockeys noticed, observed, and copied him. Before you knew it there were jocks bobbing in the monkey seat on all the tracks, large and small, of America. As sometimes happens: when a venerable and seemingly unshakeable tradition disappeared, it did so in the twinkling of an eye.

Origins are tricky things. Innumerable nameless others had groped toward this change but it was Tod Sloan who did it, and who deserves (and in his day richly received) full credit for doing it. However, there was a good deal more to it than simply an isolated change in technique made by one autonomous individual. Though he didn't know it and didn't write about it in this way, Tod Sloan was part of a deeper, wider series of changes which were altering more than a style of riding. Tod Sloan was associated with the evolution of a different *kind* of racing.

The monkey seat style of riding was an additional impetus to what had been happening in American racing for half a century. There was greater and greater emphasis on speed. The monkey seat helped force the pace of the race from start to finish. The old style had been leisurely. Horses and their jockeys ran against each other. Now they ran against the clock. American race tracks were built, and were being continually modified, to increase speed. Racing on a dirt track was faster than racing on the turf. The fundamental reason for the emphasis on speed had to do with the social and economic context of American racing. This had long been, since Jacksonian times, a commercial sport. It was dependent on attracting people who paid to watch it and who bet money while watching. The Sport of Kings of traditional Europe, while it too had always been connected with money and with material rewards, was rooted in an aristocratic style of life where racing seasons went on whether few or many came to watch. So English race courses were in the country, away from cities. American race tracks, by contrast, were generally very close to cities by intention. They had to be. That's where the people were who had to be attracted to the track to make the meeting a successful proposition. Everything was geared toward increasing attendance. More races were run each day than was British practice. Races became shorter. More days were added to the season. In fact, the season had no natural limits at all. It was determined by attendance. The emphasis in American racing was on speed, not endurance. Speed became one of the essentials of American sporting entertainment—speed kept people interested, amused. We should remember, in these days when baseball seems to some too slow a game to compete with football or basketball, that the heart of baseball's early popularity was precisely its sure-fire, slam-bang action. By these means thoroughbred horse racing became more than ever an important spectator sport, an important form of mass entertainment.

*   *   *

In Tod Sloan's pages, American racing is contrasted with its counterpart in Great Britain—that ubiquitous transatlantic theme which was one of the preoccupations of American high culture in this period, witness the novels of Henry James, the paintings of John Singer Sargent. Unusually, we have it here at the level of popular culture. The conventional elements are here: the contrast between the brash and vulgar materialist New World and the confident, cultivated Old World of higher values. Innocence confronts cynicism. The New World is raw, but also energetic and innovative while the Old pays for the richness of its traditions by an unavoidable rigidity and complacency.

This is a very old theme, and one still present in Americans' contemporary view of their relationship to the world. And while it was thought of as a relationship imposed by history and therefore inevitable, it is important to emphasize that Americans have relished their role in this cultural drama. Of course they and their culture were the object of snubs and of disdain, but on the whole Americans gave as good as they got and they were buoyed by the unquestioned assumption that history, in the not-too-long run, was on their side. The superior refinement of the Old World concealed a loss of vitality and power. The biological metaphor of youth versus old age meant that the future belonged to America.

Tod Sloan's picture of the meeting of the Old and New on the turf, while it contains elements of the conventional vision, is in other ways different. Naturally, his depiction has nothing in it of sociological analysis or theory; it is a mosaic of personal impressions and incidents. He was clear and undeluded about the pervasive role of class feeling in British life. His reception was a very frosty one at first. People there, as everywhere else, laughed at the way he rode. He was a bizarre curiosity. Yet there was a paradox in the British response to him. In everyday terms he found that he was treated with far greater civility in the class-bound United Kingdom than in the democratic United States. The British aristocrats he met treated him much more nearly as an equal than had the American plutocrats for whom he had ridden. Jockeys were not ridiculed in Britain while "there was a time in America when they tried to treat jockeys like a lot of monkeys." Lord William Beresford, a leading English turfman, befriended him and spent countless hours talking with him about horses. "The more I saw of [him] the kinder he seemed to become to me and the more interested he became in what I was doing." Tod Sloan became celebrated for his success with sulky and bad tempered horses and Lord William was intrigued by Sloan's ideas about horses' instincts and dispositions. Everywhere in his memoirs one encounters Sloan's yearning for respect, for self-dignity, for love. "Lord William used to say that I never seemed to do so well when he wasn't with me. He was right." By himself, on his own from a very early age, Sloan searched continually for parental authority, haunted by the unappeasable sense of loss "when I was left alone by those I have never ceased to grieve for."

What it comes down to in Sloan's account, is that there still remained in Great Britain vestiges of an older style of horse racing, of a sport in which participants were bound together by something beyond the betting and the money. In the United States Tod Sloan had learned about the horse-racing world in conditions of harsh struggle. While he occasionally encountered an American equivalent to Lord William Beresford—for example a sportsman like William C. Whitney, who "would have tried if necessary to keep racing going without a single wager on a single track"—horse racing was mostly a business, and a tough and unsupervised and unscrupulous one at that. Sloan didn't idealize British racing culture. Ordinary British horse players made him their hero, and he liked that very much. "All the way back to London," he wrote, "I heard that crowd calling to me—'Tod,' 'Toddie,' 'Sloanie,' and everything they could twist my name into." But he also knew really why they cheered him—because he won money for them. He remembered that when he had first arrived in Britain "there was no body to speak to me, [but] after I had made a few successes there was no end to the people who came up and claimed me."

In this transatlantic cultural drama of wickedness and innocence in which Tod Sloan figured, the roles were reversed. The Americans represented cynicism and an awareness of evil. They brought dope and unprecedented amounts of betting money across the Atlantic with them. Dozens of American gamblers and con men came with Sloan or followed in his wake. This American invasion was made up of a largely unsavory crew of inside operators. And at the center of it all, the gamblers' hero and instrument, was Tod Sloan. He openly bet a tremendous amount of money, always on himself and his horses, he said. That had been perfectly legal and accepted in America. It wasn't in Britain. Sloan ignored that fact or pretended not to know it. Clouds of rumor and speculation and loose talk swirled about him: "Well, there was the usual talk about my having done this, that and the other." Lord William Beresford had taught him the expression "Save me from my friends." But who were his friends? "The truth was that I could never find out, to the extent I wanted to, who really were those I should be with." Maybe he didn't want to find out. Certainly there was more to British racing than the unaffected social affability of some of its sporting aristocracy. The reversal of cultural roles in the transatlantic drama of Innocence versus Evil had its limits. There was a fist of iron beneath that velvet glove of British aristocratic amiability. Perhaps on *both* sides of the Atlantic there was wickedness, cynicism, evil enough, with innocence finishing dead last. Tod Sloan would find out.

* * *

If there was innocence anywhere surely it was back home in Indiana. Another of the sources of interest in reading this book is to recapture a sense of the rural, insular culture of the Ohio Valley in the years right after the Civil War. In some ways Tod Sloan lived the classic life of rural boyhood, the idyllic world of James

Whitcomb Riley's poetry of wimmin' holes and barefoot boys. Certainly Sloan's life was largely unconstrained. He wandered about the countryside, playing hooky from school, fishing and hunting. His mother died when he was five. His father, a Civil War veteran, had been psychologically demoralized by the war. He ran a barber shop and a real estate office—shaving his customers both ways no doubt. He let Tod and his brother and two sisters fend for themselves, while he retreated into some interior world of his own marked by an unrelenting indifference to what happened to his kids. Tod was taken in for a time by a neighboring family but when they broke up he was on his own. He was thirteen.

He failed to grow physically. His father called him "Toad," from which came "Tod": James Forman Sloan was his real name. He knocked about the countryside taking odd jobs to support himself—cleaning out a livery stable, a saloon, working in the new oil and gas fields. He was terribly burned in an oil well explosion: "it seemed to shrivel me even smaller than I was before." He hooked on with Professor Talbot, an aeronaut, who toured with his hot air balloons, which he demonstrated at county fairs. Everything was punctuated by an endless stream of jibes directed at him because he was so small. Eventually he found his way into the kind of work that seemed to everyone to be destined for him—racing. What else was there but to be a jockey? But he feared and hated horses, and the chapters in which he discusses how he learned to ride are a deeply moving and marvelous picture of a boy overcoming terror, internal and external. Another American success story? Yes. In a way Tod Sloan's story is certainly the record of astonishing, fabulous success.

However, there is another way to look at this picture of the barefoot boy who becomes a champion. That is to pay attention to what is usually left out, the restlessness and dislocation of the culture in which Tod Sloan came of age. We have here a picture, absent from most of our history books, of the American family in dissolution, and a picture, too, of a society with little room in it for the unconnected, the homeless, the powerless. These people fill the pages of Tod Sloan's memoirs. They worked in the circuses, carnivals, small-town race tracks; they were the legion of hustlers, con men, promoters and imposters. They are forever cutting corners, cheating and tricking everyone else, and being cheated, conned and tricked themselves. There is a quality of desperation in these lives, and an equal sense of tenacity, a prosaic, gritty refusal to go down for the third time.

It is in fact a picture of rural and of small town America which goes a long way toward explaining why millions of young women and men did everything they could to escape and move to the city. (You will learn almost nothing about women's lives in this book. The sporting and entertainment world Tod Sloan moved in was exclusively male, suspicious of women, hostile to black people. Sloan's pages are dotted with unselfconscious racism.) They escaped from the small towns and went to the big cities—to Chicago and to New York City. In the anonymity of the city they found escape and some freedom. The great example of this novel of escape is *Sister Carrie* by Theodore Dreiser, also a Hoosier, born three years before Tod Sloan, also cut adrift at an early age, and also with a father, once prosperous but finally demoralized, who turned inward and closed himself off from his family. When he was famous, Tod Sloan returned to Kokomo. Like so many others he found out that he could not go home again. Nor did he want to. He had been permanently cut adrift in a culture of atomized individuals. Tod Sloan had escaped from Indiana by enacting another of the prevailing American myths, by going West, to California where he invented his own bonanza, the "monkey seat." And then, like so many with ambitions, he headed back east, to the Big Town. American racing's capital was New York City. That was where the crowds and the money and, increasingly, the publicity were. The small town was claustrophobic, stifling, narrow, bigoted. Big city culture had its pitfalls too, of course, as Sister Carrie and Hurstwood—and Tod Sloan—found out. From New York City there was only one path to greater fame left, across the Atlantic, from the society of millionaires to the society of lords and kings.

* * *

The climax of his career, really, was meeting Edward, the Prince of Wales. "He smiled as I came towards him and shook my hand very warmly. Never in my life have I been put so much at my ease nor treated so splendidly. After all I was only a visiting American and only a jockey at that." More than anything else, this was Tod Sloan's vision of the attraction of British culture:

> I used to think to myself how pleased they would be at home and how they would ask me all about it, and what the American papers would say. I can tell you that although I come from democratic America, there was a wonderful impression left on me by the great personal attraction of that royal gentleman.

Tod talked to him, man-to-man, and gave him advice about betting and rode some of his mounts, and won for him. Soon there came the greatest compliment of all. Tod Sloan was asked to ride for the Prince's stable, as contract rider, in preference to any English jockey.

He was at the summit. Then the storm broke. The rumors about betting and inside information and doping horses grew more insistent. Sloan believed that many were inspired by jockeys jealous of his success. The stewards of the Jockey Club sent for him, asked him questions, reprimanded him. That seemed to be the end of that, but Lord William Beresford, who knew how things worked behind the scenes, warned him: "Things look pretty black, little man, but we must hope for the best." Sloan came to America and while there read in newspapers that the Jockey Club had intimated that he ought not to apply for his license to ride in 1901. The action of the Jockey Club effectively closed all race courses in Great Britain to him, and most American race tracks as well because few of them were willing to oppose the British action or to disregard it. Racing was becoming more uniform and systematized. Sloan apparently believed that everything would be all right the following year. But it wasn't. Not in 1902 or in 1903. Not ever.

Tod Sloan was not formally suspended or disqualified. He was allowed access to any race course. He could warm up horses and ride them in workouts. He could own horses and train them (and in later years did own and train a few). But he was refused a license to ride. He was never formally charged with any transgression or given any explanation of the action taken against him. Of course it was understood why he had been denied his license. He openly gambled and associated with gamblers. He had done so ever since he came to Britain. Why then did this happen to him when it did? When the Prince of Wales asked him to be his contract rider Sloan was put in a position at the center of British racing. His conduct could neither be ignored nor could the Prince openly be persuaded to change his mind. It was an awkward situation but probably an endurable one—for a time. Then came the event which sealed Tod Sloan's riding fate. In January of 1901 Queen Victoria died. Edward was now King. The "little man" got caught up in the machinery of a mighty state. The presence of the disreputable and bumptious American jockey in the royal stables could no longer be ignored or endured. The betting (and allegations) of doping were blatant and insupportable that close to the Crown. Anyway, racing had to be cleaned up. Where better to begin than with Tod Sloan?

All efforts by Sloan and his friends to change the decision or to modify it were futile. The Jockey Club was unyielding. As a last resort he wrote and got published the book we have in our hands, a final effort at self-explanation and self-justification. And at restoring his career. In that respect the book failed. But what can we make of it as explanation? Was Tod Sloan guilty? And of what? He admitted in his memoirs that he had acted unwisely, that he had done things that he ought not to have done, though details are not presented. The entire affair is obscured by the fact that no legal action of any kind was ever taken, no specific charges were ever filed. Who now can say whether the penalty was appropriate to the transgression, whatever it was? No reader, however, will be able to avoid coming to some conclusion about the meaning of all this in terms of Tod Sloan's reputation. As much as any book I know about American sporting culture *Tod Sloan* raises painful, distressing issues. What if a champion is also a cheat? Can we separate talent and technical proficiency from ethical and moral considerations? It is not a sufficient response to say that it is right to distinguish between private and public realms for the sporting life is always and essentially public. Tod Sloan asked for the judgment of his readers and now they can give it.

*   *   *

The first fifteen years of his banishment from riding are covered in this book, the last part of which seems to me a depressing record of his efforts to find something else to do. The cocky tone cannot disguise the sadness and demoralization in it. There is no question that the interest of the book tails off in many ways, into a restless and trivial accounting of once-famous names, celebrated places, forced high spirits and good times that seem mournful as one reads about them now. What sticks in one's mind is the ironic way in which this last part of his life recapitulated the restless, aimless years of his boyhood and early maturity. It had taken Tod Sloan a decade or more to find what it was he could do. It took him almost two decades to realize that he would never be able to do it again.

In the book he predicted that he would spend the rest of his life in Europe. That turned out not to be so. Perhaps life there was too closely associated with what he had lost. He had never given up his American citizenship, and so in the 1920s he came back to the United States. He managed a billiard room in New York City with John J. McGraw. He had a short and unsuccessful fling in vaudeville. He married twice and both marriages failed. He lost all his money and dropped from public view except for occasional short notices about bankruptcy and law suits and divorce. He returned to the anonymity he had rocketed out of thirty-five years before and came full circle, too, in ending up where his racing career had first taken off, California. Broke and broken, he died in Los Angeles on December 21, 1933.

* * *

Henry James and Theodore Dreiser have made their unlikely appearance in these pages in connection with Sloan's career and his Indiana boyhood; but there is a direct connection between Tod Sloan's racing fame and fate and another major American writer—Ernest Hemingway. This is a final claim of his to our attention.

Tod Sloan was the inspiration for one of Hemingway's short stories, "My Old Man." Literary critics and biographers have argued, from the time the story first appeared, about whether or not "My Old Man" was influenced by Sherwood Anderson's stories about horses. Hemingway was annoyed by this and, in this case at least (whatever the general influence upon him of Anderson's prose style) rightly so, because he knew where this story came from. Inevitably transformed in many details by the requirements of Hemingway's imagination, "My Old Man" bears a striking resemblance to numerous aspects of Tod Sloan's life and of his racing history. And most of all, it captures unforgettably the moral ambiguities of that life. A passionate sportsman, a one-time sportswriter, Hemingway knew second hand about Tod Sloan's career and racing significance and about the disastrous end of his days as a jockey. It was this last which must have intrigued him, and he may have had more than second-hand sports-page knowledge of it. Even though Tod Sloan had left Paris by the time Hemingway got there in the 20s, there would have been lots of Sloan's racing contemporaries still around, and many stories about Sloan no doubt circulated among the racing fraternity at the Parisian race courses Hemingway frequented. And who knows?—he might have read *Tod Sloan, By Himself*. That Sloan's infamous reputation remained familiar even a quarter of a century after his riding demise, and that the American style of racing was also a matter of some notoriety in the minds of Europeans is clear from one of Hemingway's letters—written many years after the story—in which he described riding to hounds with a regiment of British soldiers. "All the officers were measuring my stirrup lengths and comparing them with how Todd Sloane and other notorious American characters used to ride," Hemingway wrote, and concluded: "There were many comments on the American seat" (letter to Charles Scribner, 19 August 1949).

Tod Sloan's life was a natural subject for a Hemingway story. It brought together several of the themes which preoccupied him as a writer, especially in his sports stories. There was the fascination with technique, the desire to describe precisely how something worked; the pathos of the one-time champion at the end of his rope, trapped within an aging body but still able to summon up a lifetime's experience and cunning; the tension between the athlete's private code of honor and the need to cheat or lie, especially in that most horrific form of betrayal, the double-cross. Treated with varying emphases we find all these in "Fifty Grand," "The Killers," "The Undefeated," *The Old Man and the Sea*. They are realized poignantly and with more delicacy than is usual with Hemingway's "My Old Man."

Hemingway's remarkable intuitive grasp of some of the aspects of a character like Tod Sloan is embodied in the dualities which form the structure of the story. The story is about Butler, a once famous jockey, whose career is now on the skids, and his son Joe, and it is told in Joe's words and from his point of view. Father and son lead a marginal, rather precarious but also pleasurable life, in the years immediately after World War I, wandering about Italy and France from race course to race course. The boy is unaware of what his old man is really up to, and the emotional center of the story is the boy's ultimate loss of innocence about his old man, just as its ethical center is the ambiguity between the father's public corruption and personal kindness and generosity. Even when he learns the truth about him Joe says, "I don't know. I loved my old man so much."

This dualism is paralleled by the contrast between the external idyllic atmosphere of the race courses and of the countryside which surrounds them compared with the sordid and ruthless dishonesty concealed within the actual racing itself: San Siro in Italy "With that big green infield and the mountains way off," and Maisons-Lafitte in France: "about the swellest place to live I've ever seen in all my life. The town ain't so much, but there's a lake and a swell forest that we used to go off bumming in all day, a couple of us kinds, and my old man made me a sling shot and we got a lot of things with it. . . ."

The boy is fitfully aware that his father's professional career is shaky: "It seemed like everybody steered clear of giving my old man many mounts." He knows that his father was worried about losing his license for some reason and he has overheard the bitter comments directed at his father by accomplices with whom he has fallen out. But it isn't until his father wins a lot of money on a race that the truth comes home to Joe about his old man, and about racing. Butler gets inside information from a friend, another jockey, named George Gardner, who is riding Kzar, the heavy favorite. Hemingway gies us a beautiful description of Kzar as a kind of fabulous incarnation of the thoroughbred, and a wonderful account, in its energy and clarity, of the race itself, allowing the reader to share Joe's excitement and heartbreak when Kzar is beaten by a nose after a pounding finish.

"'Wasn't it a swell race, Dad?' I said to him.

"He looked at me sort of funny with his derby on the back of his head. 'George Gardner's a swell jockey, all right,' he said. 'It sure took a great jock to keep that Kzar horse from winning.'" Joe's disenchantment is distilled in one sentence: "That sure took the kick all out of it for me and I didn't get the real kick back again ever...."

With the money won on that race Butler buys a horse which he begins training, works himself back into condition and starts riding again. Hemingway subtly suggests to us that he is riding honestly now, riding to win. This adds to the pathos of the description which follows of the race on a rainy Sunday at Auteuil in which Butler is riding, and winning. There is a collision, jockeys are thrown and Butler is killed. Joe is left entirely on his own except for George Gardner who comes to take him away. While waiting together they hear two men talking about the accident. "Well, Butler got his all right," one says, and the other replies: "I don't give a good goddam if he did, the crook. He had it coming to him on the stuff he's pulled." Gardner tries to help Joe out, without pretending to deny the truth of what they've heard. He says what remains that can be said. "Don't you listen to what those bums said, Joe. Your old man was one swell guy." Joe's own final reflection, the conclusion of the story, serves, as I am convinced Hemingway intended it to do, as a kind of epitaph for the life of Tod Sloan and for the ambiguities it leaves for us. "Seems like when they get started they don't leave a guy nothing."

Once they got started on Tod Sloan they didn't leave him much, and maybe that was fair enough. In fact, though, something of Tod Sloan does remain. What that is, readers can now find out for themselves.

Contents

PREFACE	V
INTRODUCTION	XXV
I. TOD SLOAN'S REMINISCENCES	1
II. MAKING BAD AS A JOCKEY	5
III. "MONKEY ON THE STICK" IN PRACTICE	16
IV. START IN NEW YORK	21
V. W. C. WHITNEY'S LIBERALITY	25
VI. FIRST TRIP TO ENGLAND	29
VII. TALKS WITH LORD WILLIAM BERESFORD	34
VIII. SECOND IMPRESSIONS OF ENGLAND	38
IX. A GLORIOUS WIND-UP	41
X. HOLIDAY INCIDENTS	45
XI. SOMETHING ABOUT CLOTHES	50
XII. THE LATE KING EDWARD	53
XIII. NUNSUCH'S CAMBRIDGESHIRE	57
XIV. A PERIOD OF SUCCESS	63
XV. TRAINERS—AND TRAINEES	69
XVI. ENGLAND AND AMERICA	73
XVII. KNIGHT OF THE THISTLE	78
XVIII. HOLOCAUST	83
XIX. FLYING FOX AND CAIMAN	87
XX. JOCKEYS AND JOCKEYSHIP	92
XXI. THE BIG PLUNGER	97
XXII. A VISIT TO AMERICA	102
XXIII. THE ASCOT INCIDENT	106
XXIV. MERMAN'S GOLD CUP	110

XXV.	CODOMAN	114
XXVI.	DARK CLOUDS	119
XXVII.	NABOT	126
XXVIII.	AT THE TRAPS	129
XXIX.	"SLOAN'S CHANCE HOPELESS"	135
XXX.	DOPE	142
XXXI.	MY MARRIAGE	146
XXXII.	HOPE DEFERRED	151
XXXIII.	THE THEODORE MYERS STABLE	156
XXXIV.	SOME MINOR SUCCESSES	159
XXV.	MY DOG PIPER	166
XXXVI.	A LITTLE FIGHTING	171
XXXVII.	MAKING A BOOK	175
XXXVIII.	SUGGESTIONS	186
XXXIX.	PRACTICAL JOCKEYSHIP	189
XL.	MORE SUGGESTIONS	195
XLI.	FINIS	200

List of Illustrations

In 1900	xxii
Tod Sloan: From Spy's Caricature in "Vanity Fair"	7
Mr Charles F. Hanlon	15
George E. Smith: "Pittsburg Phil"	18
Lord Marcus Beresford and Mr Richard Marsh	32
King Edward—then Prince of Wales—driving at Newmarket	59
My First Year in England	62
Beaten on Caiman by Flying Fox	81
Winning the Jubilee on Knight of the Thistle	82
In King Edward's Colours	89
Lord William Beresford on the Road to Epsom	91
Lester Reiff	93
Returning to Scale after Merman's Gold Cup	111
Walter Davis	116
"The Flying Bird" and Tod Sloan	130
Prince Poniatowski and Tod Sloan	133
M. Charron's First Lesson in Riding	137
Rose de Mai	140
Lord Carnarvon and Tod Sloan at Longchamps	144
Miss Julia Sanderson	148
At the Carlton Hotel, Nice	155
The First Time an Aeroplane carried Four People	161
After the St. Moritz Annual Billiard Tournament	164
Shooting Clay Pigeons at St. Moritz	167
With my Dog, Piper, at St. Moritz	169
In Algiers	178
Mr. Theodore Myers's Training Quarters	180

Working for the Ambulance 182
Two Pirates: Milton Henry and Tod Sloan 184
"Henry" 185
A Hospital Garden Scene 199
My Editor 202

TOD SLOAN

BY

HIMSELF

EDITED BY

A. DICK LUCKMAN
AUTHOR OF "SHARPS, FLATS, GAMBLERS AND RACEHORSES"

WITH THIRTY-TWO ILLUSTRATIONS

LONDON
GRANT RICHARDS LTD.
MDCCCCXV

In 1900
My last English photograph

TO

MY FRIEND

FRANK C. JACOTT

WHOSE SYMPATHY AND ENCOURAGEMENT

IN MANY TRYING MOMENTS

WILL BE A LASTING

MEMORY

July 1915

Introduction

FOR MANY YEARS I have had a wish to collect the incidents of Tod Sloan's life. The opportunity never seemed to arrive. However, with the strenuous times of the Great War, and soon after Paris had been threatened by a German occupation, I found my chance.

There is a double purpose in writing Sloan's life. I had heard him telling so many good stories about himself, and about others, that I thought it would be a pity that they should be lost to the present-day public and to future generations. I was sure, too, that many phases of his career would typify life preceding 1915, and that this book might be as interesting in the years to come as it is to-day to those who know Sloan personally.

Tod Sloan is one of the best-known individualities in Paris, London, New York and other great cities. He has been caricatured by the best-known artists, and written about in newspapers, magazines and books. His career has been such a varied one that even a single chapter of his life could be elaborated without undue padding into a most readable volume. My endeavour has been to get Sloan to recount the story of his life in chronological order, at the same time not missing little sidelights and stories which cropped up as we went along, and which could be inserted here and there without breaking off the story.

There are certain things which I can say about Sloan which he is too diffident to allude to himself except in the barest fashion. Years ago in a series of articles in *The Daily Express*, I endeavoured to lead an appeal to the stewards of the Jockey Club for the renewal of Sloan's licence, but unfortunately it came to nothing. One heading I remember began, "There should be no such thing as a life sentence." In those words is the gist of the whole matter. It has always seemed incredible that after years of punishment, Sloan should not be reinstated. It is not so much a question whether he would be able or would want to ride again. It is rather that a stigma is attached to a great artist in riding when an intimation is given to him that he must not apply for a license for it would be refused. Two wrongs don't make a right, and it is no use comparing Sloan's alleged offences with those of other riders who have been put on foot and then given their ticket in less than three years. Fifteen years is indeed a terrible time for any intelligent man to be living in hopes and to find those hopes cast down as year follows year.

It is a common mistake to think that Sloan was ever warned off. The number of times I have been asked, "What was Sloan warned off for?" I cannot reckon; all that happened to him was that he was told that he had better not put in his application. He has been allowed to ride at exercise, and he has received direct information that there was no objection at all to his going on English racecourses. Indeed, racegoers can testify to the many meetings he has been to ever since the time he had perforce to retire from the saddle. Now a jockey who is warned off, or even suspended, is not allowed to frequent any enclosure on a racecourse. However, that is only a little point which this book will make clear.

It is an interesting coincidence that Tod Sloan first made the acquaintance of racehorses in 1886, the year in which poor Fred Archer made his exit. Opinions will always be expressed and will always differ about the comparative merits of Archer and Sloan as jockeys. The comparison is unnecessary: the former was the greatest exponent in the last fifty years of the old style—and Sloan discovered the new. That this pair were the finest jockeys ever seen by living racing men admits of no doubt. Perhaps the two of them shared equally the faculty of judging pace. In strength of finishing, the style of Archer may have been more impressive, but the gift of knowing the peculiarities of an animal, and wheedling a horse of doubtful courage to do something for his jockey, has been possessed by Sloan to a greater extent than by any other jockey the writer has ever seen. One has only to see Sloan with cats, dogs or horses in a yard to realise that he might have done anything he wished as an animal trainer. The way he can make friends with a horse who will not let others come near him is remarkable. Not only that, but he will make a horse do whatever he likes. There was one animal in particular at Maisons Laffitte which Tod Sloan could induce to eat anything he liked. It didn't matter whether it was a potato, bread or fruit. The grimaces that old horse would make scrunching up an orange was the greatest comedy possible. As long as Sloan would eat some of it himself then the horse would follow his example. There was another animal who would lift him up by the jacket in his teeth and put him down as gently as a lamb, never hurting him in the slightest. I merely relate these two incidents to show the almost hypnotic influence Sloan has over horses. Does it not suggest, therefore, that there may be some extraordinary sympathy between man and beast which contributed in a measure to Sloan's racing successes?

Sloan is a man of super-intelligence, and his views about most things suggest that had he gone into another walk of life, he would have been equally successful. But it was too late after that downfall at the end of 1900 to shape himself seriously for other pursuits. Nevertheless, his intelligence has enabled him to live—and to keep up the extravagance of a dozen or more of the best cigars daily! The number of people he has known and the countries he has lived in should make the narrative which follows appeal to a far wider circle of reader than is comprised by merely racing people.

That well-known sporting editor of books and magazines, Mr. Lyman Horace Weeks, wrote some years ago:

"Successful as Sloan has been in his riding and in his personal fortunes, it has all been deserved and worthily supported by the conscientious discharge of professional engagements and a constant adherence to honourable turf methods. In this he has set a laudable example to the members of his profession. At the same time, his record is a shining example of the certain reward that the turf holds forth to men of his calibre."

The same writer also said of him in 1897: "One striking feature of his riding is that his judgment never deserts him at any stage of the race; from start to finish he uses headwork, placing his mount in a way to secure every possible advantage."

Frankly I have had some difficulty during the preparation of this book to get Tod Sloan to speak sufficiently of himself. While as a private citizen he has retained absolute confidence in himself, and can be quite as assertive as the next man about what he thinks, I have had a difficulty on occasions in getting him to speak out sufficiently as to what big things he has done. And yet he will be quite talkative as to his weaknesses!

An American trainer, after this book was finished, called my attention to various little episodes which have not been dealt with by Sloan himself. For instance, from the records my friend the trainer possesses, it appears that in 1895 Sloan had 442 mounts, of which he won 132, or about 30 percent, and in the following year he scored over 36 percent of his mounts, and he placed over 130 times. It was 1895 that he first rode four winners in a day. That was in California. None of the riders in 1897 came near him for average. It was in 1898 at Gravesend (U.S.A.) he won five races—in fact all that he rode in—in one day; and on three successive days at Coney Island he won all three races he rode in.

It seems strange to hear and read that Sloan was at one time a "very prudent fellow," but does it not strike you that his imprudence in later years may have been caused by his always being surrounded, especially in England, by many who were not the best of companions for him? Sloan makes no excuses for himself; in fact, he would take the whole burden of responsibility for his faults on his own shoulders. But there is no doubt that the fuss made of him gave him an exalted idea of his own importance—and, mind you, this is from his own lips. There are scores of people who read this book who knew Sloan intimately when he was riding in England, but none of them need take it personally when I say that there were many in this country who simply spoilt him. That is the reason why Sloan during that period, and the months which led up to his downfall, was more to be pitied than scorned. As he has sat in his parlour smoking a big cigar and chewing over his past, while doing the same to the cigar, he has reviewed those days from 1897 to the end of 1900, and also some of the incidents afterwards, especially his regret that there was no one to stop him taking that ill-advised action against the Société d'Encouragement. Mind you, it must be admitted that Sloan is not the easiest proposition to lead, but personally I can vouch for it that he is easy enough to lead when the advice given is sound, even though it may be opposed to the first views he has taken. I do not mean to say that I have a monopoly of wisdom, but many of us who are very weak about the management of our own affairs often develop with age a striking insight into what is best for others, and on no single occasion can I remember whole-souled friendly counsel being ignored by Sloan.

A. Dick Luckman.

I

Tod Sloan's Reminiscences

My Christened Name – Beyond the Dreams of a Black Dog – Ignorance and Fear of Horses – First Time in the Saddle – Men I Have Met

AFTER THE DEATH OF MY MOTHER when I was five, and of my adopted parents, or rather the people who adopted me, under their own name, Blauser, I had various designations. My real name, that which I was christened by, James Forman Sloan. The name Todhunter came from my father nicknaming me "Toad" (because I was so small), and then shortened to Tod, and the "Todhunter" was the variation of someone, I forget whom.

When I was left alone by those I have never ceased to grieve for, my faithful friend was a black dog, Tony. We would sit trying to entice fish out of the water, where they were not before I came around with my rod, and I felt he looked at me as if he thought something of the very small boy beside him. He would gaze at me when I played chequers, for I was seldom if ever beaten: it was a sort of gift handed me by Nature to be a phenomenon at the game. In fact, I had an uncanny vision for the game known in England as draughts.

But neither Tony nor I knew what was before me. There was never an idea round about my home in Kokomo, Indiana, that a horse was anything but a curiosity. My father had never driven even a donkey. How could Tony know – scared as I always was at the idea of a horse – that I should some day shine in the world Tony and I knew only from picture-books, and that I should be shaken by the hand and talked with by the Prince whose coloured picture was given to us by the local grocery store at Christmas? That prince was to be King of England.

There were, too, lesser lights of American growth. I would have the weekly paper, and see the picture of John L. Sullivan, and when we looked at the portraits I would murmur: "Gee! Tony, we have expected this paper to-day, shall we ever have a handshaking acquaintance with him? What a pride it would be to meet 'John L.'! And if only he would notice me some day!"

In my humble way I was to come out of obscurity. From playing truant from school I was to show the world how weight could be properly distributed on a horse; I was to be the possessor at one time of nearer half a million dollars than a quarter; I was to meet almost every celebrity in the world they and I flourished in. I am suggesting Tod Sloan myself – the boy, the man, the jockey. Then came the reverse of fortune, the facts of which shall be told; the grim battling; hoping against hope; the procession of years full of incident; but with the constant open sore of disappointment.

A sense of humour can save our reason and the jokes of existence can make me laugh, and perhaps you will laugh with me—who knows! A jockey's tears are for himself, his smiles can be shared with the next fellow. All the same, who would have thought, when I was run away with, on an old horse, with me grabbing him round his neck, that, later, I was to sail in for race after race for the great owners of England and America.

I have said I was frightened at the sight of a horse. It came about like this. We had to follow the funeral of a boy who was drowned in a flood through being reckless. I wanted to see him buried, but as the cemetery was a long way off, and I was late, I "stole" a horse—that is to say, I borrowed him out of a livery stable near where I was working. In the last three months I had no knowledge of anyone having ridden this horse. I got on the horse—he was a grey, I remember—and the stirrup-leathers were shortened by a chum of mine to the last hole, and even then were too long! So I had to tuck my feet into the leather loops. How I got round my corner when the grey wanted to go round his is something I shall never forget.

That horse knew he had a kid of under forty-five lb. on his back. I am sure of it, although I hadn't learned horse language in those days. However, it was ordained that there were not to be two corpses at that funeral, and we did arrive at the graveyard. I know I didn't look three feet high when I got off that horse. He was quite young. He just sniffed at me, then shook his head, and champed up the grass. When I got back to him his contempt seemed to have increased. Whether it was the sour grass, or that he really wanted to be stretched out at a gallop, I don't know. The other visitors to the funeral had gone on ahead, and how to get up on the saddle was licker to me. I tried to get him to a fence so that I could climb on his back, but he wouldn't have it. I wanted my way, but he had his. At last I made one dash for it, but before I could get either on or off he had raced away with me. I was embracing his neck! I got my right foot through the leather, but the other hung down. I did not dare to drop off, for that would have been certain suicide.

People could see me now. Everyone yelled to me to stick on. Part of the journey was over rough cobbles, and the grey must have stumbled half-a-dozen times. I swore to myself that, if I ever got off alive, I would only look for a horse after that in a zoological gardens. He seemed to go faster with every furlong he went. At last he hesitated and slackened, and I steered him to a fence and a fellow rushed out and grabbed him.

"You're all right now, Tod," he said. "I'll lead him home; but you stick in the saddle just to show 'em that you didn't come off."

"You take him home," I said. "I've done enough jockey business for one day. You don't catch me on a horse again in a hurry."

It was a darned funny thing that, years after, when riding in a big race in England, having had already two successes that day, the whole incident of the grey broncho came back to me. I was showing the way home on that English track on another grey, and the memory suddenly came into my head so vividly that I began to laugh. The fellow who was on the horse running second, just at the shoulder of mine, shouted: "You're laughing: you haven't won yet." He thought I was jeering him.

This is all a sort of start to my life's experiences, but here the introduction will not bother you. There will be many other things to say about all those I met, for, before I came to England and saw for the first time the Prince of Wales and all the nobility and great owners of the country, I came next to many celebrities in my own land. The great Buffalo Bill (Colonel Cody) nursed me on his knee when almost a baby, and it was he that made me crazy for firearms of all kinds. I remember that he let me try one of his revolvers one day, and all the time even till now I have had a longing for rifles, sporting guns, Mausers, and have even tried my hand—quite recently with some success with the latest quick-firer.

Others with whom I came in close touch were Frank James, the brother of Jesse James. They were both among the notorious bandits of America; the latter was killed by a pal, but Frank, after he received a pardon, used to hold the forward flag on several racetracks. However, there is no need to give a list, for they will come up in due order as the story of my life progresses.

Little did I dream when I saw one the Valkyries compete for the America Cup that I should meet and ride for Lord Dunraven. Lord William Beresford, one of the greatest of friends to me, had only been heard of: there will be such a lot to say of him. There was my acquaintance with John L. Sullivan and James Corbett. I shall recall how I referee-ed one of the first matches the great French billiard expert, Fournier, played in America. Then reference must be made to the well-known Riley Grannan, who came near bringing off one of the greatest betting coups at Newmarket. I have played bridge and talked till I was tired to the late John W. Gates, the Chicago millionaire—"bet-you-a-million Gates." George E. Smith, at one time a simple cork cutter, and who as a millionaire backer was known to the world as "Pittsburg Phil," was a constant companion of mine. He made a huge fortune backing horses in America. I have never known two men more alike in their living and character than "Pittsburgh Phil" and Charlie Hannam, who has had much the same kind of success in England.

There are scores of others too to write of.

I must also discuss how from close observation and from constant visits to the starting-post I made sure in my own mind that I could get a start and beat well-known English jockeys.

It's right here that I want to give the exact reason for ever leaving America, and how it came about. All the details of my arrival and early sorrows and joys will be told in due order. In the winter of 1896-1897 the late Tom Loates, who, as everyone knows, was one of the English crack jockeys, came out to New York for a vacation and to have a rest for a time. He was a good deal about with Jack MacDonald, the poor fellow who was killed in a railway accident at Salisbury a few years back. When Tom Loates had been in New York some time I put myself at his disposal to make his stay there a merrier one if possible, and we spent a considerable time together. I was in a position to show him round, for not only was I saving about fifty thousand dollars a year but was also busily engaged in spending about two-thirds of that sum! Loates and I saw a good deal of each other, and with the early opening of the racing season at Morris Park I got the idea that I would like to do Tommy a good turn. There were two cinches that I was engaged for, a brace of real good things I thought any kid could get up on and ride home, so I went to him and told him that, as the Stewards were also anxious for him to ride, I could arrange for him to have the two mounts. The American public were very interested to see England's crack jockey, and I can say with all sincerity I wanted to give my pal a chance to show himself on a New York track. But I couldn't argue him into it. He said that as he was in America for his health he was afraid of what Mr. Leopold de Rothschild would think if he got in the saddle. However, whether he was fit to ride or not makes no matter. He backed my two mounts and both of them won. We had dinner that night and he thanked me. He had won a nice bit of dough. A few days after, on the eve of his leaving for England, he was interviewed by one of the newspaper men, and was asked who he thought were the best American jockeys. He answered Fred Taral was a good rider, and also the coloured boy, Willie Sims, while among the younger crowd he had noticed a promising boy in the little kid Winnie O'Connor. It didn't matter much, for I was doing too well financially, and riding too many winners to need a booster, but here was my friend giving a story to a leading paper, and not only did he put a coloured boy before me, but left my name out altogether! I wasn't exactly sore, but from that time I had a fixed determination to go to England to see what I could do against him.

II
Making Bad as a Jockey

Start as an Aeronaut — Peddling Balloons — "Who's the Boy for the Parachute?" — Joining a Stable — Worse and Worse — More Runaway Rides — Become a Cook

MY FATHER, who had been an officer in the United States Army, first had a look at his latest kid on 10th August 1874. I had two brothers and one sister, and my first appearance on any track was on the date just mentioned at Bunker Hill, twelve miles from Kokomo, Indiana. Father, who had fought in the Civil War and was made prisoner at Gettysburg, never drank, and didn't feel called upon to buy drinks for the boys who came to congratulate him. Some time after I was born he started in business at Kokomo. The combination of the two shows he ran seems funny to us now, although it was quite serious at the time. At one entrance to the building he occupied was a swell barber's shop, and at the other door, to the left, was his real estate office. He made a good living out of both. He used to play the violin very well, and I suppose we got the habit of whistling from following the tunes, both my brother "Cash" and I have often been cuffed for the habit. I have mentioned that I was a champion chequers player; they said that I used to whistle my opponents off their game: I'd never stop. After my mother died my father was a bit too easy with me; in fact, he was too lenient altogether. I would go out in the fields with Tony and fish, fish, all day long, instead of going to school. At least it gave me a taste for the open air. I was captain of the baseball crowd in our small town, giving orders to fellows four and five years older than I was. In fact, I took it on myself to boss them all, and they stood for it. Sometimes I got near getting a licking, but I suppose I was too small for them to take very seriously, although I could sting them a bit with my tongue, which was bitter even then.

I had stayed away from school so much, roaming about with my dog Tony, that one day the folks at home threatened to put me in the Reformatory School. Tony and I both cried and I asked him what he would do, and he sort of pointed away to the west where the sun was setting, and I took him as a pointer and determined to make for my aunt's house, about twenty miles away. Tony seemed to understand and at daybreak we set out on the train. It seemed a fearful journey to me then — but remember I hadn't been out of Kokomo and that I was only about thirteen years old. The Reformatory had scared me and I kept thinking I must help myself somehow; I'd surely be the butt of the town if I had to be sent to be "cured."

Tony and I therefore "hiked" it off for "aunt's" — my real aunt, my real mother's sister. She wasn't altogether all over me when I arrived and asked me what I'd come for.

"Come on a visit," said I.

"And yer dog, is he a visitor too?"

"Neither he nor I go where the other doesn't" was the best way I could put it. Then I looked round to see if dear auntie had any grub for me, and Tony put on a sort of inquiring sniff too, all the time trying to make friends with aunt. But she wasn't having any. Later she pulled out some bread and butter and some pie and told me there were rats about the house—that was for Tony's benefit.

She kept on putting questions, asking me this, that and the other about my schooling and what I was going to do for a living, and I had to make the best answers I could.

Then she began to ask whether I was going to stay the night and I repeated that I had "come on a visit."

I soon began to feel that we were outstaying a welcome and after two days my aunt was glad to turn me and my dog out: we *had* outstayed our welcome. She was a good churchwoman and never could hold with my not being the same as all the other folk she knew. Her husband worked on the Pennsylvania Railway and I got no sympathy from him either. Tony and I camped out for a night or two, then I went back home and my adopted mother (Mrs. Blauser—Aunt Lib) asked me, without letting me in the front door, whether I had come for my trunk. Never having had either a trunk or enough clothes to fill even a small bag, I could see also that she meant it. What was I to do?

There was no question but that the situation spelt W-O-R-K, or at all events earning enough to board me, and buy myself a chew and tobacco for my pipe—for I had begun early at the habit which led to sixteen or more coronas a day. Don't forget I was only thirteen years old.

I went to work at the gas and oil wells, and Mr. James Neil took me in. Neil was a foreman master driller and I soon picked up enough knowledge of the engine-work. Two serious explosions in which I nearly lost my life made me get a bit "*fâché*" with the oil-well graft, and when the No. 4 well drill was finished, and Neil got ready to go back to his home in Pittsburgh, I looked out for another job too. It was time: I had been two weeks in linseed oil and lime water after one of the terrible burns from the explosion: it seem to shrivel me even smaller than I was before.

I knew Callaway, who kept a livery stable in Kokomo—the same town, my native place—so I went round to him. He put up and I was handy boy about the yard, doing this, that and the other, sort of general utility turn. But I was so small for the work, and although I was willing enough they were always telling me about my helplessness. Two months therefore saw the end of that.

Down on my luck again, I went on to my real father's place in Marion, also in Indiana, but I could see that there was not enough to support *me* about the house: they were too poor. However, work turned up in a carriage factory. But it was the same old cry—"too small," and I had to beat it from there. They said I was too light for the work: I only weighed fifty pounds. I was an apprentice without pay so there wasn't much lost; naturally I couldn't help support the family.

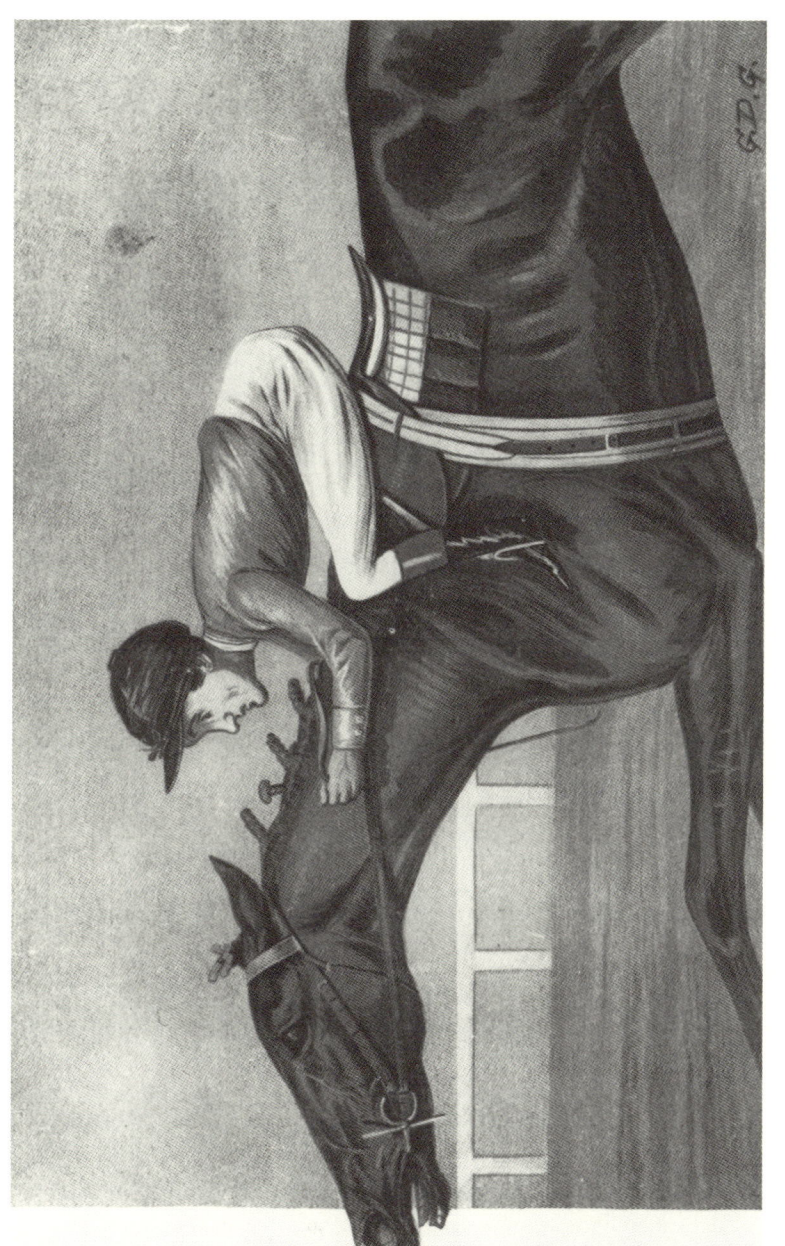

TOD SLOAN
From Spy's caricature in "Vanity Fair"

Then a job turned up in a drinking saloon. I had to sweep up, attend to the glasses, close the shutters and all the time pick up swear words from the customers. I was a useful boy at light jobs but was told after a bit that I was not heavy enough for the sweeping! It was a bit of a knock-out—for I used to put in a lot of elbow and wrist work for what my back couldn't do; in fact I reckoned myself quite an artist with the broom. Still there was nothing else for it but to up and away and get back to Kokomo. I thought I had a better chance there.

Things went on until there was a very important period of boyhood. There was a "Professor" A.L. Talbot, a sort of aeronaut who went about the country going up in his balloon and with all sorts of side shows, including ringing the sticks and pocket knives. He had booths for various things. He had one big balloon on a dray drawn by a team of horses which I always used to admire when they came into "Doc" Callaway's yard.

"Professor" Talbot saw more in me than others had done. We had struck up an acquaintance some time previously, and this time I went along with him. We travelled around and made our own balloons, and when the game got slack we had to hustle and earn our board by making toy balloons for kids. It was my business to go round and peddle them. I tell you I was some salesman, and often think I could have managed a department store if father had taken me by the back of the neck and forced me into business.

I shall never forget the first place we struck—Legrange, Indiana. I was a mite walking beside the hefty fellow that the "Professor" was, and a boy sang out: "Hallo, Talbot, where did you get this one?" Certainly I must have looked a bit comic carrying a big chunk of meat while Talbot had an armful of bread.

The "Professor" shouted back, "Don't you ask sassy question; he can lick you anyway," and then he looked towards me. But I didn't want to fight and I was making myself look smaller than ever, when Talbot said, "Look here, you, if you don't lick him, I'll lick you." So there I was on a hiding to nothing anyway. Well, I sized up the other chap and saw he wasn't much bigger than me. I went for him sharp and, having been a bit of a wrestler among the boys at home, managed to throw him, but he wouldn't let me hit him, rolling over on his face just by a big cedar-tree. I tried to get a fist round by his ears, but he dodged me, and all I could do was to rub his face against the cedar-tree singing out, "You won't be so fresh after this." Really, I don't believe that I had much of a temper before that day but that scrap developed it—or rather started it.

We were quite a happy family with Talbot. We used the horses for riding half-mile races against other horses at the Fair. Talbot used to be the jockey, and afterwards he would ride in circus dress two of them barebacked. He gave capital exhibitions of riding and was a good all-round showman. I never knew where he came from but I should say at some time or other he had been a clown in a circus. He would fight on the slightest provocation and would sometimes suggest by the look of his face that he had been through a pretty rough gruelling the night before. But he wouldn't talk much about all this. It wasn't that he used to get drunk and fly into a brawl at a saloon, but would scrap for the love of it. One day I remember at a country fair he sent me down from the ticket office with a dollar to get small change. I was passing one of the stalls where they were doing the three shell and pea trick. I watched for about ten minutes and at first they took very little notice of the small kid. At last I couldn't stand the temptation any more and I called out, "I'll bet you a dollar that I know where the pea is."

The grafter answered, "I can't bet with you, you're too young and small, but this gentleman can, if you like to give him the dollar."

Of course the "gentleman" was the booster or buttoner—as the tour for three-card game is called in England. Well you can guess what followed; I pointed to the shell and the pea wasn't there. I went away whistling, walked about for a time and then back to our show. Talbot didn't say anything at first; he didn't remember where I'd been, but at last he sung out to me:

"Where's that dollar I give you to get change?"

"I've lost it."

"What do you mean—lost it? How could you do that?"

"Well, not in the way you think: it didn't hop out of my pocket." And I plucked up courage and told him all about it.

Talbot put on his hat and ordered me to follow him. He walked straight over to the shell game, keeping his temper until he said, "You had a bet with this kid here and he lost a dollar."

The man started to deny it, swearing that he had only one bet that morning and that it was with a gentleman who put a dollar on, but Talbot stuck at it and there was a dangerous look in his eye until the man forked up the money. Then he let his fury go. He smashed up the shells, kicked the bench into pieces, shook the guy by the collar, gave him an open hander and a parting kick as he was running away, and added certain injunctions in certain language to the effect that he would do quite a number of things if he saw him at those tricks again. As a matter of fact, we never did see him again.

Of course Talbot's balloons were not filled with gas. He couldn't always get it for one thing, and anyhow it cost too much. They were inflated in the old original way that Mongolfier discovered—with hot air. Talbot was good enough to tell me that I was the best filler he had ever seen. I was very handy with pine logs and oil barrel staves that we had to use in order to get enough hot vapour. One day he was going to make an ascent when a bit of the balloon showed signs of fire. I could see it was smouldering and I sang out to everybody not to let it go. But Talbot was already on the trapeze ready to ascend—he used to do all sorts of monkey tricks in the air on that same swinging bar.

I cried out to him, "Don't go; the balloon's on fire," but he didn't hear and shouted still louder to the men to let go. Just as he started the flames burst out. With the extra heat he went up all the quicker of course, and we could only wonder how soon he would come down. I never thought I should see him alive again. When he got up about fifteen hundred feet the thing was all afire and collapsed, and he came down very swiftly in a field about a hundred and fifty yards away—not exactly with a crash but at a pace at which it might be thought no man could be alive to remember the tale. But he wasn't dead! He was only knocked out. He soon showed signs of life. The scrap of the balloon which was left had broken the fall somewhat. We took him round to the drug store and gave him some brandy. He got up about an hour after and went to a dance. By the way, this all occurred at Cullum, Indiana.

My first experience at building a real new balloon was at Washington, Indiana. I liked the job better than anything I had done, and soon got expert at it. It was after this that Talbot signed a contract to give an ascent and got an extra twenty-five dollars for doing a parachute act in connection with it—neither Talbot nor I had ever seen a parachute, and he told me so, but we got a picture and started in making one. Then he told me that he had promised the public a surprise—to slip his boy out of the balloon. He sprung it on me one morning.

My first ascent was to be at Boonesville Fair. The Professor had promised the people who ran the show a surprise. As a matter of fact he had contracted for an extra twenty-five dollars to "slip his boy" out of the balloon in a parachute! He sprung it on me one morning.

I asked: "Who's the boy?"

He said: "*You* are 'the boy'!"

I answered: "Oh, I am!"

But he saw my face.

"You don't seem to like it, Tod," he said.

"It's all right," I answered. "But what sort of thing is the parachute, the umbrella thing I am to come down in? Shall I be heavy enough to make it open out?"

"Oh, you'll be all right," said the Professor, just as if he were saying "Pass the butter," but I began thinking it over, and the more I looked up at the sky and began to think of having to slip down from the clouds the less I liked it. I began to think how I could dodge it. My brother "Cash" had left home some time before, after a scrap with father. Cash ran down the railway track faster than the old man, and when he stopped it was with a stable of horses.

I had heard from Cash that he was overseer and head jockey of a stable, and he said that if I wanted to join him and become a rider I was to leave Washington, Indiana, at once.

Well, I had to cough a bit and think over what I should say before I told the Professor, but he was very sporting about it; and, as it meant only twenty-five dollars' difference in the pay for the show, he said: "Perhaps you're right; go and join your brother."

And so we parted, and with my "trunk"—about a foot square, easy to carry under one arm and containing a shirt-waist and a pair of stockings, not more, for I was just a kid in knickers—I went off on the railroad train.

I came upon the "stable car," and Cash, midway between Washington and St.

Louis. I saw a little fellow ahead of me hiking a mile down a railroad track as hot as a furnace carrying a pail of water in each hand. He had a long peaked trotting driver's cap, and looked the funniest guy I'd ever seen. I walked up behind him to see who he was, and I heard him whistling—and then, of course, I knew it was Cash.

We embraced like brothers should; I was glad to see him and he me. We sat down by the track and talked things out. We had plenty of hope—but I couldn't focus that talk quite properly through looking at that darned cap of Cash's. I burnt it one morning.

It was here I got hold of another dog. I whistled to him, and was going to steal him, for I'd taken a fancy to him, but the owner came out, and as I had actually got hold of the animal's head there was only one thing to say:

"Do you want to sell this dog, boss?"

He stuck out for half-a-dollar, but I whistled him into taking a quarter. And I had a new companion.

I hadn't by any means got over my fear of horses, but Cash put me at odd jobs, and when we got to St. Louis he made me ride a little, and gradually I got used to it. The stable belonged to Tracy and Levy, and they had two horses called Surprise and Biddy Bowling. It was a pretty easy job to start with, and all I had to do was to lead one of them round after he had done a gallop until he stopped sweating. Then Cash taught me the art of rubbing a horse's legs, and generally "doing" him; but how tired I got! I don't think that ever in my life I really knew what weariness spelt until then. I would hunch myself in a corner with every limb aching. I suppose I got a few muscles to work which had never been asked to come forward and do their bit before. Then they told me that I should have a little bit of exercise jobs, "riding work," as they say in England. It was at Kansas City, and my! how cold it was. I felt frozen, for recollect that I was only thirteen and weighed four stone.

"Up you get on Biddy Bowling and let her walk round the track," someone said, showing me a horse rather like the grey that had given me such a fright. Biddy took a peek at me, and I often wondered what she was thinking of when "Shrimp" Sloan was on her back. At all events she must have thought there was an insect worrying her. She made two or three little Wild West movements, and after I had picked myself up and rubbed the bruises I walked back to the stable. She got there long before I did!

I still hated the whole business, but, as I had gotten into it, I didn't care to slouch off. In any case, to my reasoning little mind, it seemed better than being jerked out of a balloon, for sometimes, when I'd eaten too much supper, I would dream that I was dropping down from the sky with the parachute just out of clutching distance.

I had a chance to go into the stable of Colonel Charlie Johnson, who owned a horse named Jim Douglas. My first ride in public was on this horse, at Pueblo, Colorado. All I had to do was to walk around the ring. Now, Jim stood well over seventeen hands, and was a pretty mean horse, I can tell you. When they hoisted me up he began to walk, then he trotted, and then he broke into a canter. I yelled my loudest for help and lay back tugging with my small arms at the bridle reins. Some of the stable boys came running after me, but Jim must have thought that they were other horses, for he stretched himself out and did a furlong inside thirteen seconds. He swung along until he came to a mud bank, where he shot me off, and then turned round and allowed himself to be led quietly back. We all know that dogs can smile and that tears come into their eyes. I am not sure to this day whether Jim was laughing at me or whether he pitied me. In any case there was no half-and-half idea about what they thought in the stable-yard. One thing was quite certain: I should never make a jockey. They told me so, and I agreed that it wasn't my work; but I was a handy boy, and, instead of getting rid of me, they put me on to cook. I could hardly reach the top of the stove, but the coffee I made was all right, and I got fine and dandy at frying bacon and cooking eggs for the bunch. I remember that I tried my hand at a few other things, but generally had to smuggle the result away to a corner and eat it up myself, until one day I found I could make hot biscuits—like your Scotch scones or small soda cakes, but hot. *They* were some success, and the neighbours would send the ingredients from miles round for me to make them. So we muddled along. I was always thinking that something would turn up, for, although cooking can be a fine art, I was not actually qualifying for a chef. Now at that time I was quite sure that I should never be a jockey, but all the same I would sometimes sit down and ask myself how it was that I was frightened of a horse when I was not scared of other things. But the talk with myself generally left off where it began. I didn't get rid of the idea at the back of my mind that I would like to learn to ride. I kept on figuring to myself that I ought to be able to do as well as the next fellow, but somehow it all left me in a bit of a whirl. Yet I was always coming back to the subject. My brother Cash lost his job with Johnson, and in the spring we went to Denver, and he got a position with a big fellow, named Hank Combs. Then the desire to ride again came back to me. But it took me longer to learn than anyone I ever heard of. I did have another chance of showing what I could do in this stable; but it was the same old story. They found a little chestnut colt for me to exercise, but he threw up his tail and ran away with me into the woods, getting rid of me against a tree. I nearly broke my neck! I didn't remember anything until I found myself lying in one of the attendants' cots. My Denver debut had thus ended in disaster, and I wanted to clear out; but how to get away presented certain difficulties. We had nothing except a little handbag each. Luckily Cash, thinking he was going to be a jockey, had bought about forty dollars' worth of saddlery, caps, etc., and had paid for them. They were coming west to him through the American Express, and by showing the receipt and the way-bill to a fellow in the town he got ten dollars. They didn't put up the bar against youngsters going into pool-rooms and gambling saloons in Denver in those days, and with two dollars of the ten I went into one of them and began to win. I ran the two dollars into fifty. What would have happened next I don't know, but Cash suddenly came to me saying: "For God's sake, give it up; I've lost all my eight dollars, and we shall have to walk if we lose what you've got there." I had a little sense—and we cleared out.

I then found my way to Kansas City and began to work for the trainer Johnny Campbell, whom many may have met in Europe. Campbell had a sort of idea that I was going to be a success. At all events he expected a great deal more from me than I did from myself. He had what he thought a promising colt named Viking. I fear I may have ruined the animal, for as soon as I got on his back, he cleared out with me and ran three and a half miles before he stopped. Well, I ask you—he was only a two-year-old, and a gallop like that was liable to spoil any young animal's career. Johnny Campbell was furious, in fact the maddest man I ever saw in my life. They advised me to keep out of his way, and I was wise to the fact that he'd choke me if he caught me. But I owe a good deal to him, and he was really a kindly soul. Once more I had to have little words with myself and wonder whether it was all worth going on with.

I suppose I screwed up a little more courage gradually. At all events, I wasn't thrown quite so often in next few gallops I had. At last I actually got a mount in a race—at New Orleans, on Lovelace, for the Beverwyck stable, and I finished third. I rode in four other races at the same meeting, but didn't win any. I hated myself, for I didn't seem to improve at all. I may as well be frank about it: the truth is that I was so bad until 1893 that I was byword among trainers. They used to say that if a man didn't want his horse to win he needn't have him pulled. All that he had to do was to send for Sloan. His riding would be handicap enough. Of course, I heard about it all, and it didn't upset me as much as it might have done, for I knew I couldn't ride.

One little sentence however kept mysteriously ringing in my ears: "*You may be able to ride some day.*" Still, this was poor consolation, and, as I was a thinking sort of kid, it hurt me some when the papers made fun of me. I should like to have had a go for two or three of those newspaper men, but I bided my time, without much hope, however. I just kept my tongue between my teeth and didn't talk so much then as I do now. But those papers! When "By" Holly signed me on at the Bay District Track in San Francisco one race writer said that Holly must have engaged me because of the loud clothes I used to wear instead of for any merit I had as a rider.

It was the same old story. I tried and tried and seemed to get worse. I was growing older too—although I never grew up—and I really began to wonder whether it was worth going on with, and in 1894 I decided it wasn't. In thinking about what I should do after determining to give up riding for ever, I made up my mind that I'd go on the stage. I looked about and actually had something in view. At that time, however, I had an unknown friend who took a good deal of interest in me. I found out about it afterwards. It was he who told me to stop all the nonsense about the stage and to go on trying to be a jockey. I shall always be grateful to him. Charlie Hanlon and George Rose really shaped my career. Hanlon made me study horses, and I began to stand better with myself and not wake up in the middle of the night and think I was already a hopeless failure. It wasn't in the stableyard only and on the gallops that I tried to find out all I could. As a matter of fact, I discovered the "monkey-on-the-stick seat" quite by accident at the Bay District Track.

One day, when I and Hughie Penny, who was then a successful jockey, were galloping our horses to the post, my horse started to bolt, and in trying to pull him up I got up out of the saddle and on to his neck. Penny started laughing at the figure I cut, and I laughed louder than he, but I couldn't help noticing that, when I was doing that neck crouch, the horse's stride seemed to be freer, and that it was easier for me too. Before that I had seen a jockey, named Harry Griffin, riding with short stirrups and leaning over on the horse. As he was the best jockey of the day, I put two and two together and thought there must be something in it, and I began to think it out, trying all sorts of experiments on horses at home. The "crouch seat," the "monkey mount," or the thousand and one other ways it has been described, was the result. Then the time came when I determined to put it into practice. But I couldn't screw up enough courage the first time I had a chance. I kept putting it off. At last, though, I did really spring it on them. Everybody laughed. They thought I had turned comedian. But I was too cocksure to be discouraged. I was certain that I was on the right track. I persevered, and at last *I began to win races!*

In the whole the experience I have found that a boy with a nervous temperament makes the best jockey. He is quick and alert to take in a situation, and he becomes a human ferret, finding out things for himself. The Tod Sloan of that day was a bundle of nerves, and he discovered new things every day. I will give you an instance. It was at the Ingleside track at San Francisco that I learned that a horse runs better when "pocketed." Of course it is rough on the nerves of a rider, but the horse breathes in a space where the air doesn't come to him in a rush, and all a rider has to do is to watch his chance and slip through when he thinks the time has come for the effort. He will find his mount fresher and quicker to put it all in. Another thing which I learned about the same time, was that, however tired a horse may be in a race, and no matter how hard it may be for his rider to keep his position, the horse will take on new energy if he gets the chance to go through a gap between two other horses or between a horse and the rails. I have studied horses all my life since the time I have just spoken of, and I am quite sure that it's a kind of compelling instinct.

Mr. Charles F. Hanlon

III

"Monkey on the Stick" in Practice

*Friendship with "Pittsburgh Phil" — Cork Cutter to Millionaire — Qualities
Which Helped Him to Make Three Million Dollars — American
Tick-tacking — Determination to go East*

AFTER THE SUCCESSES SPOKEN OF at the end of 1894 I fell sick in 1895, and Mr. and Mrs. Rose brought me back to Indiana to recover. I had a long bad time of it, but I got well enough to start riding again at the State Fair at Sacramento and beat everything which was fancied. Everything I touched turned to gold; talk about "Get-Rich-Quick Wallingford"; he was nothing to me, and I had chances of making money in speculation right outside racing.

In the autumn of 1895 I went to San Francisco, and it was there that I first met "Pittsburgh Phil." A straighter man never existed on the Turf. I have mentioned that he began life as a cork cutter; his real name was George E. Smith, and in his early days, when putting in all he knew at his work, he could never earn more than one dollar twenty-five cents — that is, five shillings a day. "P.P." occupied a place among racing notabilities that has never been filled, and probably never will. He made a vast fortune despite the fact that he was never liked by the Jockey Club members and was made to feel that he was not desirable to them. He stuck it as long as he could, despite all the terrible difficulties put in his way. The Club's argument was that he was a bad example and did harm to the standing of racing. Years after I remembered all this. Things happened that were kind of echoes!

Now I was always a great friend of Phil. All the same in common with others, I took the same view as the Jockey Club. There is not a man living, however, who could say that "Pittsburgh Phil" was ever guilty of a dishonest action. I was never tired of studying him, and could find new points about him to interest me every day. We would travel together and stay together, but I never knew of his bets, and very few others did either.

It was rather curious that autumn, that all the other jockeys were up against me. It was all the better for me though, because they lost races through watching me too much and not attending to their own and other horses. I had already heard that "Pittsburgh Phil" had been noting me, and had been backing my mounts. Now, Sam Doggett was one of the two jockeys riding for him. Evidently Phil wasn't satisfied with him for some reason or other, for one afternoon he asked me if I would ride his horse next day. I did, and I won, and ever after that "Pittsburgh Phil" was my friend. It was a serious set-back for Doggett though.

I rode many other horses for Phil, and although we lived together, I never knew beforehand if he had backed a horse I was to ride, or whether he had laid against me. He would never tell, me nor any other man, whether he had won or lost, and, as I have said, he was altogether very much like Charles Hannam, in England. He kept his own counsel. You could never tell from his face or from his manner after a race whether things had gone as he wanted them to. He could read a race better than anyone I ever knew. Many a time he would notice something about a horse which finished down the course, and after the race he would say quietly to me: "If you can get the mount on that the next time he runs he'll win," and I cannot call to mind any instance when he failed to be a wonderful prophet.

It was absolutely wrong to believe one of the stories—and there were thousands of them about—of his "method." All those who spoke and wrote about him said he betted entirely on information and could "fix" races and riders—and trainers too. In fact, he was said to have been a perfect bunch of tricks. But it was all untrue. I was closer to him than any other man. He would think and talk nothing but horse, and no one knows better than I do that his success was entirely due to his judgment and level-headedness. He devoted all his hours to a study of racing, didn't smoke and only drank a little white wine.

He had a memory also, which was always an envy to me; in fact his mind was a film from which nothing could be blotted out. He simply was his own handicapper, and it is all nonsense about his employing an army of men to get news. The only people he employed were those who did commissions for him.

We would sit down night after night and talk about such a lot of things, and I enjoyed drawing him out about his early days, and then he would get everything out of me that I had to tell; and he would encourage me to go on and on. He had a quiet way of convincing me, and somehow after a talk with him I would go to bed happy, and dream that I was to go east to New York. In those days, that was as far as my ambition reached.

Phil's own early story—I got it in snatches from him—was that when he was following his humble employment he used to read the papers always, and saw a picture one day of some horses, owned by the Brothers Dwyer, which had won. There was a lot about them that morning, and then the next day he saw that another horse owned by the same stable and ridden by the same jockey, Jimmy McLaughlin, had won. This gave him an interest in the subject and he would never miss the racing news. He noted what owners and jockeys were winning, and he determined finally to have a try at betting himself and went to a poolroom, which may be described, for those who don't know, as an open betting "Club."

Well, Phil backed the Dwyer horses, and at the end of the first week he had cleaned up over a hundred dollars. After that, he told me, "I came to the conclusion that betting on the races was a hell of a game, and a darn sight better than cutting corks, so I threw up my job and told my mother I was going to follow the races."

The way Phil got his nickname came about as follows. In those days in America it wasn't usual to give in betting more than just a short anything in the

"Pittsburg Phil"

way of identity, so he gave his name simply as "Phil," and when he landed in New York with fifty dollars in his pocket, and went to the pool-rooms, the name stuck to him; on the race-tracks he was known as "Phil from Pittsburgh." He went right ahead, and left over three million dollars when he died. For fifteen years he was always plunging, and in his time he pulled off the biggest strokes in the country, betting as much sometimes as fifty thousand dollars on a race. Bookmakers became afraid of him, and he had to be a bit clever in the way of putting his money down. One day out in California, when he wanted to make a big bet on a certain horse, I saw him climb up behind Johnny Coleman's book. "I want to bet a thousand on this one, Johnny," he said; "so if you'll take it, I'll place it all with you instead of going round and causing a panic." Coleman looked round and seeing better prices marked than he was giving didn't hesitate to take Phil's thousand. Then he sent his commissioners out to hedge it off, but beforehand Phil had posted his men at other books and had arranged the signal of raising his hat the minute he got the money down with Coleman. Off went the hat, and his men helped themselves, and when Coleman's runners went to lay it off, the odds had shortened very much. They rushed back and Coleman was hopping mad, for he'd seen through the game right away. Of course the horse won, and that day Phil cleaned up about one thousand dollars.

As I have said, Phil would never tell anyone—not even me—what he was going to do. An instance of this, and of how he could hug judgment to himself, was when we went to see the Fitzsimmons-Corbett fight at Carson City. We went on a special train, and I had no idea what he was going to do until we were at the ring-side. Then he told me he was going to back Fitz. I begged him not to, and the others agreed with me, but he stuck to his opinion, and after the men got in the ring and started fighting he took all the money that was offered him—and there was a lot of it, I can tell you. Johnny O'Neil bet him a thousand dollars where I wouldn't have given him five cents for his chance, and I told him so. I even wanted to bet with him myself that Corbett would win, but he wouldn't bet with me. I shall have a great deal more to say about Corbett when I come to deal with my friendship for him. In this fight it will be recalled that Corbett took a strong lead in the early rounds and drew a lot of blood from Fitz. In the fourteenth round, after Corbett had landed a left-hand hook on Bob's jaw, Fitz got his right in, and them a little later Fitz gets in what was described by the referee as a "sort of cross between a hook and an upper-cut to a point nearer to the pit of the stomach than under the heart." Jim's face was terrible with the agony he was suffering: he was beaten. "Pittsburgh Phil" won "enough."

* * *

I could never get away from the idea that I ought to go east. I had been doing so well where I was. I would discuss it with Phil, and in after years it was said that it was he who had brought me to New York. As a matter of fact, in California, after I had ridden for him, he gave me strong advice *not* to go to New York.

"It's a different game there, son," he said. "You are known here, and you have confidence in yourself, but you'll find it a cold proposition there."

"That's all right, Mr. Smith," I told him; "I have made up my mind to go, and when they begin, and the flag falls at Morris Park, you'll find me on deck."

And he did.

IV

Start in New York

A Westerner Grafting—Meeting Jack MacDonald—A Three-handed Match—"Mac's" Suspicions—Getting Even—Days and Nights with Mr. Fleischman—Control of Stable.

WHAT WAS PRACTICALLY MY PERMANENT ARRIVAL in the East brought no brass bands on the scene, and the newspapers took no kind of notice of me. Although I had been successful in other places, they saw no reason to believe in me.

To begin with, I went out to live at the Woodmanstone Inn in Westchester, near the old Morris Park track, and hung about living quietly on the off-chance of getting a mount; but no one hurried to offer me one. I was comfortable about money, at all events, for a few months ahead. The people in the neighbourhood gave me the cold shoulder. They thought I was simply there hustling and trying to get a chance ride. In fact one of them described me as a "bum jockey from the West who was grafting."

At that time there were six or seven hundred horses being trained in the district, and I would go out in the morning and keep myself fit by riding some of them. Nothing turned up for a time, but I gritted my teeth and determined to get there. One day two odd rides came my way. I knew nothing about either of them, and didn't see the owners. The first was a horse named Runaway. I won on him and then got up on the second, a filly belonging to Mr. MacDonald. She was an outsider and I got her home comfortably. That began a good season.

A day or two after, I was going by train to Westchester from New York. I was reading the paper taking no notice of anyone when a man opposite me and leaned over and said: "How did that filly run with you the day before yesterday?"

Hardly looking up from my paper I cut him short by answering: "All right, I suppose," and went on reading, intending to be silent if he put another question. I had previous experience of being asked things by strangers and I wouldn't have minded showing a little bad manners if this stranger had become too inquisitive. When I got out at Westchester, the stranger got out also.

"I want to speak to you," was the next thing I heard. It was the stranger, who then took a roll of hundred-dollar bills out of his pocket and slipped three of them into my hand: "I'm Mr. MacDonald, that was my filly you rode."

I was taken aback of course, and began to apologise saying: "If I had known who you were of course, I wouldn't have been so rude."

In reply, Mr. MacDonald put his hand on my shoulder: "I like you all the better for it, and you can ride for me whenever you like."

That was the beginning of a long association, and I think it was a regret to both of us when we fell out two years later. It came about like this: There was a three horse race at Sheepshead Bay. MacDonald had a mare called, I believe, Intermission, and she had to beat Hamilton and another named Clifford, a 100 to 1 on certainty. MacDonald thought he was sure to be second with his. He got wind that "Pittsburgh Phil" was wagering heavily on Hamilton to beat his mare for second place, but as I have already mentioned Phil never told me what he was doing, and I had no more idea than the dead which he had backed. As I learned several days later his money, thousands after thousands of dollars, was piled on Hamilton to be second.

Thinking that I knew all about it, MacDonald went to the Stewards and asked permission to take me off his mare and put up another jockey; but was told that they saw no sufficient reason why they should, but they would watch the race very closely and if they saw anything peculiar, they would be the first to take action. He argued, but all his talk was no good; they had spoken the last word. Nothing was said to me by "Mac" and I won the place for him.

"Mac" came to me directly after the race: "That's all right, Tod; you did ride a good race! I thought she'd beat Hamilton, but if it hadn't been for your riding, she wouldn't have done it."

Five days after, two prominent owners went to my principal employer, Mr. Fleischman, and told him to put me wise about what Jack MacDonald had done, adding that before Mac had gone to the Stewards he had told one of them that it was quite certain that Tod was not going to do his best. And all the time I had it all dead set to beat Hamilton! Mr. Fleischman did as was suggested, and as a consequence I went up to "Mac" on the race-track directly afterwards and asked him why he did it, and he tried to explain to me that the race had meant such a lot to him, and as "Pittsburgh Phil" "your intimate friend" had put so much money on Hamilton, he was afraid it might be a great temptation to me to do my pal a good turn.

I told him that I didn't want to know him again, and asked him not to speak to me, and that in any circumstances, I would not ride for him any more.

All the same, I determined to get even with him in some little way if it took me a year or two, and one day I had my chance. I ran him up seventeen hundred dollars over something he had won with in a selling race. He had a lot of niggers working for him, and one of them who was standing by bleated: "Don't run him up, Tod," and Charles Quinn, who was near, said the same thing. My answer was: "Why shouldn't I go against that policeman? 'Mac' would be a dead cop if he had his club and star; he looks lonesome without a uniform."

Of course "Mac" was wild, but I felt satisfied.

I never knew what Phil lost over Hamilton, but as there were about two hundred bookmakers there that day, and everyone went mad gambling, I should say that it must have been a big order. However, I can remember many good things about MacDonald and only tell what I have, because many in America will remember all about it.

It was later in the season when I first met and rode for Mr. Charles Fleischman, a wealthy owner with a very large string of horses in training. He secured first call on me. His patronage to begin with, and his friendship and intimacy with me afterwards, make one of the happiest memories of my life. He was a man of about sixty-six, owning a beautiful yacht, the *Hiawatha*. He had two sons, Julius and Max, who at that time did not take any active part in racing. Mr. Fleischman would glory in sitting up half the night gambling. His peculiarity, or rather amusement, was to be taken for a mug, and when he was gambling and had perhaps won seven or eight thousand dollars he would never stop playing until he had lost all he had won, or had given it away. We used in those days sometimes to play at Daly's gambling-house in 29th Street, New York, and sometimes I would be three or four thousand dollars to the bad, but it would never occur to him that he should help me out at all, although he was always most liberal in other things. Apart from a personal regard for me — in fact, he treated me like his his own son — he liked me for sitting up all night with him and not wanting to go to bed. Sometimes I would go to the length of saying that he couldn't expect me to do my best on his horses the next day, but he would answer that it didn't matter a bit. We would drive down at three or four o'clock in the morning to the bay in a buggy or wagon, and go aboard the *Hiawatha* for three hours' sleep.

In that first season I was with him, I found that he had determined to quit racing before I joined him, for he felt he wasn't getting a proper return for his money. But all the time he was dead keen on the game. He would talk it out with me all the time we were together. I remember him as the dearest old man and so amiable that my affection for him grew every week. One day he told me that he would go on for another season if I would sign on again as first jockey for the stable, and I agreed on certain conditions.

"The conditions being money?" he asked.

"No, it isn't that," I explained.

"Well, let's deal with the money first: I'll give you twelve thousand dollars retainer. Is that enough?"

"More than enough, Mr. Fleischman; but my conditions are that I have full control of the stable and that a new trainer shall be brought in."

He agreed at once, and I engaged Tom Welch, a real honest trainer of horses — now located in France — and a number of new hands. Mr. Fleischman had got rid of his agent for the stable, and his nephew William Fleischman came to me saying that I might suggest him for the job and he got it. We had a splendid start the next season, winning race after race, and everything went as smoothly as could be wished. Unhappily, however, the poor man didn't live to see the big things we did with his horses. With his death there was a doubt for a moment what would happen with the stable, but luckily his sons decided to carry it on.

At one time Mr. Fleischman, and all the rest of us, thought that Max would turn out a regular "sport," but he never carried out the promise. He took most interest in the business and the yacht.

Old Mr. Fleischman, apart from his gambling in the Faro banks, would bet on every race of the day on the course, and no matter what he was told, he would seldom back another horse if I had a mount. I put it to him that a man was liable to go broke doing that, but he would never pay any attention. He would answer: "Look at the fun I have had! Never mind, if I have lost to-day, I'll bet like hell on you tomorrow." I never went to see him in Cincinnati, but I have been to his country home in the Catskills.

When he came to New York for ten or twelve days for the racing he would smoke a little and drink a little and would order a good dinner, but he would never give the cook a chance; he'd hurry over the meal too much, looking again and again at his watch. All he wanted was to get to the gambling-tables. Little did I think when I used to go to the grocery store when I was a kid to buy a tin-foil packet of Fleischman's Compressed Yeast that later on I should be riding for him and be his intimate friend. His firm made a deal of money out of the wastage from the manufacture of yeast. Especially vinegar and alcohol, I believe. I know the stable used to be able to get a demijohn of the alcohol—two or three gallons—the stuff they use on horses after gallops, for the equivalent of a shilling.

In spite of his gambling, Charles Fleischman left between fifteen and twenty million dollars.

V

W.C. Whitney's Liberality

His First Good Horse—Heavy Bettor—A Wonderful Futurity—Fourteen-Thousand-Dollar Present—Getting Me Out of a Bad Deal—Cablegram from Lord William Beresford

I FIRST MET Mr. William C. Whitney at the time that he had second call on me. It was in 1898. He had first call on me the following year after my contract with Fleischman and Featherstone.

W.C. Whitney will be remembered as having been the most popular man in American racing. As far as racing was concerned, I want to say right here that he knew very little about horses and he must have sunk a stack of money in his racing ventures. He didn't become interested in the Turf until late in life, and his career did not, after all, extend over so many years. I have always said that to know horses intimately, you must be raised with them. Of course, his son Harry Payne Whitney has forgotten more than his father ever knew, for he has been round among horses, hunting, driving, riding and racing, ever since he was a boy.

It was John E. Madden who was principally responsible for Mr. Whitney going on the Turf. Madden has bred and raced more good horses than any other man in America, excepting James R. Keene. Madden saw to it that Mr. Whitney started well. If I remember correctly Hamburg was the first big purchase Mr. Whitney made, and that was due to Madden, although I can take some credit for it, for I told Mr. Whitney when he asked me that Hamburg was worth any price he would pay for him; and, although it may sound funny to some people, I do not hesitate to say that Hamburg, with the possible exception of Santoi, was the only great race-horse I ever rode. He was one of the sweetest-dispositioned horses that ever raced. You could place him anywhere you liked and he would always do his best. He loved to race, as every good thoroughbred does, and you never saw such a beggar to do his level best under all conditions, and he had none of that devil you meet with in some of the greatest. I was never beaten on him.

When he had been on the Turf a little while, Mr. Whitney, although he loved the sport for its own sake as much as any man I have ever known, began to bet very heavily. He liked to win, and would say so, but he never talked of winnings or losses, and not a soul could tell how he stood after a race.

Another purchase I advised Mr. Whitney about, and one that made a bit of history, was a little mare named Martha. He would pay any price for a horse that I said was worthwhile, and I had told him at Saratoga that Martha was sure to win back her purchase money, and he answered: "All right; go ahead and buy her." I did, and she more than won herself out. The sequel of it may as well be told here. Martha turned out to be one of the best brood mares in America. Two or three years afterwards, I had been riding in Liverpool—in England of course—and on returning to London I found a message telling me to call on Mr. Whitney at the Bristol. I had just ridden a mare called Maluma in the Liverpool Cup, and got the only real bad fall of my life. My right ear was almost torn off and my face so scratched and cut that it looked as if someone had used a currycomb on it. A great surgeon at Liverpool, Sir Tudwell Thomas, had sewn my ear on again, and I appeared before Mr. Whitney with my head in bandages and one eye closed. He looked at me for a minute and then laughed and said: "Well, how does the other fellow look?"

It appeared that he had sent for me to ask if I would like to go to America to ride his horse in the Futurity, the richest race in America, but seeing me in such bad shape he said he supposed there could be no chance of my caring for such a journey.

"Never mind about the chance," I answered. "I'll go all right and I shall be able to ride."

He persisted in saying that he didn't think I would be able to manage it, especially as the Futurity was only about two weeks off, but he gave me five thousand dollars for my expenses and I went aboard ship.

Well, I rode his colt Ballyhoo Bey and won the Futurity. It was a great regret to me that Mr. Whitney was on the ocean at the time and didn't see the race. Then I rode the same colt in the Flatbush a week later and won agin. It was not until after that that I heard that Martha, the little mare I had bought for him at Saratoga, was the dam of Ballyhoo Bey. Speaking of that same Flatbush, it was about the funniest race I ever rode in or heard or. Some of the other jockeys had framed it to "do me up." I had more than an inkling of it myself already and Winnie O'Connor, who did not have a mount in the race, came to warn me. "These boys think you are a buttin, Tod," he said, "and they are going to try and fix you; be on your guard." I told him I could take care of myself and when we went to the post I asked the starter, Christopher Fitzgerald, about it.

"I have heard a rumour of some such thing," he said. Then he made a little speech to the jockeys: "If I see the slightest thing out of the way here I'll report the matter to the Stewards and I tell you it will go hard with the boys who are guilty." The start was good, and I dropped in behind two other horses, with Spencer on Tommy Atkins just a little behind me. I stayed in the "pocket" taking my time, and I saw through the trick by the way the two in front kept looking back at me. On we went, and just before we crossed the main track, I moved up as if I wanted to go through. They parted immediately, but instead of going into the opening I pulled out to the right and dashed ahead. Spencer fell into the trap laid for me: he tried to dash through the gap and with the two riders in front closing in on him, Tommy Atkins went down on his knees with his nose to the ground, and I was away off in front. Tommy Atkins was the best horse in the race and should have won without an effort, for although he lost twenty-five lengths by that stumble, I only beat him by a head. When he got home after that race Mr. Whitney was one of the most delighted men I ever saw. He and I walked around the lawn behind the club-house and he made me sit down with him on a bench.

"I haven't given you anything for winning the Futurity," he said, "except that five thousand dollars you had in London for travelling expenses. See, I'll give you all I have in my pocket," and he pulled out a roll of notes and handed nine thousand dollars to me, and then, after a pause, he took out his watch and gave me that too. "Now you have all I've got," he added, and shook my hand. What a man!

Mr. Whitney was the most even-tempered man I have ever known, and he had keen judgment. No wonder we all liked to serve him well. While he was the soul of geniality he was no "handshaker," and everyone who had dealings with him knew that he wasn't to be "buncoed." I have spoken of his great generosity, and one instance of it was when one day I went to his house on Fifth Avenue. After a little casual talk and looking round at his pictures and furniture, I told him I was in a hole: "I have been gambling in stocks and I'm in bad." A man had told Ned Gilmore, Charlie Hoyt and me in the Fifth Avenue Hotel that sugar would go to a certain point. I had taken the tip and as a result I was pretty nearly fifty thousand dollars to the bad.

"I didn't know you gambled in stocks, Sloan," Mr. Whitney answered; "and I am sorry to hear of it now. That is a game you should keep away from. You musn't expect me to approve of it; stick to your own business." Just as I was going away he added: "I don't see how I can help you, but if you buy about five thousand shares of American Tobacco and go to sleep on the deal until there is a ten points' rise, I think you may pull out all right, but, mind you, I guarantee nothing. Cut it all out is my advice to you."

I bought the Tobacco stock, leaving a limit of ten points and went to California. And then one day when I was standing in a duck marsh during a day's shooting, I was handed a telegram telling me I had made a hundred and ten thousand dollars. My luck was talked about and much exaggerated at the time. I was reported to have cleaned up half-a-million dollars, but the figure I give is exact.

Although he became so keen on racing Mr. Whitney never came out to the stables in the early morning at the hour when Mr. Keene and other big owners we all know, like to see the horses gallop, but he loved to be around horses, and would drive over in the afternoon and loaf about, looking over the boxes and chatting with the stable-boys. Every one of them would have done anything for him. I think his favourite track was Saratoga and quite early in his racing days he determined to build it up. He often told me he intended to make a Newmarket of it, and it was mainly due to him that it became so successful. He built up the Turf after his experiences in England; he was always talking of the English ways of doing things.

The whole story about my first experiences in England will be told later, but in 1897, before going away from Liverpool, Lord William Beresford said he wanted me to come over for the autumn of 1898. I answered: "If you want me to come, cable to Mr. Whitney." They did not know each other. The result was that one day at

Saratoga, in 1898, Mr. Whitney sent for me: "Sloan, I have just received a letter from Lord William Beresford asking me if I can let you go to England." He read me a sentence: "'The opportunity looks big for Sloan to come: we have some good horses.'"

Now I was carrying a cable from Lord William in my pocket but I had felt backward about asking Mr. Whitney to release me and I told him so. "Well," he replied, "Lord William is a fine fellow, and I would like to oblige him, so if you want to go, we will try and get along without you. Stay for the Futurity, and after that you can go if you are still of the same mind—that is, of course, if Mr. Julius Fleischman gives permission."

I thanked him and he wished me good luck, saying he might go to England himself. And he did, and I introduced Lord William and Mr. Whitney to each other at Newmarket. He bought out Pierre Lorillard's interest in the stable, and he and Lord William went into partnership and I rode for them. I am always thinking of him, and everyone knows what racing lost in America when he died. Racing might not have had the set-back which it did had he lived.

While I have said that Mr. Whitney was fond of betting, I must add he was one of those men like the late King Edward, Lord Dunraven, and others, who would rather any horse of theirs won a race purely for the pleasure of beating the other horses than win thousands simply by betting. I believe that Mr. Whitney would have tried, if necessary, to keep racing going without a single wager on a single track. But of course it is difficult to imagine that racing could go on without betting.

VI
First Trip to England

*Misery in London—Cold Shoulder at Newmarket—My First Gallop—
Preparing St. Cloud II—Covering Fifteen Miles—First Appearance on a
Course—Beating the Gate—Losing Yet Winning the Cambridgeshire—
Lord William's Kindness—A Week of Successes*

LATER ON there will be scores of characters I have met and horses I have ridden to talk about, but as I finished up my last chapter by writing about my English career, it might perhaps be a good thing to tell here how I made my first start for London and my innings as a jockey in England and France from 1897 to 1900.

In the summer of 1897 Mr. James R. Keene sent for me to his down-town office in New York. "Sloan," he said, "I've got a horse, St. Cloud II, in the Cesarewitch and the Cambridgeshire. My trainer, Pincus, thinks he has a good chance. I have been thinking over the advantage of getting you to ride him. Would you like to go over to England?"

It didn't take me long to answer: "I certainly would."

"How soon could you go?"

"To-morrow."

"Well, I don't want you to decide so quickly."

However, the matter was settled then and there, and I sailed on the following Wednesday, 17th September, on the *Majestic*, and landed in England with Ed Gains, the walking man, whom I took with me. There was no one to meet me, and feeling as lonely and out of the swim as a fish on land, I went to the Savoy Hotel. I knew absolutely no one, not even Mr. Keene's trainer, Jake Pincus, who although American, had by long residence been turned into a regular Britisher. Pincus, of course, was the man who trained Iroquois, the only American horse who ever won an English Derby. He was at one time a rider himself.

How well I remember roaming round that hotel! It all seemed so cheerless and I was so homesick that I nearly cried. I felt better when I went and had dinner at the old Simpson's Restuarant. It was the food, I think, which made me feel a bit as if I was having a home meal. In those days, especially when I was working, I could have eaten a horse, I had such an appetite, and I didn't put on extra weight through it, either. When the time came for going to bed, everything was so lonesome that I nearly found myself looking at steamship time-tables.

However, I had found out where Newmarket was and how to get there, and went there two days after my arrival. On arrival, the first thing I did was to go straight to see Mr. Pincus who lived in some rooms over a public-house kept by

Martin. He had heard of my coming, but at the same time I can't say that he was inclined to take any particular interest in me; in fact, the name "Tod Sloan" spelt nothing to him. We talked a bit and I found he had become more English than American. They were going to gallop St. Cloud II the next morning, he told me, and added that I had better be out on the heath to meet the horses. I told him that I thought it would be better if I walked the horse out myself, so as to warm him up myself.

He took a good look at me and answered: "You aren't used to Newmarket. There will be a lot of other horses about. The horse's usual lad had better be on him until the time came for the gallop."

I could see that he didn't think much of me, so I said quietly: "If that's so, then the boy had better ride him in the gallop too."

He seemed a little annoyed, but finished up the talk by saying: "Just as you like. You had better be at the stable at seven in the morning."

He was a great big devil, St. Cloud II, standing about seventeen and a half hands, but he walked out all right to the gallops. The boys were sniggering, and when we did a light canter they tried to guy me. The horse went sweetly with me. Then the boys started whispering. I heard one of them say: "Wait till he comes the other way." Presently they put Quibble to lead me a gallop, and St. Cloud II seemed to like me even better, for he stretched along and I found out he was no end of a nice horse. That was all which was done.

I hung about Newmarket making the acquaintance of a few people at the Rutland, and got up on St. Cloud once or twice again. It was all very dull, and no one seemed to want to make friends with me.

The following week was the First October Meeting and not a ride came my way. I went down to the post on a pony I had got hold of and I watched the starts and felt as if I could beat the best of them. At last, I had a mount or two on bad horses without any chance at all. I shall never forget the way all those in the ring and on the stands behaved to me the first time I cantered out. It was my first appearance. They had seen no one riding with what they called the "Monkey-on-the-stick" seat and a big laugh went up. It must have been mighty funny to them. I know I didn't appreciate it myself. However I stuck to my colours, although as I didn't win, I began to think that I might, after all, be wrong, and I even commenced to ask myself whether the English sporting writers weren't right when they said I couldn't ride at all. Lord William Beresford spoke to me kindly, however, and said I *could* ride, and he let me know he believed in me. I dare say he realised how much his words bucked me up and made me determined to show them a thing or two. The first race I won was on the horse named Quibble. It was the first time they ever tried the starting machine, and one of the people who were exploiting it got it into his head that I was against it and had been doing all I could to queer it. So I thought I would show him! Now I had had experience with the new invention in America, and, as I say, it was only an experiment on the part of the Stewards. The other riders were strange to it, and while they were getting ready after the barrier flew up, I was 'way off and nearly quarter finished before they started. I am afraid my win in that race came very nearly finishing the chance of the starting machine in England. I know that it was not taken up until two years after.

Meanwhile I had been riding St. Cloud in preparation for the Cesarewitch. A few days before the race came his winding-up gallop; it was out on the Limekilns. What with walking to the course, and trotting round, we covered quite a lot of ground before being told to canter for a distance which must have been over four miles. By the way, these canters in England I found out to be in many cases really half-speed gallops! The horse went well, and I thought on pulling up that his work was surely finished for the morning, when after about ten minutes, Pincus said, "Now we're going to gallop him." "Going to *gallop* him, Mr. Pincus? Why, look what he's done already!" I felt like getting off, but thank goodness I didn't, for if I had, they would have put one of the lads up and the horse would have been ruined. As it was, I spared him, although there was a horse to take him along and another one to join in when half the distance had been covered. With one thing and another, he must have covered 15 miles that morning, and in my opinion his chance for the Cesarewitch four days later was ruined. I know that in that race he was the tiredest horse you ever saw. It was a pity! Luckily for the horse, he was eased up after the Cesarewitch until the Cambridgeshire, a race I shall always think that I won.

In this second race, my theory was that I was winning all the time and that I led all the way. The big fellow travelled with me as if he knew exactly what he had to do. I saw one after the other drop out, and from the Bushes home there were only three of us: I had to watch Sandia, who I always kept almost clear of; Sir William Ingram's horse Comfrey was on the other side of the course. I was confident that I had the race in my pocket, but I kept the big horse going nicely all the same, and the charge against me of over-confidence was not merited. As a matter of fact, I shall always believe it—in fact I *know*—that Comfrey, who was given the race, was only third, Sandia being second, three quarters of a length from me. There was no one more surprised than I was myself, and, in my trouble, I may have said that the race had been "stolen from me." But I made no charge whatever against Mr. Robinson, the judge, a gentleman I have always had respect for. What I did say in my disappointment was certainly twisted round. The next day Mr. Robinson came with a newspaper man to the jockey's room and asked me exactly what I did say about him. I told him frankly that I thought I had won, but I never uttered one word against his honest conviction that he had seen the race in the way he had placed them. My opinion, as I told him, was that the width of the course and the fact that the judge's box was set so low between them made it almost impossible to judge a finish correctly. He listened very pleasantly to me and said he was quite certain that I had not been outspoken about him personally. Of course, it's a long time ago and makes very little difference now, but that race has always stuck in my gizzard, and I shall always wish that someone had taken a photograph of the finish.

I was very upset, but Lord William Beresford came up to me afterwards and said, "Don't worry yourself; we think you won, and perhaps you shall ride for me on

LORD MARCUS BERESFORD AND MR. RICHARD MARSH

Friday." I should explain that Cuthbert, who was a book-keeper or secretary to Lord William's stable, had already told me that there might be a mount for me on Meta on Friday, for Wood didn't want to ride her, as he had had the offer of the mount on a semi-certainty in the same race. But it was clear that he did want to ride Sandia, in the same stable, on the same afternoon. I dare say Cuthbert thought that when I found I couldn't ride Sandia in the bigger race, I would refuse the mount of Meta. I had more sense. "I'll ride her all right," I said. I did, and I beat Wood a head on his hot favourite!

Lord William was so pleased with me that Friday afternoon that he announced: "You shall ride Sandia too. Let Wood hunt up another mount." And I won the Old Cambridgeshire on him. Those were the days when that race used to finish at the top of the town.

Mr. Martin, above whose bar I used, as I have said, to live with Pincus, had been kind to me, and he had made up a shooting-party for the following day, Saturday. I was very anxious to have a go for the first time in my life at the pheasants. Well, just after Sandia had won, Lord William came to me and said, "I want you to ride two for me at Hurst Park to-morrow."

"Impossible," I replied in my "fresh" way. "I'm going to a shooting-party."

"Never mind your shooting!"

"I can't put it off. Mr. Martin has got it up specially in my honour," I said—and I meant it.

Lord William put his hand on my shoulder and said quietly, "Now, little man, you have to come to Hurst Park; I'll see Martin."

I was going to stick to my guns, but Lord William had a sort of way with him, and in the end I went to Hurst Park, and I think I actually won both races. One race I won readily enough, and the other they didn't give me, saying that I had lost a short head! Mistakes will happen.

Now that was a pretty good week's work. My reputation in England had begun. For my own pleasure, I may as well add, that although Lord William chaffed me about that party with Martin which didn't come off, he made it up to me by letting me shoot with him and his party in Deepdene, Dorking.

VII
Talks With Lord William Beresford

Character and Disposition of Horses — A Take-down at Leicester — Buying a Trotter — Myself Against the Horse-swapper — Diddled Warwick in a Fog

THE MORE I SAW of Lord William Beresford the kinder he seemed to become to me, and the more interested he became in what I was doing. He was always anxious to know what rides I was getting, and to influence others to put me up. In 1897, he was staying at the Adelphi Hotel at Liverpool for the Autumn Meeting, and several times he asked me round to his apartment, where he would sit "talking horse" to me for hours together. Sometimes others would come in but I think he liked better to chat alone. Especially he was interested in the instinct of horses — not any particular English horses that I was just then riding, but those whose characters or dispositions I had really studied. Some of the things about which he drew me out may be put down here, for as the topic interested him, so it must others.

I have always had rather a reputation for doing more with horses who are bad tempered and sulky than other jockeys, but I don't take much credit for this. I told Lord William that it was simply because I knew that horses don't like to be bullied, and I also told him that I had managed to find out the peculiarities of one or two of his own horses, and that I would play up to them accordingly. For instance, I remember a colt named Lake Shore on whom I won four races straight off the reel. He was considered an awful sulker and sluggard. As a matter of simple fact, he was nothing of the kind. He got his bad reputation because the boys made the mistake of trying to keep him up to his work by riding him too hard. I found out that it was necessary to fool him. He would not be bullied. He became angry directly anyone on his back started — as they generally did — by kicking and pulling at him and whipping him too. My way with him was, just at the start, to behave as if I were trying to control him. I would tug at his bridle a bit and then I would relax. That made him think I had given it up — the struggle I mean — and he would strike out for all he was worth under the impression that he'd conquered me. He nearly always won when ridden that way, because he did his best — *on his own account.*

One day at Liverpool there was a bad mix-up and two horses came down. Now, from what I have seen, I am quite sure that nine times out of ten when a horse falls, it is the fault of the rider. When a jockey gets in a scramble or a tight place, he is apt to pull his horse's head about from sheer fright until the animal loses control of his action. Then, if he strikes into another horse, down he goes. But if he is allowed to fight out his own battles, he is most apt to win out. Talking about falls and a horse's instinct, only in few cases have I known a thoroughbred to step on a jockey who had fallen in a race. If a boy will lie quite still when he is thrown, the chances are that he will escape without a scratch from a horse's hoofs. I found this out once when riding in a field of seventeen at Nashville. I fell and nearly all the horses actually went over me and not one of them ever touched me.

While I am writing of my attempts to get horses to take to me, I may as well tell of the only one that wouldn't. He was an animal named Little Silver and I knew him first in California. Somehow I couldn't stand the sight of him. I never knew why it was, but sometimes I thought it was because I was afraid of him. I hated it every time I had to ride him. I only won on him once for he wouldn't try with me. But a kid named Eddie Jones, an exercise boy, could take him out and win on him. He knew Jones and they liked each other, just as two men do. It must have been a case much like that of Diamond Jubilee and Herbert Jones in England. Of one thing I am quite sure: you can get a real friendship with a horse, and some horses, as we all know, develop real affection for men, or boys, or goats, or dogs, and even cats, and they are jealous and nervous when the objects of their affection are away. I remember discussing all these points and instances with Lord William at Liverpool that time. I shall have some more to say about the question later on.

Lord William would often laugh at some of the experiences I had that autumn (1897) when I was riding and when he didn't happen to be there to help me with his knowledge and advice. For instance, I was induced to go down to Leicester by an owner-trainer who had a horse called—Well, never mind. He was very serious about it. I just had to go. Well, when I got to the course, I found that he told some of my friends that they could bet on his horse. This made me so mad, then and afterwards, because if I had chosen, I could have ridden the winner, who, by the way, started favourite. The small man kept me to my promise, and I know he had a bet himself, and that he succeeded in influencing my friends. Judging from the manner we went down to the post, I wouldn't have taken a pound to a penny on my mount's chance. Before we'd gone the first two hundred yards, I was half the distance behind the others and the lot had passed the post before I was much more than half-way home. All the boys laughed at me. Rickaby and Sam Loates were the worst! The owner came to the jockeys' room after the race, but when I saw him I couldn't help saying, "You had better get away from me."

I wouldn't even look at him, I was so mad.

"I'll sell my horse, for I've got another one, ten pounds better than he is," he said after a time.

"Then sell him," I answered, "at whatever you can get for him. If you have any relations in the meat for animals line of business, you'll know what to do."

I acknowledge it now: I couldn't stand the ridicule: Fancy Sloan not being able to get a gallop out of a horse! I was properly taken in—in fact it was the worst takedown of my life, with one exception, and I may as well tell that story here too.

I was living at Redbank in New Jersey, with Johnny Campbell. It was the ambition of all the boys about a stable, and especially those who had a little bit of money, to possess a trotter and a buggy. I had a bank roll of about seven hundred and fifty dollars. Well, one day when I was idling about, a fellow I had never seen before went past me slowly in a buggy. A boy who had come to our boarding-house two days before—he was "planted" there I fancy—said that he knew him. "Here's So-and-so," said the boy; "he's a big horse-dealer."

The guy called out to me, "Like a spin?" and having nothing to do that afternoon in I hopped. We went off at a fine lick; that horse could trot. After a while I said to my new friend: "Look how he's sweating; my! it's pouring off him."

"Well it ain't to be wondered at," he replied, the trotter goin' faster all the while; "we've been to Long Branch and back this afternoon, and that's going some!"

I didn't wonder any more, for it was a big journey at the time. He shook the horse up then, and I kept feeling how much I should like to be behind him again.

After another minute or two—for I was thinking and he didn't interrupt me—the horse-dealer said to me: "Yes, he's a fine horse: there's a feller been after him and I've sold him for four hundred dollars."

"How old is he?" I chipped in.

"Well, he's really about eight or nine, but I said he's seven," and he winked and shook the animal up again. "I'm going to deliver him to-morrow," he went on, "with the buggy and harness thrown in for the four hundred."

That was too much for me. "You're going to deliver him today," I jerked out in a commanding sort of way; "you are going to sell him to *me*."

"I can't do that," he explained, as if he were apologising already to the other man; "what would he think of me?"

"Never mind what he thinks of you, the horse is *mine* I tell you"—and so he was. I paid over the stuff that night.

Before the dealer left he said, "There is only one thing I want off that harness: it's those little plates with my initials on the blinkers," and he added, "I'll be round in a day or two to get them: my wife would never forgive me if I didn't get those plates."

I had asked no one's advice about the horse, and the next morning I started to take my pride and joy out for a spin on my own. I felt proud of my choice and really I didn't think it worth while to consult anyone else about it. Hadn't I been in a livery stable and didn't I know as much as the next fellow? Well my brother Cash turned up just as I was going to put the horse in the buggy. The first thing he did was to start laughing. My horse could hardly stand, let alone walk! He was eaten up with rheumatism! Of course, the dealer had warmed him up the day before. He had never let him stand still a minute, but jogged him one way and the other when I got in and out, or whenever we ought to have stopped.

I think I got forty dollars for the harness and buggy, but where the horse went to I forget. He never was any good. I never saw him again. His age was not a day less than seventeen.

Lord William used to say that I never seemed to do so well when he wasn't with me. He was right. Another time was when I was induced, much against my will, to go to Warwick. At first I had refused, but some of those around me who would bet on anything I rode, argued about it: "Tod, we hear that one or two of those mounts you are offered can go a bit; you may as well ride." Still I stuck out. At last, however, I did agree. It was foggy when I arrived near the place. I had been to Stratford-on-Avon that morning, wanting, as all good Americans do, to see Shakespeare's birthplace. I remember we drove over from Stratford to Warwick. Getting near the race track the mist got thicker and thicker; I had never seen the course before, and it was a case of groping one's way to the starting-post. I thought to myself that I'd stick behind some other fellow in the race and depend on his knowing the way. The starter told us all to get as near to him as possible so he could see us. We hunched in together and at last he got us off. I stuck to the jockey guide, a small boy that I had selected for the purpose, but he didn't know the course either! We struck a patch of fog so thick that you could hardly see your hand before you. At last the two of us landed in the middle of a field somewhere and had to walk back to the paddock, about twenty minutes after the others.

I was just inside the jockeys' room when the trainer, a man with a very small stable, rushed in saying, "Hurry up or you'll be late to weigh out; you know you're to ride mine."

"I'm not to ride again; it isn't riding at all out there," I answered.

He began bullying me, and threatened to bring me before the Stewards. Indeed he rushed out to do so, but in less than a minute came the notice that the rest of the programme had been postponed or abandoned!

VIII
Second Impressions of England

Officials' Kindness – Liverpool Jumping Course – Never a Drink While Racing – Laid Out at Kempton – My Opinion of Democrat, and – Lord William's

I HAVE OFTEN BEEN ASKED for some of my other impressions on my first start in England in 1897. I certainly noticed the jockeys were very nicely treated, and one thing I had never seen in America were the luncheon tickets which were given to us. The officials were pleasant too. Mr. Joseph Davis of Hurst Park, Mr. Manning, the Clerk of the Scales, and Mr. Arthur Coventry and several others were particularly kind to me. There was a time in America when they tried to treat jockeys like a lot of monkeys. I remember one man over there who was promoted from one job to another until he became a sort of superintendent of the paddock – Paddock Judge they called him. This man was always suggesting to the Stewards something new which would, in his opinion, prevent this, that and the other "abuse" and keep the Turf with regard to jockeys "clean." One day, as the result of his suggestions, an order came that all the boys had to be in the jockeys' room at one o'clock, and that they were not to leave it until it was time to go to the post, and that they had to come right back after the race until it was their turn to ride again. In fact, they were to be caged up like a lot of monkeys. I wouldn't stand for it. I said I wouldn't ride if I had to. The idea of such a fool thing preventing any fraud if fraud was intended!

That reminds me of a certain trainer who, in the autumn of 1897, saw me walking about the paddock at Lingfield instead of being in the jockeys' room. He came up and said, "Aren't you going to ride? I want you to get up on one of mine."

Now I knew he was a fellow who had written a newspaper article a few days before, in which he had said that I should be penalised, that I ought in fact to put up extra weight, because my "seat on a horse was unfair." But he didn't know that I knew about it.

"Am I to carry a penalty," I asked him, "for riding as I do?"

"No, of course not," he replied, affecting to laugh, but looking rather foolish.

"But didn't you write an article saying that my seat was unfair?"

He answered that that was all newspaper stuff.

"Did they pay you for the article?"

"No, they do all my business for me."

"Then get them to ride your horse for you, too."

I told Jack Watts the story. I remember that he never stopped laughing about it. By the way, I shall always think that Watts was the best English rider of the old school I ever saw. I liked him very much, really liked him. I don't say it because he was hospitable to me.

They used to think that when I first arrived in England, I was fogged with the English money, but I had gotten used to it coming over in the *Majestic*. Before that, I had only seen it—bank-notes I mean—once. It was when Charlie Mitchell was in America. I had just met him, and I was going out in a carriage to the old Guttenburg track. I picked up Charlie Mitchell and took him with me. He asked me what they charged to go in, and pulled out a bunch of English notes. They still look to me like writing-paper. I hadn't any money with me, I remember. Mitchell gave an English fiver to the gate-keeper, but that worthy wouldn't take it: he had never seen one before. We asked several people if they could change one of the notes, but without success. It looked as if Mitchell would be shut out till after the first race. After a time I left him. I went inside and found a bookmaker named Ike Thompson to change a bundle of notes into American money for Charlie. As a sequel I think he had a tenner on the only winner I rode that day and came out well to the good, for mine, a horse name Osric, was an outsider. Mitchell was delighted.

A novelty to me in England was the sight of the steeplechase jockeys at Liverpool. I saw them for the first time at the Liverpool Autumn Meeting. I had never seen cross-country riders so tall and big. I didn't know any of them, but I didn't let that prevent my staring. Not one of them offered to make friends with me. Perhaps they looked upon me as a curiosity, a kind of monkey. In the morning, I had gone out on the course and had a look at the fences. It was all so colossal that it almost took my breath away. Of course, the jumps were greater and stiffer than anything I had ever seen in America. It was in the Grand Sefton I first saw them. To see the horses going out into a country looking as if they were never coming home again, is the greatest sporting living picture imaginable. I didn't have a chance of seeing the Grand National till 1899. That, of course, was more wonderful still.

Lord William would sometimes wonder at my appetite in the evening at Liverpool and Manchester. He had heard of my good work with the knife and fork at Simpson's. There I could eat three orders of beef with vegetables, and then switch off on to the saddle of mutton. In hotels like the Adelphi in Liverpool, the Queens in Manchester, and elsewhere, I could eat a tremendous meal, and couldn't bear to go out to dinner where I couldn't be sure of getting what I wanted. I liked best a big cut from a joint of lamb with new potatoes and salad, but it must be remembered that dinner was my one meal of the day. One must confess that the luncheon-rooms open on a race-course are generally no very great temptation. I can say, too, that I never took a drink when I was riding until racing was over for the day. This self-imposed rule was never broken during the whole of my career in England, and for years elsewhere, not even under what might be called really necessary conditions.

One case in particular that I recall was at Kempton Park—I think in 1898— when I met with an accident through Mr. Sol Joel's Latheronwheel rearing up and falling back on me in the paddock. I had shouted out to the boy to loose his head but he wouldn't, or didn't hear me, and I was crushed under him. The horse tried his best to get off me with the true instinct of the thoroughbred not to do injury. At last he got clear. If I had not known how to respirate I shouldn't have had any life left in me. As it was, when they came to examine me they found that my pelvis was injured. The race-course surgeon put the joint back in socket and as I laid there the doctor said that I had "better have a little neat brandy."

"I will—after racing," I replied.

Lord William, who was standing near—he had come to see how I was—immediately broke in with: "You've done with racing for to-day."

"Then who's to ride Democrat?" I asked.

"I shall put Cannon up," he answered.

"No *I* am going to ride Democrat," I replied. I think if any other jockey had been mentioned I should have been content to lay there, but as it was I got up soon after *without the brandy*. The next race was for two-year-olds. Forfarshire was in the field. I was only beaten a head. Lord William always thought that it was my unfit condition after the injury which cost him the race, but I can confidently say that it was the best race I ever rode in my life. What is more, Forfarshire had 28 pounds in hand that day, but he was messed about a bit in the race by a horse ridden by Madden. Sam Loates, who rode Forfarshire, blamed me for it afterwards and there looked like being a fight, but—leave it at that. Lord William always had too great an opinion of Democrat. As a matter of fact, he was a very ordinary horse, and I am sure that had a jockey of the old-fashioned school ridden him on that day he wouldn't have been in the first six. I am not taking too great credit for myself in saying this, for if a rider like Johnny Reiff or Frank O'Neill or Milton Henry had been up they would very likely have done as well as I did. Later on, by the way, Democrat was given to Lord Kitchener for a charger. The next race that day was a two mile or a two mile and a quarter affair—I forget which—and the doctor, Lord William, and others were all furious at my attempting to ride. But I had my way and I won the race, all the time suffering such tortures as I never had known before. Altogether that day I won three races—*without brandy mind you*. However, I was paid out for my foolhardiness by being kept in bed for eight days, and I wasn't able to get about properly for two weeks. I really think that what prevented me breaking down altogether directly after the accident and taking to my bed as soon as I could get there was Lord William's saying that Cannon—then my great rival in winning mounts—was to be put up on Democrat. It is wonderful how much pain can be stood when the blood is up!

Lord William was very sympathetic during my illness, but it made me feel worse when he came to see me and wouldn't talk about Democrat. I would say to him, "Democrat could never have beaten Forfarshire, my lord," and I would almost have a relapse, and would start feeling all my pains over again, when he answered me, "We won't talk of that, little man, you did your best." It made me feel like hell. Lord William would never discuss the race afterwards. I know that to his dying day he was convinced that Democrat was the best horse in the race on that day at Kempton.

IX

A Glorious Wind-up

The Baby in the "Pram"—Nearly a Tragedy—Dining with an American Owner—I Have a "Follow"—The Record at Manchester— Four Winners and One Second—Police Protection—Dodging Swollen Head—Those Who Claimed Me—How Molly Plumb Nearly Spanked Me

I RODE VARIOUS WINNERS in the last three weeks of the season of 1897: Amhurst in a big field at Lingfield, and a horse named Bambini at that dangerous place, Northampton. I heard afterwards that the course was done away with, and quite right too, for it was certainly about the trappiest track I ever struck. I shall never forget that race, but the danger that particular day didn't come from the galloping itself. Right down beyond the turn, with no idea that the horses were so near, was a woman trying to get a baby carriage with a baby in it over the low rail—a bit of gas-piping or something—to the other side of the course! She managed to get the front wheels over, or half the "pram," and then it stuck. As we came along, we could see it. To whoever was on the rails—and I was there—it meant certain destruction—destruction to the baby and the baby-carriage or to the jockey and his horse—or both. _____ was on my whip hand and he was keeping me pinned on the rails. I looked at him but he wouldn't catch my eye. I shouted but—nothing doing. There was only one course to take to save life and limb and I took it. I barged into him and nearly knocked him over. But the baby was saved and I was too. And what's more I just beat him. Of course _____ was mad, and he was going to report me to the Stewards, but I got to them first. If I remember rightly, he was fined and put down for the rest of the meeting. The Stewards had seen the whole incidents of the race, fortunately for me.

I rode winners at Liverpool and remember a rather funny entertainment after that meeting. One of the owners—an American, with one horse only, I heard afterwards—who had won a nice little bit over a race he had won kept on saying to me, "Now don't forget when we get back to London *you* are to have dinner with *me*. I had dinner with you the last time." As a matter of fact, I think all the exchange of hospitality had been pretty one-sided up to then. I went to dinner and we sat down all spick and span, feeling good, and my host took up the card to order the meal.

"What do you want? Like some fish?"

"Just what you like," I replied.

"Do you want any meat? Well all right, perhaps we'll have some soup. Ah! *petite marmite*—if we have that there's meat in it; we can eat that and we needn't order any other meat afterwards. Then we'll have some Camembert cheese. Ever tasted that? No? Oh! you'll like it."

I hadn't put in a word and he seemed quite satisfied with himself. We had the soup and then the fish—one small sole between the two. He took the head and had finished his Camembert before I had looked at it.

"That's all right," he said as he lit a cigar.

Paying no further heed to him, I asked the waiter for the menu: "Now I'll have something to eat. I've dined with *you*, now I'll have something on my own." I ordered a steak, fried potatoes and a big salad. He tried to put himself right, but he was a cheap fellow at anything of that kind, and I repeated his words: "That's all right. I've had dinner with you: now I'm just getting in to a little fancy work."

When I'd finished, he made no move to pay. But as a last little try he said: "How do you expect to ride if you eat all that?"

"How am I going to ride if I don't eat *once* a day?" was the way I ended the conversation.

There was no particular feature about the three winners I rode at Derby, but after Derby came the biggest thing I had done in England. It was at Manchester. On Thursday I won on Bavelaw Castle in the Rothschild Plate. On Friday I got Sapling home in a very big field for the Ellesmere Welter: I had been on him at Liverpool and had won on him there, too. When I went out to the old New Barnes track on the Saturday it was raining and the going heavy. I had only one idea in my head—to get away to London after racing was over, for I was going to Paris and to Monte Carlo. I would have gone anywhere to get out of such weather! I was thankful that it was the last day of the season. That Saturday afternoon crowd rather astonished me, and some of them laughed at me as the crowd had done the first time I was seen at Newmarket. Little did I think what was waiting me later on that afternoon as I cantered down to the post on Captain Machell's Manxman for the Farewell Handicap. There was a field of fourteen. I got the run of them and won it. I heard afterwards the horse had been well backed. In the next race I was on a favourite, Mr. Wm. Clark's Le Javelot, and I was expected to win. They gave me a bit of a cheer as I won it. I wasn't riding in the next race. Then came the Saturday Welter with a field of twenty-two. Neither the weather nor the mud could shake my confidence: we slopped along and at the distance I felt I had them all whipped. The mare I was riding, Martha IV she was called, seemed to like me and I *got there*. That black mass of people set up a roar when I passed the post. Lord William was delighted and I had to dodge the people who wanted to pat me on the back. I rode Keenan in the November Handicap, but couldn't beat Asterie, who was better class. Then followed the Final Plate and I rode Bavelaw Castle, whom I had won on two days before. I knew exactly what to do and made the horse to put in his best, but I hadn't seen one or two who were thought to be dangerous. You get, however, into a kind of feeling that you *must* win when you have begun, and Bavelaw Castle had to do it. He did.

Four wins and a second! I didn't get a swollen head that day; that I *can* say, whatever happened to me before or after. My only idea was to dress quickly and to get into a cab, but it wasn't so easy. It looked a bit dangerous in fact, for they were waiting there in the hundreds and thousands either to shake my hand or pat me on the back or to grab a souvenir. All the stories I had read as a kid about those who used to wait just to touch John L. Sullivan came back to ME! Ed Gaines and I went out to look for the cab, but it was impossible to get at it. The crowd was closing in. Gaines's face was as white as a sheet: he thought we should be trampled on. At last they got a dozen policemen who formed a square round us. All the same I *should* have liked to shake hands with a few of them. I should have risked having all the breath pressed out of me and I was such a little fellow that I might have been dead while they were looking for me on the floor. However, there it was: I was the proudest kid in England or America that day. Apart altogether from what I had done before, I had just made good in England and let them know that there was such a jockey as Sloan.

All the way back to London I heard that crowd calling to me—"Tod," "Toddie," "Sloanie," "Sloan," and everything they could twist my name into.

In that short month I had forty-eight mounts and won twenty-one races. Lord William sent me immediately a splendid gold cigarette-case with the names of the four Manchester winners engraved on it and the second, Keenan. On the other side was a reproduction of his own writing.

I was tickled to death at the idea that people were beginning to know me and to talk about me a bit more. Oh Yes! I plead guilty! Nothing is going to be kept back. I intend to write about all the times I got a bit above myself. I confess that it ended in that serious complaint, "Swollen head." At the same time it was not unnatural at my age to be a bit fresh when I had actually shown those who had laughed at me and who didn't believe in me that I could do something they couldn't.

Now with regard to what I made. I had paid all my expenses and had at the end of the season about two thousand pounds over; of course this was through my presents. For the time I was at it, this was equal to, or even better than, in some other years in which I rode. In this connection I have just realised—and may as well put in here—that in all the years I rode, I never asked for nor charged any fee or expenses for riding trials or gallops, nor did I charge my railway expenses to meetings. This will be borne out by owners and by Messrs. Weatherby and others.

While, when I first came to England there was nobody to speak to me, after I had made a few successes there was no end to the people who came up and claimed me. Often it was impossible to remember having met them before, let alone having talked to them! But I would go though the handshake and the ordinary greeting: "Glad to see you." Some of them would say, "Don't you remember me? I was," etc., etc. Sometimes they were just as funny as the man who rushed up to Jim Corbett once saying, "How are you, Mr. Corbett, don't you know me? Surely you remember when you left Jackson, Mississippi, all the inhabitants came out to see the champion pass through. Well, I was the little fellow with the brown Derby hat standing in the crowd."

I recall one man, a year or two after, who came up to speak to me at Doncaster. He started telling me that he had to thank me for giving him a winner at

Goodwood. He had had a tenner on and wanted to thank me, for he had pouched a good win. Having nothing to do at the moment, I humoured him, but I told him that I had never met him at Goodwood to begin with. He insisted that I had, and offered to bet me fifty pounds that he was right.

"Show me the fifty," I said, kidding him.

"Well I haven't got it on me—" he began.

"You don't look as if you had," said I, and drew him on by adding, "Would you like to bet me ten dollars? Show me that amount. Eh! What? I don't think you've got even that." The truth was that he had tried to get up a conversation for his own ends, perhaps in order to use my name, but I knew by the way he had started that I had never spoken to him. Fancy Willie—that's me— saying I was going to win a race to anyone—especially a stranger on a race-course! "Let me tell you something," I went on: "I have never been to Goodwood in my life, and the only place I think I've seen you in before was the waxworks."

As a matter of fact, I never rode at Goodwood in my life, and have never been near the place.

That was only one of a hundred odd incidents of the kind, but speaking of being claimed, I think the funniest of the lot was when I made a trip to Kansas City a few years after I gave up riding. I was in the paddock when someone came to me and said, "There's a lady wants to speak to you over there; she's sitting on the stand among the people there: she says it's very important."

I asked who she was and whether she was old or young, and her name, but the man didn't know. He had received the message from someone else. So I fell for it. There were a lot of people sitting near a large lady who would have had to diet and waste to ride twelve st. When I got to her she threw her arms round me, while I struggled to get away. Then she pushed me away from her to get a good look at me, holding me by the shoulders with her strong hands.

"Don't you remember me? I'm Molly Plumb. I used to carry you in my arms when you were six years old. I lived next door to you."

Now it was only twenty-five years before that I was six years old. I remembered her very well and added that I'd see her again when I came back, but that I was very busy that day. That didn't please her and she called out at me, "Tod Blauser"— Blauser was my adopted mother's name—"for two pins I'd turn you over on my knee and spank you."

What a shout went up from the people round! I laughed with them but she didn't, so the only thing to do was to shake her hand in both mine and to say, "I'm glad to see you, Mrs. Plumb"—she may have been Miss—and to make an exit. She called after me, "I'm disappointed with you, Blauser. Mind you come back and see me."

It was lovely to see her but she didn't realise I had my business to attend to: she thought she was on a fair-ground, I think. Mrs. or Miss Plumb must forgive me if she sees this in print. One is liable to forget after so many years. But I could never forget the name; she had been kind to me. Yet we'll hope to have that promised supper some day, with nice baking hot biscuits.

X
Holiday Incidents

My Aunts Visit Me—At the Races—"When do you perform?"—At the Grand Hotel, Paris—Cost of an Illumination—Winning $12,000 at Monte Carlo—My Present of Pointers

THE INCIDENT I TOLD JUST NOW about Molly Plumb and her absolute ignorance of the race-course reminds me of how I once gave an invitation to my aunts Lib and Min—two sisters—to come and spend a week or ten days as my guests in New York. They knew of my fame at the time, and were tickled to death at the idea of visiting me. Aunt Lib was really my adopted mother, but I called each of them aunt, and Aunt Lib's husband, Dan Blauser—a man of Dutch extraction—Uncle Dan. I believe Aunt Min had once been as far as Cincinnati, but the other had never journeyed more than sixty miles away from home. They were types of real good country people when they arrived at the old Pennsylvania station on the New Jersey shore. I had taken a nice suite for them in the Imperial Hotel, great big rooms where they could roam about and admire everything—and themselves too if they wanted to, for there were plenty of mirrors and decorations.

They spent their time running about New York, and I did the best I could to entertain them, taking seats for theatres and vaudeville shows galore. They were peacefully happy.

Then came the races at Sheepshead Bay, close to the sea. Neither of them had ever seen the ocean or a ship, and how they did stare with delight! I had a place just then down near the course, at Jerome Cottage, and I gave them a whole floor to themselves.

On the first day after their arrival, Sousa's band was playing at the races and I got them two seats just in front of the conductor. They were in raptures. After settling them I had to leave them alone until after the fourth race, but I had been told that they were getting on very well. I had ridden three winners in succession, and I put my overcoat on over the colours I was to wear in the last race of the day and went off to see how they were getting on. To begin with, I peeked at them from a distance and saw them beating time to the music with beaming smiles on their faces. I didn't interrupt at once, but when the tune was over, I went up and asked how they were getting on.

"When do *you* perform?" asked Aunt Lib, for all the world as if she were on a fair-ground—like Molly Plumb.

"I've *been* performing—only three winners—and I shall *perform again* in the last race," I answered, and I opened my coat to show the colours. "All you've got to do is to keep your eye on this jacket. Didn't you see my performances earlier in the afternoon?"

"We saw some horses go by," said Aunt Min; "were you that little feller performing in front?"

"That was me, and you must look for me on the track in the race after the next one."

They promised that they would, but I am sure they were much more impressed with my importance when, on leaving them, I went up to shake hands with Sousa and several of his leading men. They looked at each other as if to say, "See the people our Tod knows!"

I left them to their contentment until after the last event, in which I finished second.

"We couldn't see that jacket of yours," said Aunt Lib when the racing was finished, "you weren't performing in front that time."

"No," I answered; "it was a friend of mine's turn."

Poor dears, that one day gave them enough of racing. They never wanted to go again. I often wished that I could get an exact impression of what they thought about it all. I confess that it took a little moral courage to stand the smiles of all the people round during the loud talk of the two dear women, especially when one of them embraced me warmly—a thing she was quite liable to do—bless her!—several times a day. No one was rude, however, or ridiculed us, but I dare say many will understand my very mixed feelings when they asked me in the hearing of scores of people when I was going to do—my circus turn! Anyhow, they went away very happy. It must have been funny to hear them telling all the folks at home about their trip.

I think they would have come to Europe if I'd asked them. They had so much to learn—and so had I, for the matter of that!

Perhaps I was a bit green when, towards Christmas in 1897, I left London for Paris and Monte Carlo. Ed Gaines was still with me, and I had another man, too. On arriving at Paris, we went to the Grand Hotel—that was before it was altered of course. I asked for a bedroom with a bathroom off, but was told that they hadn't got one; then after a bit of whispering I found that they only had one such private bathroom and that was in a swell suite costing something like a hundred and fifty francs a day. I took it and the boys accommodated themselves in two bedrooms which belonged to the "apartment." We intended to entertain a bit, but as a matter of fact, we didn't do much in that way, for no one knew me and I knew nobody. With the exception of going round to Maxim's, which didn't interest me then, and the Café American, where there were no Americans that I could see, life was pretty dull for those few days.

I got tired of it all one night about ten o'clock, and we all went back to the hotel, where there was a bright fire burning in my sitting-room. Now on the mantel-piece and the walls there were large candelabra chockfull of candles and I thought to myself, "If I'm paying all this money for these rooms, I may as well make the place as bright as possible, light the candles and have a little party"—although there was electric light and gas, too, if I remember right. So out I took a box of matches and lit the whole lot—several dozens there were. Gee! didn't that room look dandy? I began to feel warm and cozy and I was much more cheerful, until when I got the bill next morning just before leaving I found thirty-six francs charged for those candles! I tried to fight them about it but—nothin' doing. After that episode I felt inclined to cover candles over with a cloth when I saw them at other hotels for fear the temptation should be too strong for me.

At Monte Carlo, roulette was nothing new to me. I played twice a day for the six days I was there and won about sixty thousand francs—about two thousand four hundred pounds. I never had a losing sitting, and I was mighty pleased with the packet I took away. On the way back, I stayed in Paris again for a few days and had a much better time, for I got to know a few people and rubbed along more comfortably with the French customs. Then going back to England I sailed on the 15th January from Liverpool by the *Campania*.

Crowds of reporters met me when we arrived off the Quarantine Station at New York. I tried to avoid them, but there were the usual interviews, and I remember that the reporters I didn't say a word to, or even see, wrote the longest stories. A good deal had, of course, appeared in print in New York during the month of my success in England.

Mr. Charles Fleischman had bought a hundred copies of the *Inter-Ocean* of Chicago whenever anything had appeared about me, and he had mailed these to all his friends to show "how well his boy had been doing." When I got to New York itself, the reporters didn't leave me alone: some of them from whom I scurried burnt me up with mock interviews full of jokes at my expense. They described my palatial apartment and made out that my room was littered with cigar ends and cigarette stubs and that the carpets and furniture were all burnt and spoiled—the room of me, Tod Sloan, who cannot help being neat and who loves tidy rooms!

They also talked about my coloured servant—a black nigger named Dick Keys. He was my valet in town, while I had a white man, Frank Garrett, for my race-course valet. The two used to quarrel like blazes. Sometimes I thought I would have a secretary to manage them, but I never reached that pinnacle of success. At the last moment I would think that I couldn't afford the luxury. Thinking it over now, I fancy that, with the way I was spending money then and afterwards, a secretary would have been jolly useful, for I was very careless about banking and other business. Here is an instance: I went in to my bank one day—it was years later than the time I have just been writing about—in fear and trembling to try and arrange an overdraft. I was afraid that there was only a sum of three or four hundred dollars to my credit. When I had worked up to the suggestion, the manager asked: "How much do you want?" "Five thousand dollars," I answered. I knew I was good for that sum.

"Let's see how you stand first," he said, and in a minute showed me a slip of paper with nine thousand dollars odd written on it—to my credit, mind you.

"What do you want to draw fourteen thousand dollars for?" he demanded.

I was taken aback and told him I only wanted to take five thousand, but that I had made a mistake in checking my pass-book. As a matter of fact, I never went through the items in my life!

Before leaving New York I received two fine dogs, pointers, from England. One was given me by Lord Charles Beresford, and the other by Lord Marcus. They were brought over in a private cabin and were looked after by poor Andrew Latimer, who was then Chief Steward of the *New England*. He was a great friend of mine and of many of those who may read this. It will be remembered that, after several changes of boats, he lost his life in the *Titanic* disaster. Such a real good friend to me he was, open hearted and generous, in fact an all-round good fellow.

I took the two dogs out to California. I was greatly pleased with the present and it is a pleasure to me to know that there is hardly a good pointer in California to-day who does not trace back in his pedigree to Wisdom or Whisper, the names of the two. Breeders in California owe a deep debt of gratitude to Lord Charles and Lord Marcus.

I rode for a while in the very early spring on the Californian track, especially at Ingleside, and was in fine form, winning about 40 per cent of my mounts and having on two occasions five winners. It is curious that the number of times I reached this score in a day was exactly the same in three places; three times in England, three times in New York and three times in California. I have often been asked how many times I have ridden four winners in an afternoon, but I cannot answer this. I should guess the figures at something like fifty.

I spent two days at my home town, Kokomo, soon after I came back. There was a ball at Logans-Port and scores of Kokomo people wanted to go, but they didn't know how to get there. I settled the question by ordering a special train and as many as liked to go had to only step aboard. I put them up at the hotel, too, as my guests. I was "some fellow," they thought—the poor boy who had once run about the town. It was "Blauser this" and "Blauser that" until they found there was no special to go back by. I told them I hadn't bought the train, and that they had only to wait till the next morning for ordinary cars. They didn't like it.

I also went to Chicago, where I had many friends, for I had spent a long time there with my sister and Cash when I was quite a little kiddie. It was when living in Chicago in 1888 that Johnny Campbell came to where we lived one night to take me out with him to New Jersey.

Cash was making the living for the family in that fall of 1888—ten years before the time I have just been speaking of. He was employed in building; that is to say, he hammered laths on unfinished walls. He'd fill his mouth with tacks and I was certain with the faces he made sometimes that he would swallow a few. I used to go with him very often and hand him the laths, and we would eat and drink what sister had put up for us. Sometimes I'd pull Cash's leg:

"That fellow working over there is a goer; he's put up two laths to your one."

Then Cash would set his teeth, take a pull at his belt, fill his mouth with a fresh lot of tacks, slap at the laths and would look round every now and then to see how his rival was getting on. He'd nod to me, for he couldn't speak on account of the tacks, as if to say, "What do you know about him? I'm beating him; in fact I'm leaving him standing still."

The other fellows would see the joke and they never hurried, for there was no piece work about the job, and it made no difference to their pay, however many laths they hammered on during the day. But Cash couldn't think of that: he was always ready to sweat and always out to beat the other guys. Cash, in fact, was some worker, and at week-ends, as there was a great rush time at the barber's, he got a job for several hours on Saturday night and for four hours on Sunday, shaving. He got five dollars for that. Of course little Tod couldn't be out of it, and he used to go with him and lather the customers. I would give them five minutes of it sometimes while waiting for Cash to come along with the razor. I had to stand on a stool to get at their faces with the brush, and I used to put in some fine fancy work. My, it was funny! I used to laugh then, and I laugh still more so now when I think of it.

XI

Something About Clothes

Wanting a Fit-out — Johnny Campbell's Order — He Gets the Bill — A Fancy for Shoes — On the Ocean without a Stitch

I SPOKE JUST NOW of going off with Johnny Campbell from Chicago to New Jersey. About a year after I first went to him, we were at Long Branch races, and I determined that I must get some clothes: I wanted a suit badly. I figured it out that I could go to Powell, a tailor in New York, and give him so much down and have enough for my expenses and a bit left in hand. I knew the suit would cost sixty dollars and thought the balance could be paid when the things were finished. I hopped into the train and in the parlour car the first man I saw was Johnny Campbell. He looked me up and down with surprise: "And where are you going, my lad?"

"Going to New York to get some new clothes," I answered as bold as brass, while looking for a seat.

"You're going to do what?" he asked again.

"Get some clothes," I repeated. "I'm sick of going about like this."

The train had moved off and Johnny seemed amused. Presently he called me over to him, and said, "That's all right and I'll help you," and he wrote on the back of a card to Powell:

"Make Sloan what he wants and send the bill to me.

"J.CAMPBELL."

I thanked him and on arrival in New York I went straight to Powell's place, then at the corner of 12th Street and Broadway. I gave the tailor the card and then looked at the materials, chose one I liked and was measured. Now I only weighed 4 st. 9 lbs., and when Powell told me the price — sixty dollars — I said, "Surely you're not going to charge a little feller like me that figure! Why, I sha'n't take half the stuff that would be required to make *you* a suit."

Powell started to explain to me how much more difficult it was to fit a little man and handed out all the "guff" about the amount of stuff it took to make some of his fat giants' clothes. He had to average up, and so on. Besides, he added, cutting for me took just as much time and labour as for anyone else.

Now comes the joke:

"Summer's coming on; surely you want something lighter for the other suits?" the tailor suddenly asked.

"What others?"

"Well Johnny Campbell says, 'Make Sloan what he wants and send the bill to me,' so you had better fit yourself out properly and have a couple more suits and an overcoat while you are about it."

I laughed at what Johnny would think and say when he got the bill, but the temptation was too strong; I let myself go. I can tell you that when the things came home, I didn't half fancy myself and swelled it about to the envy of all the boys at home. But you should have heard what Campbell said to me when he got the bill for two hundred and seventy-five dollars: he didn't half let me have it; but he paid it all right, and afterwards he would laugh and shake his fist at me. In recent years, Johnny and I have often laughed over the incident. Anyone who reads this and who knows him should ask him to tell it his own way; perhaps it will sound better than the way I tell it. By the way, from that time on, clothes were always a great fancy with me, and boots too. In fact, it may be said that these were my real extravagances, but when I was making money freely there was always a pleasure in looking at something in value I had for it. Some of my earnings in 1897 were left with London tailors, and after 1898 I nearly always had my clothes and boots built for me in England.

In the newspaper interviews, when they wanted to poke fun at me, the reporters would say that I never travelled without more than a dozen trunks and that they were all full of clothes. As a matter of fact I never took more than three; but considering the size of the garments I wore there could be a lot of clothes stowed away in them! Certainly I was fanciful about shoes and would carry a dozen or eighteen pairs on a journey of any length. I had a joke one night when there was a supper-party in my apartments at the Imperial Hotel in Broadway, New York, where I lived for some years. A parcel had just come home and had not been unpacked: brown shoes, evening pumps, and a lot of other shoes. The company, especially the girls, were anxious to see what was inside the big cardboard box, and I let them open it to satisfy their curiosity. My size was and is about one and a half. Of course, the girls at once wanted some of these new shoes as something out of the ordinary, something quite different from anything they had had, but I was quite safe when I said to them: "Any of you who can get a pair on her feet, is quite welcome to take them home with her."

They all had a try, but by no sort of persuasion or by use of the shoehorn could they get their feet into a pair. However, there was no need for them to feel hurt or put out, for I have only met two women in my life who could wear my shoes, one— of her later—the other a friend I cannot focus at the moment.

Speaking of clothes, I remember that, when I crossed to England in 1898, I had to travel without a stitch of belongings. My brother Fremont, who by the way does not come in much in the story of my life, and will not, for he died in the autumn of 1914, had the knack of doing everything wrong in any little commissions he had to undertake for me or others. I was due to leave by the *Deutschland* from the Hoboken Pier, and Fremont and my nigger valet must go and put all my things on the *Kaiser Wilhelm*, an opposition German boat sailing the same day, but an hour earlier. They waited on and on for me to appear, and then when the *Kaiser Wilhelm* had sailed it occurred to them to rush down to the *Deutschland*. We were almost off when they arrived and I spotted them. You should have heard what I said when I learned what had been done! They tried to explain that they thought I might possibly have been somewhere in one of the state rooms on the other boat, and that they had waited on the chance. In the middle of my rousting them the *Deutschland* got under way and they had to slip ashore in a hurry. Apart from the inconvenience I suffered I worried all the way across about an unlocked suit-case which my brother had deposited at the last moment with the other baggage on the *Kaiser Wilhelm*. It had about five thousand pounds' worth of tie pins in a leather case inside it. But I never lost a single thing. All the baggage was delivered to me at Southampton. It was the eventful journey when the two ships raced each other across the Atlantic, our boat getting in first by hours. It wasn't funny, though, to be all the time without a single thing except what I stood up in. People helped a little. There was a nice girl on board who lent me a pair of shoes and a pair of stockings so that I could have a change. Willie Sims, the coloured jockey, who was on the ship, let me have a few collars, and I borrowed a tie, a new one, from someone else, and I shall always remember that I have never returned it. I got hold of a shirt from someone, too, a flannel one, and managed to turn out fairly respectably for dinner, but I felt a bit out of it all the same. Of course, everyone dressed for dinner at my table on that voyage; they would.

The story got about in New York, and, of course, there were some funny pictures published. One showed me beckoning to the *Kaiser Wilhelm* to come alongside; and great piles of baggage were drawn on deck in a pile as high as the funnels of the big ship. My luggage of course! Just about this time, too, a cartoon appeared in one of the dailies showing "Uncle Sam" at Sandy Hook pulling me one way, and "John Bull" on Land's End, England, hauling the other.

The papers were on the whole kind to me in those early days, but, as I have said, some of them used to roast me a bit, trying to tear me down by ridicule. For instance, Jean De Reszke had said he would like to see me, and one day I called on him at the Gilsey House. The next morning, one of the papers made out that I said when I went into his apartment, "Hullo, Jean."

"Hullo, Tod," they made him reply.

"Who do you ride for?" I was supposed to have continued.

Jean de Reszke answered—according to them: "I'm not a jockey: I'm a singer."

My answer was the limit: "You'd better quit singing if you want to make any money. Being a jockey is the only way to get it...." All lies of course.

XII
The Late King Edward

Preparations for Second Visit to England—Getting Fit—The Yacht and the Horse Belmar—My Brother as a Fighter—Presented to the Prince—His Personal Magnetism—His Wager of £200—Taking my Tip about Encombe—"Why didn't you take your hat off?"—Promise of a Ride in Royal Colours

I OFTEN TALKED ABOUT ENGLAND to "Pittsburgh Phil," but he never showed any wish to go over, preferring to stay where he knew pretty well all that there was to know. All the same, he liked to discuss England and English ways with me, and, without any wish to flatter me, he used to say that he had always considered that I was about the only rider he knew of at the time who would make a success abroad. Several times he thought of sending a man over, a journalist friend of his, to back my mounts, but it came to nothing.

Phil did very well over my riding that season—1898—in the East, for I was in great form, riding two, three, and four winners every day. I kept myself so fit, too. I had a boat—we called it a yacht. I named her *Belmar*, after a horse belonging to Phil I had ridden with great success. I was living at that time in a cottage down at Sheepshead Bay. William Fleischman, who was agent for the stable, was nearly always down there with me, and Mr. Julius Fleischman, who owned it, would often come and see us. We spent a lot of our time in fishing on the *Belmar*. And I used to have as much pleasure in sailing the boat as I had in riding the horse it was called after.

I won five or six handicaps on Belmar off the reel. I have never come across a more intelligent horse: he knew the winning post just as well as I did, and I had the sense to trust to his wisdom more than once. I learnt to give the credit for my wins on him to him. I won several events by a head, in which I know if they had been run a second faster, or if he had had ten pounds more weight to carry, I believe the result would have been the same. I learnt all his peculiarities. How that horse just loved to race! He would line up with the others as quiet as a lamb; then he would break away and take his position. He always came along about three furlongs from home and—won. As soon as he passed the post his ears would change. Surely, if there is any real expression about a horse it is in his ears. No matter how hot the finish had been Belmar would relax after he had finished his gallop, and would hardly even make an effort to walk to the paddock. He would lick my face like a dog and never kicked or bit anyone.

I have always claimed that the horse is the most intelligent animal in the world. I have argued it out again and again, especially in connection with the old-time rivalry between horses and dogs. It must be remembered that a horse never gets the same chances that a dog does. A dog is about the house, is talked to, sees what human beings are doing from morning to night, gets familiar with the sounds of words, and generally is trained or given lessons to like a child. But the horse is so much more alone; he is left to himself. If you could get a thoroughbred as small in size as, say, I am compared with Jack Johnson, and let that little horse run about a house, well—Heaven knows what he couldn't do in the way of parlour tricks. I only put this down by the way. Yes, people should always remember, when placing the dog in front of the horse for intelligence, that we do not take the horse into bed, and into our living rooms; we do not let them sleep on our sofas and chairs.

Altogether, in that 1898 season in America, up to August, I rode about 190 winners. Just before I left, in that month, I began to feel tired, extraordinary as it may seem, and I was even thinking of retiring for two or three months in order to go shooting or something of the kind. I had got as far as I could get in the way of riding success, and I was longing to achieve something in another walk of life. That was why I wasn't sorry when the message came for me from Lord William and I got permission to sail. A lot of American sports had made up their minds to follow me across in order to back my mounts. Indeed, they went by the same ship, and claimed me on board—that is to say, they lost no time in striking up an acquaintance. I didn't own the ship, so I was in no way responsible for what people afterwards called the "American invasion."

I didn't take Ed Gaines with me this time, but for a day or so I had an idea of letting my brother Fremont have the trip. However, I altered my mind. He was making his living training a few horses for Mr. Fleischman out West and I thought he had better stick to that—for the present at least. I also had it in my mind that he might be developed and get a match on fighting, for he was about the hardest hitting bantam weight I have ever struck. Jimmy Berry, the champion bantam, remembered my poor brother, and used to tell me several times that Fremont had a bigger thump for his weight than nineteen boys out of twenty he had fought. It will be remembered that Berry was some authority: it was he who unfortunately killed Walter Kroot at the National Sporting Club, London.

I was in Jim's corner that night, and it was not till the twentieth round that the last blow hit over the heart put Kroot out. Of course we were all very upset. I remember that Berry came to my room about two o'clock in the morning. They had told him that Kroot would get over it, but my own idea was then, and always has been—although I didn't say so at the time—that it was only a matter of minutes that Kroot could live after Berry hit him. About four o'clock we telephoned and heard that Kroot was dead. They arrested Berry, but let him out on bail and everyone was held blameless, the verdict being given as simple misadventure. I bring this in just to show that, if a man of Berry's class could think so well of my brother, who, by the way was two years older than me, it was worth my giving a thought to developing him. However, poor chap, he was so unlucky that I decided I'd better not. He cried on the wharf—partly over the luggage business and partly because he wasn't going with me.

Lord William was, if possible, kinder than ever to me when I got back to

England, and they were a good lot of horses that they had ready for the autumn campaign. It was during these three months that I was to have the greatest surprise of my life. I was to have a chance of speaking to the late King Edward, then Prince of Wales. One day at Newmarket, Lord William came for me to the jockeys' room and asked me to put on my coat over my riding clothes and come out. Getting into the Birdcage, he told me that the Prince had sent for me, and that I was to be presented to him. We walked to where the Prince was standing, and he smiled as I came towards him and shook my had very warmly. Never in my life have I been put so much at my ease nor treated so splendidly. After all, I was only a visiting American, and only a jockey at that—although I had been doing so well at my game.

The Prince asked me a lot of questions. Was I happy? How did I like England? What did I think of the racing, of the grass courses? Just before I left him—feeling all the time as if I'd like to talk to him the entire afternoon—he said that I should ride for him some time or other, and he gave me time to answer: "It would be a pride and honour to do so."

There were several other opportunities of meeting and talking to that great, kind, big-hearted man. I used to think to myself how pleased they would be at home and how they would ask me all about it, and what the American papers would say. I can tell you that, although I come from democratic America, there was a wonderful impression left on me by the great personal attraction of that royal gentleman. It sort of drew me to him in the same way that a magnetic crane in all its strength will pick up scrap iron. I don't mean to say I came off the scrap heap! But perhaps many can understand the different emotions I had, then and after, when thinking of that presentation. The impression never seemed to wear off, either, even when he spoke to me again—as he did frequently.

One day he told me that he was no gambler, and that as a rule he hardly ever had more on a horse than twenty-five pounds, but that he used to make an exception and risk a couple of hundred on anything that I was riding and that I told him I thought would win.

I remember once—it was the last race of the year at the Newmarket meetings—I was riding a horse called Encombe that I had influenced someone a few days before to buy out of a selling race. On my way to mount Encombe in the paddock, the Prince beckoned to me. He was standing with Lord Marcus Beresford, who was holding the bridle of a colt Richard Marsh had in the same race.

"Sloan," said the Prince, "what are you riding?"

I told him Encombe.

"Do you think you have a chance?" he asked, and I answered frankly that I thought Encombe was a good thing.

Lord Marcus spoke up then and told me I was wrong, and that Encombe would be nowhere. "We shall beat Encombe," he went on, "and Dundonald will beat both."

I listened of course, but before I left to get in the saddle, I turned to the Prince:

"Never you mind what Lord Marcus says, your Royal Highness. You can be a plunger here and have a bit on me."

The Prince roared; he was laughing at my nerve at speaking so boldly to him, I suppose. Well, I was thinking of what I had said all through the race. I beat Dundonald after a desperate finish.

The Prince told me afterwards that he had taken my advice and had put two hundred pounds on Encombe, who I think started at about 7 to 2.

When I was talking to the Prince, I couldn't help admiring the way he dressed. Especially did I like his overcoats, hats, and cravats. Now some of the American papers used to twist about everything I said — and didn't say, for the matter of that — and some reporters by whom I wouldn't be interviewed, would invent all sorts of things on their own. One yellow journal in particular made me say, without ever talking to me about the subject, that I thought the King of England dressed very badly. Of course, this leaked through somehow, and Lord Marcus afterwards called me over the coals for what had appeared. I was, and am, quite sure that it had only been written to cause trouble. Anyhow, Lord Marcus said severely, "You should never speak of *him* [meaning the Prince] at all."

"I never did, my lord," I answered. "The most I ever did was to answer a question of one paper saying that the Prince was a great sportsman, speaking of the pleasure all English people had in seeing him walking round like a private citizen in the paddock with no one bothering him at all."

Speaking about being presented: when the present King George, then Duke of York, was at one of the July meetings at Newmarket, Lord William came in the Plantation where I was just ready to get in the saddle, and told me I was to speak to the Duke, the Duchess, and one or two others of the royal family. The Duke of York shook hands with me and asked questions, and I bowed low, having a bit of experience by this time. I thought I was getting on fine. The conversation lasted quite two minutes, and the present King was very kind to me. I was tickled to death when I was shaken hands with and went off to mount. I looked to Lord William for approval but he hadn't got a smile, and only said quite simply: "Why didn't you take your hat off?"

This got me up and I bleated: "Why should I have to go back to the jockeys' room right over on the other side of the course, my lord? I should have to brush my hair and tie my cap on again. I shouldn't have had time. I couldn't have ridden in this race then. Remember I'm an American, my lord, and don't understand all these things."

He only smiled, but I was sore that I hadn't done exactly as I should, especially after thinking I had such swell manners. When I was presented to King Edward, I heard nothing about the cap business!

At that time I received so much kindness from all the members of the Royal Family with whom I came in contact that I should like now, while I am on the subject, to tell the story of Nunsuch, whom I rode for the then Prince of Wales (King Edward VII) in the Cambridgeshire and the Old Cambridgeshire.

XIII
Nunsuch's Cambridgeshire

Newspaper Criticism – "Boss" Croker's Shooting – Breaking the Rules

I WAS LOOKING FORWARD to riding Nunsuch in the Cambridgeshire. This four-year-old of the Prince's had been well backed, and on the day of the race she started second favourite. The race was a disaster, but in the sequel I received more kindness from the Prince and as much or more evidence of good sportsmanship as it has ever been my lot to discover in any similar instance. I heard that all the closest friends of the royal owner had backed the mare and I know the bookmakers had written the name of Nunsuch in heavy wagers to many of my own friends.

At the start, Mr. Arthur Coventry accidentally left some of the best favourites, including Nunsuch, at the post. The truth was that we were all walking the backward way of the course when he dropped his flag and in the result we took no part in the race.

One of the best-known sporting writers in England – the late Mr. Greenwood – said that "The right-hand division were scarcely prepared for the fall of the flag and four of them had their chances completely destroyed. To Mr. Coventry this failure would be vexatious in the extreme, the more so as he had been wonderfully successful of late."

My disappointment over this can well be imagined, and I felt very, very badly on returning to the weighing enclosure, and saw the Prince coming towards me smiling. I couldn't see anything to smile at myself and must have shown it, for I know that I felt all the other way! Well, the Prince came up to me and said, "Well such things do happen and it cannot be helped; I will start Nunsuch again in the Old Cambridgeshire the day after to-morrow and you shall ride her again."

I won with her then, beating practically the same field that she had met before. After this race the Prince gave me the set of colours I had worn and a diamond horse and jockey pin. That was the beginning of riding a good many winners for the late King Edward.

I should like to state here that, in the last season in which I rode – 1900 – I had the great surprise at Doncaster of Lord Marcus Beresford coming up to me and telling me that the Prince wished to have first call on me for the season of 1901, and that he was prepared to make me the offer of six thousand guineas for the claim. I accepted on the spot and looked forward with utmost pride towards keeping the contract. The English Stewards, however, prevented me from fulfilling it.

Just as I had fixed up everything with Lord Marcus, his brother, Lord William, had a cable from Mr. Whitney in America: "We must have Sloan, get him at any price, he is far ahead of the lot and worth anything for big races, even with all his faults."

Lord William showed me the cablegram and I had to tell him what had happened. I could see that he was a bit upset—I won't say annoyed—but he said he would like to try to get me out of the agreement with the Prince. He "never believed," he said, "that the English people would put up with an American jockey being first rider to the King-to-be." He added: "My little man, I am afraid you have made a big mistake. I hope not, though. Mr. Whitney and I will have to put up with a second call on you." And then he told me that he would pay me three thousand guineas for that.

Some of the English papers had a good deal to say about this matter, one writer going so far as to say that "the retainer bestowed upon Sloan caused great astonishment on account of the exalted position of the patron"; and further went on: "Owing to the Prince's great popularity as a sportsman, people are slow to criticise adversely anything his Royal Highness does; however, there can be no gainsaying that the shelving of the most representative and best conducted of English jockeys in favour of an American professional has given rise to a very painful feeling; perhaps the Prince was not altogether responsible for engaging Sloan." How circumstances led to that contract not being carried out will be told in due course.

The King often laughed over the story of my visit to Lord William's place at Deepdene for the shooting. I had taken down a new gun from a London maker on which I paid a deposit of fifteen pounds, making the bargain that, if it suited me, I would give him the balance, and that if it didn't, I would pay a sum for the use of it.

We hadn't long started, and I took my first shot. The gun burst; showing at the break jagged pieces like a saw. I know I had a very narrow escape of losing two or three fingers. I could see that all the other guests thought it was my fault, and that I was not used to firearms. The truth was that I had handled them all my life and perhaps I could have given points with any gun to the majority of those present. When the accident happened, Lord William said kindly to me, "It can't be helped," and I felt that he and some of the others were pitying me, even laughing at me!

Anyhow, I asked the loan of another gun, but Lord William answered in a sort of fatherly manner: "Oh, surely you don't want to shoot again to-day, do you?" I insisted, however, and ultimately I got a gun that didn't fit me a bit, but I went in to do my best with it. Then I heard someone say, "We'd better stop before Sloan shoots somebody!"—and when, soon after, someone else called "woodcock," everyone's idea was to get out of my neighbourhood.

I missed my first shot or two and I felt pretty sore when I heard another remark: "Sloan hasn't shot anyone yet." It made me mad. But all the same I got in a pretty right and left, which made me feel a little better, and the day finished up with my having done my share at all events.

There had been an amusing incident at luncheon that day. It was a large party,

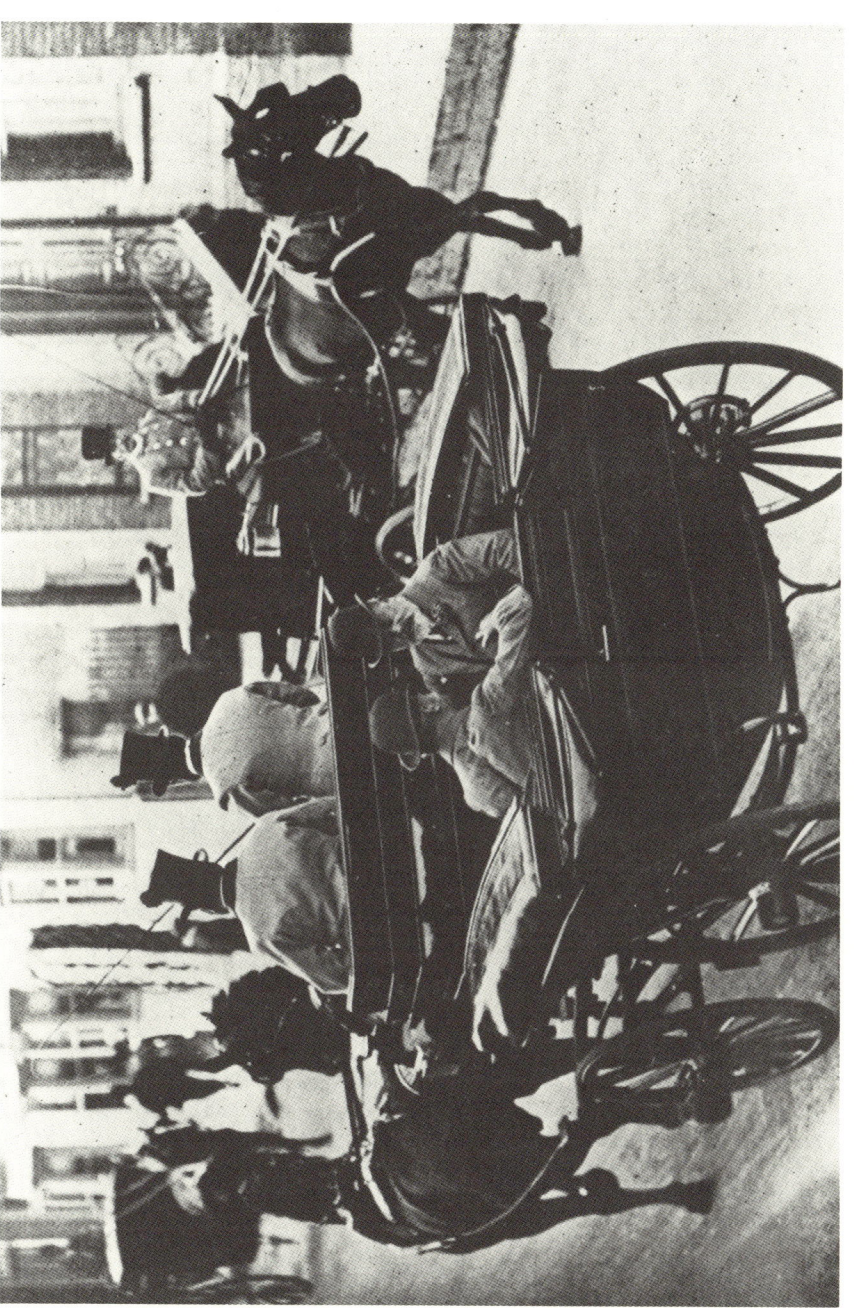

King Edward—Then Prince of Wales—Driving at Newmarket.

but it seemed a waste of time with such good sport awaiting us that an hour should be taken for the meal—and in those days I was never an eater at midday. Lord William was kind enough to press me to take something, but I told him that I "wanted to shoot," and I couldn't if I was helped to a lot of good things. But when he again suggested that I should eat a bit, I said I would have some butter with the bread I had just broken. Then it was discovered that there was none on the table, a thing which struck me as rather odd, considering that butter is always put on in America for meals. I noticed then that butter in any quantity does not make its appearance in English homes until the cheese is brought on. Anyhow, the butler was asked for butter and some little delay occurring in its being produced, Lord William asked again, and eventually a small plate of it was put in front of me. I could always eat bread and butter when having no real appetite or desire to eat anything else, and I managed to keep company with others, really lunching that day so far as my butter went anyway. When I left that evening after the shoot Lord William said, "Good night, little man. I'm glad you showed them that you could shoot birds instead of men, *and* the next time you come here to meals, there shall be dishes of butter all over the table!"

Writing of shooting reminds me of another story which Lord William told King Edward and which tickled him. It was a pure invention of mine at the expense of Mr. Richard Croker, but it was repeated from one to the other. The "Boss" had chaffed me once about something or other, so I got even with him by saying very seriously to two or three gossips who I knew would hand it about that, when Mr. Croker and I were in adjoining butts one day shooting, a bird came running towards him. According to me, the "Boss" had his gun ready to fire.

"Don't shoot the bird running," I called out. He replied (again according to me!): "No I won't, I'm waiting for it to stop!"

Mr. Croker met me after that and said, "You villain, I can't get away from that yarn you spun about me. I heard it yesterday in Dublin and it has even got over to America and has been printed from New York to the Middle West, and from there to California, and South to New Orleans. Sometimes I begin to think it's true, and most of my friends seem to be quite certain about it." Then he laughed as heartily as I did all the time and shook his fist at me.

There was one race I rode for the King in which he thought I must have brought him luck, for the animal I was on might have been beaten many a length by the best horse I think I ever saw up to seven furlongs. It was in the Portland Plate at Doncaster in 1900. Morny Cannon rode Eager, the horse I have just referred to, and I was on Lucknow, owned by the Prince. We swept along together in the last hundred yards. I was on the rails; "Morny" and I were neck and neck; Eager, his mount, was full of running: in fact he had pounds in hand. Perhaps "Morny" wanted to make a fancy finish of it and to win by a narrow margin. He didn't exactly squeeze me on the rails, but certainly I was hampered a bit. However, if his idea was just to win, it was upset, for as we passed the judge's box Lucknow's nose happened to be just in front. Frankly, I was not sure of it myself but I hoped it was so. The judge gave it a short head. I am afraid "Morny" was very upset. I dare say it was one of the greatest disappointments of his riding career. There was for a few minutes a talk of an objection, but in the end, nobody said anything, and certainly there would have been no grounds for it.

It has often been said that one of the reasons for my getting such a swollen head was that I was above myself altogether from the fact that the Prince spoke to me amiably. On the contrary, looking back to the past I certainly believe that in every respect he lifted me up and put me at my best with my own thoughts and made me hope to live up to what I ought to have been but what I was not. Had I been able to fulfill the contract for the Royal stable that had been made with me for 1901, I am sure I shouldn't have given way to the temptation to get about so much and—well, back horses. Two blacks do not make a white, and I'm not going to excuse myself for breaking a rule, but I suppose many jockeys have sinned with regard to an odd wager or two.

In fact, I have yet to know of the jockey who has not had a bet, if only a small amount. The allurement is too strong—too strong for human nature—when you are told and believe that you are on a rare good thing.

Besides, in that year, 1900, it would have been difficult for me to keep up what was, compared with other years, really a comparatively modest expenditure without betting. Little or nothing came my way except my riding fees.

My First Year in England

XIV
A Period of Success

*Caiman's "Middle Park"—What Flying Fox Was—Doggerel on—"Me"—
Disappointments—"Impossible"—Yes or No*

THE FIRST TIME that I rode five winners in one day in England was at Newmarket on 30th September 1898. I was feeling very fit that day, and I thought I might win two or three races for Lord William, but the record all round mounted to five—three for our own stable, and two for other owners. In the first event, a Selling Plate, I was just beaten a head on an animal called the Wak, Tommy Loates just getting home on Eau Gallie; they were a bad lot, all of them. Then came the Bretby Welter, where I got well away on Draco for Lord William, and won anyhow by six lengths; slight odds had been laid on the winner. I won the next race, the Scurry Nursery, also for Lord William, on Manatee, having led all the way. In the Rous Memorial Stakes the stable intended starting Desmond, but Landrail was pulled out instead. There were only three of us and the public had a big gamble on Quassia ridden by Morny Cannon, but pushing Landrail out on coming down Bushes Hill, I got home easily by three lengths. Libra was my next winner, another of Lord William's; in that race Tovaros was thought to be a good thing, and was backed accordingly, but he couldn't get a place. I brought Libra out at the same place as I had the winner of the previous race and won by a couple of lengths. In the Newmarket St. Legar "Morny" and I rode a desperate race home, he on Collar and myself on Galashiels. He had waited two or three lengths behind me till three hundred yards from home, but mine just got past the box by a head. In the Rutland Stakes, which finished up the day, there was a good thing to bet on in Santa Casa, ridden by Madden, and trained by Jarvis. Santa Casa really ought to have been big odds on instead of at even money. Of course, it was my previous success which caused my mount to be at such a false price; they actually took 5 to 2 about it—Boomer his name was. He ought to have been at 100 to 1 against, even in that field of four! Certainly he had no pretensions to gallop with the other three. Of course, I was beaten out of a place.

Still it was a pretty good day to put in five wins and a second out of seven mounts.

A lot of money went that day on Asterie for the Cesarewitch run two weeks later. Although it was reported that I was to be up on the favourite Chalereux, some of my friends who had made a packet that afternoon were convinced that Asterie could win, and that I would ride, so she was backed accordingly. But I never had any look-in at beating Chalereux—and never had the chance of riding him, either. He finished up favourite and beat me. My mount, Asterie, whipped the previous year's winner, Merman.

I shall always remember the Middle Park Plate which I won on Caiman with Flying Fox second. I should say that Caiman was one of the poorest class horses who ever won the race, and it really was a shame that a horse like Flying Fox, a superior animal in every way, should have been done out of what he so much deserved. I repeat: Caiman was one of the most overrated horses I ever knew. The truth was that I understood him and had him under such perfect control that it was possible to do more with him than with perhaps any horse of similar stamp.

Caiman had been a winner, but why they should have taken 7 to 4 about him — Flying Fox was at the same price — it is difficult for me to say, except for the fact that they didn't know how poor an animal he was by the side of the other.

In the race, the other jockeys let me make my own pace, "Morny" holding off on his crack until the place at which he generally began his run. We went slower and slower till we got almost to a walk just before striking to rise out of the last dip. I was watching him and saw him preparing to come along. So I shot mine out before he got moving and *stole* the race, Flying Fox, although going great guns, not having quite time enough to get up.

I hope it does not seem that I am claiming for myself too much judgment at the expense of others, but, without any brag or bounce, I must say that there was such a hopeless ignorance of pace among the majority of those riding in the race, that I suppose I managed to kid them and so got where I did. I always consider that, however much of a "general" I may have been in some races in my career, I can shake hands with myself in that Middle Park Plate being the greatest achievement of my life.

After the race, Lord William, Charlie Mills and others came round saying what a marvelous horse Caiman was. But they wouldn't give me any credit for the win; they kept on repeating that Caiman was the greatest of his age in training, and they stuck to it too, even though I told them he was far behind other horses which were unquestionably inferior to Flying Fox. Charlie Mills and I had quite high words about it, I remember, and I told him that in a true run race, and if I had a chance of riding Flying Fox, I would bet him anything from a thousand to ten thousand pounds that Flying Fox would beat Caiman easily. "Morny" rode Caiman once at Sandown Park after this and beat some very moderate horse quite easily, and that was taken as additional evidence: it put the stamp on the much-boosted Caiman. We all know of cases where geese have been made into swans, but there never was a better example than that of Flying Fox and Caiman.

What a great horse Flying Fox was was perhaps not quite understood by the Duke of Westminster and John Porter during the horse's two-year-old days, but I had formed my opinion of him, which nothing would shake. I was convinced that he was the best horse I had ever seen in England, and that he would turn out as good in reputation as Ormonde, whom I never saw, but whom I had heard so much about.

One day at Chester a year or two later, when I was riding something against one of the Duke's, he said to me, "Are you going to beat us again to-day, Sloan, like you did on Caiman?"

I answered, "Yes, I am, your Grace; but what a shame it was that Flying Fox should ever have been beaten! I should say he's the best you ever had."

The Duke told me then that at one time they couldn't believe it, but he added, "Mr. Porter and I have come to the conclusion that he is just as good as Ormonde, and in some respects better."

That is an opinion which should go down to future generations of horse lovers. I know that Mr. Porter will remember the late Duke saying it. When the time comes in this book for me to tell the story of Flying Fox's Derby I shall explain how he might have lost to Holocaust, but that will be no disparagement to him, for all those who saw the race will remember that Flying Fox broke away no fewer than five times— each break running from two to three furlongs. This took such a lot out of him that I had the race won on the grey Frenchman when he so unaccountably broke his leg. However, all conditions equal, Holocaust would not have had a chance. Mr. Edmond Blanc indeed deserved the success he secured when he paid what was then a record price for Flying Fox. The Turf was going very well in America at the time, and an effort should have been made there to buy him. Look what he got in France: Ajax, Gouvernant, Adam, Val d'Or, Jardy and others. The two defeats of his career? Well—these things *will* happen!

Just about this time one of the London papers ran a competition about "Sloan." I kept copies of some of the results. Here was the first prize "poem."

> "Of Toddy Sloan now let us sing,
> Whose praises through the country ring,
> Undoubtedly the jockey king,
> Proclaimed by everybody.
>
> "Unrivalled he upon a horse,
> Possessed of spirit and resource,
> One always should expect of course,
> Some spirit in a toddy.
>
> "Although of jockeys there are lots,
> Expert like Cannon, Loates, and Watts,
> It's Sloan that every backer spots,
> From Sykes to Lord Tom Noddy.
>
> "And if some unbelievers smile,
> At what they call his monkey style.
> They've got their ponies all the while,
> Upon the mounts of Toddy.
>
> "So backers cheer and bookies groan,
> As race by race is won by Sloan,

> On horses chestnut, bay or roan,
> No matter if they're shoddy.
>
> "They may be broken-kneed or lame,
> He wins upon them just the same,
> So here's to health, and wealth, and fame,
> Of Yankee-doodle Toddy!"

Here is another "beaut."

> "At Chelsea Tod should make his home,
> When he has time to spare,
> For if that way you chance to roam,
> I know you'll find Sloan's square."

Yet one more.

> "I loved Fred Archer in the past,
> I admire Tod Sloan to-day,
> Still Tommy Loates will give him beans,
> Before he goes away."

This was one *at* me.

"The best way to appreciate Tod Sloan is to put him in the Lord Mayor's show."

And the last, which was much quoted at the time, they keep framed in my home at Kokomo:

> T actful,
> O riginal,
> D aring.
>
> S kilful,
> L ucky,
> O bservant,
> A mbitious,
> N erveless.

The paper insisted on a reply from me and this is what I sent:

"I like the English people immensely—at any rate all those I have come into contact with, and those I don't know don't matter, anyhow, do they? I like your English race-courses too.

"The riding is not so difficult as in America; here there is considerably less work. I appreciate all the kind things that have been said about me. As to the criticisms that have appeared, and which I have seen quoted in one paper particularly, you may take it from me they are nonsense from one end to the other. I don't trouble about them one bit.

Tod Sloan."

Of course it wasn't always velvet for those who followed me, both Americans and the public, for, as the papers said, "There were occasional proofs that Sloan's influence on the market was independent of his average—some costly reverses might easily have weakened its potency—but that such is not the case shows how loyal and plucky are his chief supporters and how sheep-like that section of the public with whom it is an article of faith to back his mounts. One recognises Sloan to be a great jockey who has brains as well as boots, whose mounts are to an extent picked, and who, whatever and for whoever he rides, is always a trier and never muddles away a race in the manner more than one have been muddled away this week by crack jockeys. All this one freely admits, but none the less is a blind worship of the American to be deprecated."

Yes, of course there were some afternoons when some of my backers looked down their noses. It was their own affairs of course, and I had lost a bit very possibly myself, but one thing which I always look back upon with satisfaction: I *did* try to find mounts which had a chance, but I can never remember an instance of my doing somebody else out of a ride or of going behind him to get it. I simply loved to win. It wasn't because of what the papers said, for, really, I seldom read anything in the racing part except the descriptions of the previous day's running and the weights for future events. There was no special question therefore, of my liking praise or criticism. All the same, it was natural that I should feel keen on keeping the hold on the public that I had gained, and, on one occasion, just after riding those five winners at Newmarket, I was due to appear at Alexandra Park. A heavy cold kept me away. I resented very much that I wasn't able to see that Saturday afternoon crowd. There was some trouble as a result of this which took some putting right. I had asked Charlie Mills to make my excuses to the Clerk of the Scales and to explain that only ill-health kept me away. He forgot all about it. Anyhow, they were very angry with me for not fulfilling my engagements, and it made bad feeling.

Another disappointment I had about that time was when I was just beaten in the Duke of York Stakes on Mount Prospect. A dead outsider, Sirenia, a real nice mare, pipped me a head. It wasn't altogether a question of what had been won and lost, but at popular meetings, and especially on Saturday afternoons, I never tired of hearing the music of the boys calling after me when I had any real success.

With regard to amusement. In those autumn days of 1898 there were the usual odds and ends of London life—the theatres, music halls, games of bridge, supper-parties—I only looked on at supper—and there was the usual experience of meeting more people that I wanted. *Please, please,* do not think that I had such conceit that I used to put aside or be casual to those I was introduced to, but—well, I didn't always properly reckon up who they were. I know that I may have been off-handed and I may in consequence have been thought rude by those who were really anxious to do me good and whom to know was an honour and privilege. But—do you get me?—there were so many of the "also rans" who got round me, scraped introductions, and then traded on the acquaintance and used me in every way to pull their stunts and put it across the simple people who were so ready to believe anything from people who could say they "knew Sloan"! "Save me from my friends" is an expression that Lord William taught me.

The truth was that I could never find out, to the extent I wanted to, who really were those I *should* be with. I knew quick enough those I liked, and I suppose it can be said that I stuck to those whose friendship I valued. There were *others* however. A chance meeting, a cocktail, just one odd word—it doesn't matter what it was about—and I was quite liable to hear that "Sloan had said"—well—this, that and the other. These things got round and about one or two of the big London hotels, and I heard afterwards even that syndicates had been formed to back horses, and that I was supposed to supply the "information"! It made me mad sometimes. "Straight from the horse's mouth," was nothing to what I was supposed to have said on various occasions in order to do mugs a good turn. I know that there was all sorts of money torn from various people who used to be about. A few of the "steerers" didn't settle, and some were even supposed to be betting for me, but I had no more to do with them than nine hundred and ninety-nine people out of a thousand who read this book.

Round about the Savoy certain people used to look upon me as a curiosity, and I felt sometimes I would sooner be up in my room reading the papers from over home. It was the staring and the remarks which made me—now believe this—SHY. I was supposed to swank, but please don't believe all that. I won't go so far as to say that I was nervous, but didn't want all the gazing and chatting as I passed. I have heard that people who are called affected can be so from sheer shyness—they are trying to pass it off. Perhaps that was my case.

I wasn't exactly "unformed" but I was quite likely to meet those of a kind I had never seen before and I had to get to know them—and they me. Have I explained myself? I was in and about everywhere, I could do the weight and hadn't to spend night after night in Turkish baths, and because I liked clean clothes and felt that I could do what others did—meet my friends and have decent meals—my enemies began to say that I was "impossible." That was the beginning of the events that led to my being "shopped." What people said at that time was most undeserved, whatever it may have been later on.

XV

Trainers—and Trainers

George Blackwell's Ability—Byron MacLellan—How Horses Were Shod

A GREAT DEAL OF CREDIT was given to American trainers in England for some of the successes achieved by horses in their hands, and frequently this was laid on with too heavy a brush, and insufficient acknowledgment made for what American riders had done. I was often asked what I thought of So-and-so—among trainers—and others, but at the time I thought it as well to give evasive replies. One American trainer in England I should say didn't know a horse from a billy goat, although he was a good stableman! For the matter of that, there were many English trainers who were just as bad. Some of them held "proud positions." I could never understand how they got them; in fact, the thing was often one of the greatest jokes imaginable.

It was generally a case of old-fashioned methods being followed and of a refusal to pay attention to suggestions. For instance one trainer, an Englishman, had some American two-year-olds and one morning he turned up with his long rein and whip. I told him that they had already been broken, but he shouted in reply:

"They've got to be broken over again in the way my father broke them, and," pointing to his son, "that young feller over there, when he grows up will do exactly the same as I do. What is good for one generation will be for another. Horses don't change."

I used to get so bewildered with this kind of stupidity that I had no words for argument, and, in this instance I left it at that. But the hopeless ignorance in a thousand ways of some could not help striking anyone with any real experience. I am not saying that I was such a superior judge, but, looking back, I do know quite well that what I thought then and think now is correct.

I could mention many trainers of the present day—both English and American—who are really clever men. I have always thought that, of Englishmen, George Blackwell was right out by himself as a trainer. We were only just acquainted, so the statement can be taken as being quite unprejudiced. His horses used to be higher in flesh and brighter in coat after real hard work—for he didn't spare them—than those of anyone else I saw in England at that time. You see, a man may get famous on account of one or two great horses he has turned out, but the true cleverness consists in *discovering* horses. There's no reason why there should not be a Galtee More every year—he wants finding out!

There are some trainers who would sooner make twenty pounds on the cross than a hundred on the level. I remember riding good winners for one man, who unfortunately I cannot name although he had practically first call on me, and I could never understand why I didn't get a present. Owners used to look at me in such a way that gradually I got the idea that they were expecting me to thank them for something.

At all events, that's how I read it afterwards. But I never got a nickel. I know that trainer had seven hundred and fifty pounds from one man to split up with me. Yet they say that it is sinful for a jockey to have a bet!

John Dawson was a trainer who was very nice to me, both before and after I won the Manchester November Handicap for Lord Ellesmere on Proclamation. I have a souvenir Dawson gave me after I had won—some cuff buttons. It was rather curious how I got that mount. "Skeets" Martin, who was to have ridden, was dying to get back to London, and I was due to ride the favourite who, however, went wrong at almost the last moment. The day before the race was run, "Skeets," hearing that I was free, said to me, "You're a lucky swine. I wish I could get out of my mount too: he's a big outsider; the going'll be fearful."

"I'll ride him," I said, "if you get the trainer's permission." John Dawson was willing enough; he seemed surprised that I would take it on. "Skeets" was in great glee that he could go off that night to London. There were twenty-two in the field, and all those who remember that afternoon will know that the course was worse than usual. We went round in a procession with Proclamation lying about eighth. I was being clouted with mud until my two eyes were nearly bunged up and I had to keep spitting it out of my mouth, getting more and more like a nigger in appearance all the time. I am sure I was a hundred and twenty-five yards from the leader at one time but I hung around the rails, although I was nearly put out by a heavier clod than usual from the horse in front of me. It isn't so much that the mud cakes are "catapulted" at one, but one is going at a great speed and actually running into what is coming at one at a great pace too! I held on anyhow, and managed to bring up this three-year-old outsider—he was carrying 7-7—to win nicely. A lot of my friends got 33 to 1, so it was a pretty good wind-up to a season. He started at 25 to 1 and of course it was something for the public to remember me by till next year.

While on the subject of trainers, I should like to say that the greatest of all who lived in my time was Byron MacLellan, now unhappily dead. He could make a good horse out of a donkey. He did more to found a good school of trainers than any man known to the world during the last fifty years. MacLellan came from a good Kentucky family, and for the whole of his life was associated with horses. He got to know their disposition, studying them and, like some who succeeded him, believed in building up animals and making allowance for different temperaments. He would, if alive, have screamed at some of the wholesale incompetency of many trainers having the charge of horses to-day. By the way, let me say that I am rather nervous in laying down opinions so strongly, but I ask myself, "What is the good of half saying a thing and leaving the best part of it to guesswork?" I am told that it is easy to make a mistake. It is still more easy to print a libel!

What, too, would MacLellan have thought of what you and I know has been done by many English owners and trainers, and almost been boasted about, with horses which they thought were useless or which, after early trials as yearlings, they thought were no good. Often such horses are taken out and shot so that they should not lumber up the yard! It is a sin, for some of them have turned out most useful, and even great, afterwards. I could mention many instances where horses showing nothing as yearlings proved themselves later on. I am reminded of this by what my editor writes about Polar Star in *Sharps, Flats, Gamblers and Racehorses*. Mr. Hall Walker's horse was so bad as a yearling that he was not left in the Derby and was nearly gelded. The great Colin in America would not have been accepted as a present when a yearling.

MacLellan wasn't like that: he would never give up a horse in his very young days, neither would Wishard. I put down Enoch Wishard as one of the best trainers I have ever come in close touch with. I believe he started life as a blacksmith in a town called Wellsville, and from this town also came Duke, who at present trains for Mr. W.K. Vanderbilt; and John M'Graw, the manager of the New York Baseball Club. Enoch Wishard made a study of horses' feet from early days before he took to training, and he followed this up by always caring for their mouths. These certainly are two of the greatest essentials when considering a horse's chance of progressing in training. Fortunately, many trainers of the present day have given serious attention to these matters, which one must say were far too often neglected in the past. Wishard asked regularly about the mouths of his charges and he would never leave the care of their feet to anyone but himself. Perhaps more than anyone else he has proved how a man can reach the top of the trainer's calling owing to observation and taking the trouble to think about the disposition of his horses.

Wishard's, by the way, is a case that helps to prove that there is very little heredity in training. Tell me any great trainer whose son has proved as great a man at the business as his father before him. The talent is supposed to "pass down," but that is sheer nonsense. I do not think there are "born trainers" any more than there are "born jockeys." Some jockeys may have taken up riding through their fathers having been at the same, but it doesn't follow for a moment that they will achieve success. Take the list of all you can ever remember; there are a few exceptions on the other side but the vast majority goes to support what I have said.

There is a good trainer in France, Eugene Leigh. I am quite sure his father never saw a horse, and yet, what the son doesn't know about them is scarcely worth learning. One thing is pretty certain, that if the modern school of training had not been introduced by Wishard and a few of his contemporaries, racing would have remained where it was, and would have been left to a few gamblers to control!

When I first visited France, I couldn't help noticing how little horses were understood by some trainers. In fact, I was astounded. Purely from lack of care were animals suffering from thrush and the foot disease. The treatment was little understood. Then again, hardly anything was known of a horse's mouth. They had then no implements for the floating and decapping of horses' teeth, and it was only after some persuasion I got them to procure these appliances. Since then, Joe

Marsh has done a great deal in the way of looking after horses' mouths. He is a witch doctor with teeth.

The shoes, too, worn by horses at that time weighed from 1 lb. to 1½ lbs. on each foot. Blacksmiths did not even know how to trim properly the foot of a racehorse, and when I got hot about it and recommended the adoption of the American system the Frenchmen thought it would be too big a change from what had always been the rule on the French turf. France owes a great deal to American trainers. Fortunately, it can be said that many Anglo-Frenchmen have had the sense to alter their methods.

The extraordinary changes brought in by Americans caused the charge of doping being levelled against them.

One of the best horses I have seen in France, and one in which the greatest change was effected, was Mauvezin, now at Lord Carnarvon's stud. I bought him out of a selling race for eleven thousand francs in 1901. When he came to me, he could not stay more than four and a half furlongs. In little over a month, he gained nearly a hundred pounds in weight. Of course, it will be remembered that afterwards he won with big weights in France, took the Stewards' Cup at Goodwood, and proved a success at the stud.

Americans taught England a great deal about horses' feet too.

XVI
England and America

Some American Trainers – Breaking My "Drum" – Rushing "On the Road" – Talk "English"

IN TALKING ABOUT ENGLISH TRAINERS, I do not wish to be charged with belittling some really good men. Many trainers have had such extraordinary opportunities. I believe a man like Harry Batho, who trains at Alfriston in Sussex, might have been one of the most successful of the English school had he been given the same opportunities as the heads of what are known as "aristocratic stables." Batho gets to *know* a horse, and is clever in placing them too.

Mr. George Lambton proved what he could do when he had something good to deal with – and I really mean this, for I have taken a good deal of notice of what he has done in this respect. He will ask questions and, with Wootton perhaps, has been the most progressive in recent years. Despite vast experience, he will listen to sound advice.

Some men in England would never take any tip at all. For instance, when I had that terrible fall on Maluma in the Liverpool Cup, which has been referred to in a previous chapter, Robinson would run her without plates. It was a terrible day, but he said she had been used to running without shoes in Australia and he supposed she would do her best without them over here. The inevitable happened. As she was barefooted, I knew I was gone. It occurred round the turn as she slipped sideways. I always think with plates on that day, she couldn't have lost.

Charles Morton would favour me by asking me questions from time to time. If he didn't agree with all my replies (and I didn't expect him to), still, with my experience and natural "horse sense", he often found some pointer or other worth taking. Morton is a man of ripe judgment.

The strokes that some trainers put across a jockey are wicked sometimes. I remember riding an animal in one of the big back-end handicaps. Before we were out, I knew I was on a dead 'un. It was a bit maddening, and it was natural to feel furious on returning to the paddock.

The trainer said to me, "She'll run better in a fortnight," and gave me a look of intelligence.

"Not with me on," I replied. "I'm not going to ride him."

He threatened to take me before the Stewards but – not a bit of it.

The same man sent me a bill for £375 for bets, a lot of it on the dead 'un I have just referred to, and pressured me to pay him.

"All right," I wrote; "I'm going to Weatherby's, who keep all my accounts, and

I'll get them to transfer £375 for bets over to you, I suppose they'll ask me what it's for." He had got me altogether for £1400 and he wrote to me, "For God's sake, don't say anything at all about going to Weatherby's." That was good enough for me, and there was never any reason to give that claimed money another thought, for he had put it across me.

Of the modern trainers, the American Sam Hildreth, who was over in France for a time and went back when Mr. Kohler died, has been a trainer of the highest merit, and I put him next to Wishard as Wishard was in 1900. Then, too, Eugene Leigh and Tom Welch, both now training in France, and Tom Healy in America, I rank high. In France, Michel Pantall is a really clever man and has struck me as one conforming more to the best accepted American methods. Wallace Davis, who trains for Monsieur Picard, was, I think, as good a trainer as any I have met.

As I have to write a book, I feel it is necessary to give these personal opinions, but I'd like to say again that I put them down for what they are worth. They may be valuable notes for those who read years ahead some of the Turf history of my time.

One of the greatest trainers was James Rowe. He was in a class all by himself in the older school, and he adapted himself readily to the new conditions. He had been one of America's crack jockeys before beginning training.

James Rowe, after he first retired from training became a starter and was much respected for his ability. Subsequently, he trained again—for Mr. James R. Keene. It is interesting to recall one of my first experiences with Mr. Rowe. It was about the year 1892 or 1893, when I had come to New York with very little confidence in my self and hardly any prospects. There was a big race at Sheepshead Bay, and the leading trainer at that time, Rogers, told me that I could have the mount on his mare Lucania. I thought he was trying to give me a chance and took it as a great compliment, but I found out later that the truth was there was no one else available at my weight. We got down to the post and, after one false break-away, I found that my girths were loose and begged permission to tighten them. "My saddle has slipped, Mr. Rowe, can I fix it?" I said.

Mr. Rowe answered, "I'll fix *you*, you just get into line; don't you come that Western stuff on me."

Of course, it was the old flag starting in those days. Well, he tried to get us away, but there was another false break. This time I was determined to try and tighten up, so getting back to the post before the others, I turned Lucania's head the reverse way of the course and, lifting up my right leg, got at the flap to tighten it. Rowe, seeing me do this, jumped down off his starting platform and seized a whip with a long lash and, coming at the back of me, let out. It caught me from one leg across the back to the other making a great weal like a horseshoe. He was so sore with me I could see and—I was sore too.

When I got back after finishing second or third—I am sure I should have won if the saddle had been all right—I got hold of a lawyer and we laid an information that evening to the police at Sheepshead Bay. I showed the police the welt on my body, which looked as if it had been made with a half-inch rope.

Well, we began a lawsuit against Rowe and, despite all sorts of people coming up to me with offers to pay a thousand or two thousand dollars instead of the ten thousand I was claiming, I wouldn't hush it up, for I stuck to my guns that he had no right to hit me.

The action was still pending in the courts when, going into the Casino Theatre in New York one evening, who should walk in at the same moment but Jimmy Rowe and his wife. They came across to me, Rowe saying, "Hullo, Tod," and holding out his hand. I took it and we all three chatted for a minute, nothing about the trouble though. I wouldn't sell that case, but after that I dropped it on my own accord straight away. Truly I can say that no money would have squared it. Mr. Rowe and I were splendid friends afterwards and when he trained for Mr. Keene, I could always be his first jockey when I was free, and we had many successes together.

Mr. Rowe was kindness itself to me, especially when I had rather a nasty accident and split the drum of my ear. One day he asked: "Would you like to ride Elkins? I hardly like to ask you as he is not a very pleasant horse; he can run, but you'll have to be careful of him: he is up to all sorts of tricks."

"That don't matter," I replied, and they threw me into the saddle. I was no sooner there than Elkins jerked up his head, almost knocking me out and altogether knocking me off the saddle, after which he cleared the ground round him. Rowe wanted to retire him, but I was round in a minute, although in great pain, and I wouldn't hear of the horse not running, and again they threw me into the saddle. All went smoothly and I won by seventy or eighty yards. I was in the hospital for some days after that: it took a long time to dull the pain and make me sufficiently fit to have an operation.

I wound up the season of 1898 having ridden forty-three winners in three months. It was satisfactory enough, and it was with a nice sum tucked away—about ten thousand pounds—that I returned soon after to New York, where the newspapers had a good deal more to say about what I had done.

I felt rather odd on leaving England for America once more. Many a time when I smoked a cigar on the promenade deck in the morning, before the boys were about, I would look forward to meeting many of the old lot, whom I understood better and who, *perhaps*, knew *me* better than many of my new English friends, but I had it in my mind in that end of 1898 and beginning of 1899 that I would sooner have been in London fighting over certain races which I had won and lost, than be in New York. I had to answer so many questions! Some of them sounding so curious. People who did not know England a bit, nor the conditions of English racing, were very odd. The majority of the queries put to me were as to how this, that and the other backer had got on, what they had won and how far they had taken the knock "playing the races." The more delicate and interesting phases of the racing game were not inquired into. Certainly old friends among trainers used to ask me what they did in England under certain conditions but, I am afraid that generally I did not tell them exactly what they wanted to know, for I was determined not to criticise English methods—then.

Certainly it seemed strange to be back in New York. I suppose I was getting a bit Europeanised or something. I know I could not quite take the interest in some of the matters which I used to think were the beginning and end of everything.

It was curious to compare New York with London. I had heard that many Americans, and Australians too, had come to England and had drawn contrasts between everything which they had seen in London—and which at first they didn't like—and what they were used to at home. I confess that had been a little of my own idea when I went back after the 1897 season. An American may long to return if he has accomplished something; if he has not, he is likely to have only one idea: to go home and bury himself. But when I returned at the end of 1898, things began to seem a bit different; it was the life around town which bothered me. In some ways it seemed so much brighter in New York, but at times I seemed drawn towards what I had just left. I had more chances of social life in London; there seemed a sort of domestic touch even about a rubber of bridge in a private room at a hotel. I used to be asked out a good deal; it gave quite a change to the daily life. Of course I had a lot of old friends in New York who would offer me the same hospitality, but it was what I had just become accustomed to which I hankered after.

Then again, the theatres didn't seem quite so comfortable. Going out to the play in London was more like going to a party. Everyone looked so well turned out and I used to enjoy the intervals between the acts when we could talk over different things, and I had time to smoke quite a quarter of a cigar in the lobby. The plays were better, or appealed to me more, in New York, but the whole surroundings of the theatre were more attractive in the London I had just left.

On the other hand, there were many things in England that I could have done without, as I discovered when I got back. Rushing about all over the country for instance for three days or two days here, and another day or two there. It seemed to be like being "on the road" in a one-night-stand company. All American trainers who have settled in England have disliked this. It is so different from America, where one races two or three weeks at one place and then moves on to another. At Saratoga, for instance, they raced continuously for nearly three weeks, and in the good times, many horses were trained with the others of the string which perhaps were not intended to be run at that meeting at all.

Other Americans' experiences have been very similar to mine—the longing to rush back "home," a mild desire to come to Europe again, and then a great regret to leave England or France, and then, eventually, the feeling that after all, Europe was the only place to live in. One American jockey, Danny Maher, has even become a naturalised Englishman, and many other Americans might do the same, but they are slack and won't take the trouble about the papers. However, personally, I always had the feeling that if I lived and died in Europe—as I suppose I shall—nothing would make me change my citizenship of the United States, although I suppose I have just as many friends and acquaintances British as American, and throughout my career I have had as many kindnesses from our nation as from the other.

Belgians and Frenchmen, too, were also very friendly to me as far as I could judge; and I think I know now (although, of course at first, it was very difficult for me to form an estimate not knowing a word of the language, and not attempting the sort of pigeon English that some do). I suppose I have a certain knowledge of French to-day. Talking of pigeon English I think "Boots" Durnell, who I brought over to France and who is now training for the King of Roumania, was about the funniest guy I ever saw or heard when he first attempted to make himself understood in France. From the very moment he arrived at Boulogne, he began to imitate what he thought French people spoke, and after about a week he had got together certain sentences and a way of gesticulating which was all his own. It was in an attempt to speak to Charron first that he came out in his glory.

This is a specimen: "You see, Monsieur, zat ze leg of ze horse vich is swawlen and vot I do wis him zis after noon is to take ze ombrohcarshon in mon hands and zer rube 'im until he gets vell."

When he got one or two more French words in his head he would shrug his shoulders every other moment, hold his hands up, cast his eyes down, and shake hands with his left hand and always pretend that he couldn't speak English— and certainly he *was* getting out of it. One day Baron Leonino came to the stable and "Boots" started on him. I saw the Baron's face begin to broaden into a smile when "Boots" said, "Ze gallop your cheval had done zis matin is ze fastest by ze watch we 'ave 'ad for quelqeus jours. 'E'as eat up and 'e is as fit as a violin." Then Baron Leonino said, "Now suppose you tell me all this in English," and I chipped in, "Why the something, something, don't you tell the gentleman exactly what *has* happened?"

He got some of the stable hands into the way of talking too, and when the shopkeepers and Frenchmen who supplied us with things couldn't understand them "Boots" said they were fools who didn't understand their own language.

XVII
Knight of the Thistle

The "Lincolnshire"—Good Horse's Bad Moments—At Home in England

THE WINTER OF 1898-1899 brought about the usual incidents: visits here and there in America; meetings with many old friends and the introduction to new ones, especially those connected with the prize ring and the world of sport, some of whom I shall have occasion to refer to in later chapters. I had always, of course, to bear in mind that I was due back to ride for Lord William in the early spring. In fact, I heard at the end of January that I was required to ride Knight of the Thistle in the Lincolnshire Handicap. This horse was trained by Huggins, who had bought him for an American sportsman named L.O. Appleby. Two years before, when a four-year-old, he had won the Royal Hunt Cup carrying 7-5 and had figured prominently in other races. I knew little or nothing about him, but was told by letter that I had a real good chance of winning the first important race of the season. They sent me cuttings from English newspapers, the handicap, and what certain English sporting writers thought about the prospects of the race.

I had heard of Knight of the Thistle, for of course there was always the usual "horse talk" every evening and during the day—but, by the way, we would frequently, my friends and I, break away entirely from turf topics and switch on to other things, especially fights, the theatres, and—well, something not four-legged. I kept receiving letters in the early part of March reminding me exactly when the Lincolnshire Handicap was. Some of them I didn't even reply to, but I did send cables to Lord William and to Huggins to say that I was sailing on a certain date. I had timed it to a nicety, reckoning that I could arrive at Southampton and that I could get to Lincoln for the big race. There was no trouble in crossing, but I imagine they were rather upset when I didn't turn up on the opening day of the season. I was there in good time on the Tuesday.

They told me exactly what my 9 to 1 chance was likely to do. There would be a big field—in fact, twenty ran, a larger muster than there had been for a few years previously. I hadn't been on Knight of the Thistle, as I have explained, but I admired the horse when I saw him and I liked him still better when he swung down to the post with me. But at the post, I found out what a devil he was at the start. He was a very actor before he began his business, in fact a mean sort of horse, and I had any amount of trouble with him.

Lord William had said to me before the race: "Are you fit?"

I answered, "Yes."

"Have you been doing any riding?"

"Yes, in hansom cabs," and I added that I didn't intend to change my methods for I always did well when starting off a season.

"Well, there you are; if you think you are all right, I suppose you *are*."

To make a long story short, "The Knight" fiddled me about at the post, where we were for some time, with the wind blowing colder even than I had experienced it in America. Ultimately, he got going with me and, at one time, I thought I might have a chance of winning, but General Peace, a real nice horse who was receiving 13 pounds—a big difference considering the class—beat me. Of course I was disappointed, and although Lord William didn't say so at the time, I am quite certain that he was of the opinion, then and afterwards too, that had I been over and riding gallops and had I become a little more acclimatised, I should have won it. Charlie Mills, who had done the greater part of the commission, was of the same opinion, and didn't hesitate to say so to others, but I state with perfect confidence that there was nothing lost in fitness and jockeyship that day. If there had been, it might as well go down here at once. What made them firmer in their convictions was that after that day at Lincoln, I had caught such a chill right across my kidney and back that I hesitated about riding at Liverpool at the end of the week; in fact, I was knocked right out. But I went on to Liverpool all the same, intending to ride, but feeling like nothing on earth. Much against my rule, I had to take a glass of brandy at Lincoln before my dinner and determined to see what a rest for a day would do. But it was no good and I had to stay in bed in my apartment and think all the time what I might have done had I been riding. It was the weather which had crocked me up and nothing else, for I had felt quite fit when crossing the ocean and also entirely myself when getting in the saddle for that race. Next day I went to Liverpool, but there was nothing else to do but to shiver and sweat while somebody brought me in the results of the races and came in the evening and discussed what had occurred. Of course it made me feel as if I could get out of bed and take my chance the next day, but it was lucky for me—so the doctor told me—that I did keep quiet until I was able to go back to London on the Sunday and creep between the blankets at the Cecil for another day or two. When I was about and was riding as usual, of course I heard all the talk over again about what I should have done, if I had been fit—and so on and so on.

It appears that Huggins had bought Knight of the Thistle for Appleby as a type of an old-fashioned, high-class English race-horse. It was Huggins' own judgment, and in this instance, he was absolutely correct; for on his day, this animal was one of the best I ever rode. He behaved badly at the post, but he was as game as he could be. On his day of days he could have beaten anything, classic or otherwise, and such he proved when I won the Jubilee on him some weeks later from Greenan and Lord Edward II, who had finished behind him in the Lincolnshire. Mr. Arthur Coventry had all sorts of trouble with him at the post. Even on that day, he had certain peculiarities; for he was getting a bit "stalliony"—I will not say savage.

Both he and Santoi, who will be mentioned later, had their very bad moments and it was always the most interesting part of my work to try and find out what was really the matter with them. No one ever seems to have gauged the exact disposition of a horse, but I never ceased trying to "know" animals which had bad characters. They are really blamed sometimes for "cussedness" when it is not altogether their own fault. It may be stomach trouble, their teeth, or their feet. From the many thousands of horses I have ridden, my own personal impression is that there is no trouble without a cause. I sometimes begin to think that the real cause may be too much in-breeding, bringing about an extraordinary temperament, just as in human beings, lunacy can be the result of marriages in the same family. As a matter of fact, no one will ever make me think differently. I don't know whether a greater study of the thoroughbred will ever exactly enable men to know horses and get such remedies for various troubles as to make a perfectly tractable animal, but it *is* to be done; I am convinced of it.

After the start for that Jubilee, I never had the slightest doubt about the result; and for weeks after, in fact months after, I can remember discussing the horse which Huggins had been fortunate enough to acquire, and which America was lucky enough to have afterwards as a sire horse. If someone had only gotten to know exactly what was the matter with Knight of the Thistle, I am sure that he could have carried any weights and beaten the very best in training. Many of those who read this will remember all about him, and those who were connected with his early training may have something more to say than I have. In the Hunt Cup later (in 1899) he carried 9-2 and I finished third on him behind the mighty Eager, and a three-year-old, Refracto, who was only putting up 6-3. By the way, there was a Scottish firm who, after the Jubilee, started a new brand of whiskey called Knight of the Thistle Blend and sent me a big quantity of it, some of which I gave away and the rest—well, I drank it myself.

I am not going into all the races which I rode in between the Lincolnshire and the Jubilee and then on the big events at Epsom and Ascot, but I shall dip into my memory where something of more importance than usual suggests itself. I was doing as well as in the two previous autumns. I had made plenty of new friends and was learning more of England. In fact, I was getting thoroughly at home in the country I knew so well afterwards, and on the continent in which I was to eventually make my home. There was, of course, any number of Americans over to follow me and others, and I could not blame them if occasionally they were a little bit too patriotic, for the luck of the American riders seemed to be in the ascendant. I had plenty of invitations to ride, and of course my friends helped me considerably in getting me mounts. Time and again I would not know what I was to be up on during the following week, but at the end, I always found I had added many notches to my score, and as the figures got better and better, so was extra confidence given to me and to those who employed me. As the sun got warmer too, I began to feel that fitness which the trying wind of the spring had dried up.

BEATEN ON CAIMAN BY FLYING FOX
Newmarket First Spring Meeting, 1899

Winning the Jubilee on Knight of the Thistle
Kempton Park, 1899

XVIII
Holocaust

Engaged for Holocaust — Flying Fox Delays Start — What Charles Hawtrey Missed

OF COURSE, up to this time I had never had a chance either of riding in the Derby, or of seeing it, for previously no summer had been spent in England. The circumstances which led up to my getting the mount on Holocaust are, briefly, that my friend Charles Hawtrey and Miss Fanny Ward had been over in France and had seen Holocaust run in, I think, the French Derby. My name had been mentioned by one or the other or both to M. de Brémond who owned the grey. He was interested and although it was stated that Watkins, a French jockey, was to ride him, I was told that I might get the mount, and that M. de Brémond, who was staying at the Savoy, would see me if I was sitting down to dinner. Hurrying over this meal, I went from the Cecil next door to the Savoy and asked for the French owner.

I was shown into the entrance to the restaurant and M. de Brémond came out to meet me. He looked at me as I stood before him in tail coat, white waistcoat and tie and a silk hat and then he glanced over my head as if looking for someone, saying:

"Where is Sloan? Bring him in here!"

"I am Sloan," I said.

"Oh, are you? I hear you'd like to ride my horse to-morrow."

The only reply I could think of was: "Yes, I'll ride him all right, if you like."

He thought for a moment.

"Well, you can. That's arranged, eh? You've never seen him; that doesn't matter, for I hear there are many winners you have ridden which you have never seen. He's a nice sort of horse; whether he can win or not, I don't know. There's Flying Fox, of course, and that's enough without mentioning the others in the race."

I listened attentively, and when he mentioned Flying Fox, I was quite of his opinion that the big colt was enough to think of without worrying about the rest of them. M. de Brémond stopped a little while talking to me — both of us standing up — and added: "Well I'll see you at Epsom to-morrow."

The news got about through one and the other that night, but there was not much business done since everyone was Flying Fox mad. In fact, there were thousands of pounds laid on him that evening at 2 to 1 and 9 to 4 on — he started at 5 to 2 on. In a previous chapter I have mentioned what a great horse the favourite was and, even though I had confidence that my recently found mount would do well from what I had heard of him, still I couldn't pretend that I had any serious idea on that previous evening that I could win. All the same, it was nice to have a ride with any kind of chance in a race I had heard and read so much about. In America, even those who do not follow English racing results will always read anything about the Derby, the greatest race in the world. I know that I did, and I often found others doing so. American owners and breeders, too, always had the ambition to have an entry in the English Derby, and the prospects would be discussed a long time in advance. Some of the American papers would come out with big stories about the history of the race, and all that sort of stuff. I used to devour them when in a racing stable in early days with just as much keenness as I would read about Sullivan, Jackson and all the big fellows in the prize-ring. Therefore, when I met my friends that night it was with some pride that I stated I was to ride the grey Frenchman in the Derby.

I went to bed with the same sort of feeling, not a bit excited, yet feeling that I had something to do the next day. Perhaps one more personal note might be made here. If I had been engaged weeks before to ride the favourite, I might have felt exactly the same. For those who don't know, it may be said that one mount is very like another to a jockey. Of course, I have known some men to get very nervous when a big thing is at stake, but after all, a ride is a ride, and the excitement can be just as great in a selling race as in what is called a classic race in England. At all events, that is the way I look at it. I am reminded by my Editor that the late Anglo-French jockey Tommy Lane, who rode against me on Perth III when I won the Ascot Gold Cup on Merman, was of the worrying kind, and I have known others among Englishmen who felt pretty well the same. I suppose, however, that we Americans, somehow or other, are colder-blooded propositions. At all events, I have never known Lester or Johnny Reiff or Danny Maher not being able to sleep or take their food through having a big thing to think of the next day—unless they had to waste, of course.

But to get on with the story of the Derby. I had never seen Holocaust, as I have explained, and I caught the first glimpse of him when arriving in the paddock with the other boys. I was very pleased with the look of him and I told M. de Brémond so. But he didn't want to know much about that. He had backed the horse and he said to me, what I already knew, that "I had to beat Flying Fox."

He laughed a little and I smiled back at him, saying something to the effect that one never knew the luck of it.

Well, we went down to the post and it was here that I began to think a great deal more of my chance, for Holocaust stood as quiet as a sheep during those five false starts which I have already spoken of, wherein Flying Fox went a quarter of a mile to three furlongs after every breakaway. Yes, I was just tickled to death with the grey; he was beautifully behaved—as quiet and good-natured a horse as I had ever been on.

At last, at the sixth attempt, we were off. We went up the hill to the top and raced down to Tattenham corner. I was a neck in front of Flying Fox and to my delight saw that Morny had got his whip out on the favourite. Before that I hadn't really the remotest idea of actually beating him, and anyhow, I should have had no pretensions to do so, if it hadn't been for those false starts. I got Morny on the rails and I was going as easily as possible, whereas Flying Fox got the stick again.

We crossed the Tan road and had only about a furlong and a half to go, with Flying Fox well beaten by this time and Holocaust not having been called on for any effort at all. Suddenly something happened — I thought I had been cut into. There was a shock, and it was as much as I could do to keep in my saddle. The poor beggar rolled from side to side but he didn't come down as many have asserted that he did. Of course he eased up very soon to a walk. He was a horrible sight with his leg broken off short; in fact the stump was sticking in the ground. How he had gone on for even that extra hundred and twenty yards I don't know. But a horse with his blood up will stick to it without apparently feeling anything. When I got off his back he began munching grass!

I was terribly upset at the sight of the poor beast, and it is beyond question — and future generations should believe me when I say this — that I was never more certain then or now that I had another horse positively beaten than I was that day about Flying Fox. There wouldn't have been a close finish even; for, as I have said, I was going so easily, and there was any amount left in M. de Brémond's horse.

What followed is well known, the poor grey was destroyed in a quiet field soon after.

M. de Brémond took it all in a very sporting spirit and agreed with others that is was the most extraordinary accident imaginable. It was natural for Morny to think that he could have won, for Flying Fox was such a wonderful horse and would struggle on to the end. But there are limits even to what a great horse can do, especially when he had gone well over a mile before the start had taken place, and that quite apart from getting back to the post each time. Morny and I talked it over many times afterwards.

Perhaps it would have been a shame if the better horse, Flying Fox, had been beaten, but still that is all in the luck of the game. Certainly it was a disaster that M. de Brémond should lose an animal who would have been worth twenty thousand pounds if he had not broken his leg.

Mr. John Porter told his friends that he had never any doubt about the eventual result except once. He had trained the horse and knew him by heart.

There wasn't a great amount of money lost by the American division nor a vast amount by the French, but the price, with Flying Fox starting at 5 to 2 on, would have given a splendid return if only Holocaust had won. There never was a Derby I heard more discussed, and the arguments as to what would have happened had not the accident occurred never seemed to end. I was often referred to, but with the exception of telling M. de Brémond and one or two intimate friends, I never thought it was worth going over hour after hour day after day. It might have appeared, if I had given the opinion emphatically in print as I am doing now, that I was conceited enough to think that I could win on "anything" — and I was anxious not to have too many unpleasant little things attributed to me! But—just once more—*it was 10 to 1 my beating Flying Fox* after the incidents at the post. This is repetition I know, but I will add yet again, in a different phrase that it was *20 to 1 against my beating him*, if we had gotten away at the first attempt. I want to emphasise everything I have said in praise about the great son of Orme in a previous chapter.

I dare say that Charles Hawtrey may sometimes wake up in the middle of the night and think of what he would have won over Holocaust, and he has a right to. His judgment was so right in thinking he had put me on to a good thing. M. de Brémond was not sorry that he had put me up, although it was a disastrous start in his colours.

I had at one time one or two good pictures of the principal horses in that Derby parading round the paddock before the race, but I put them away some years ago and have never looked at them since. It is the ambition of every jockey to win a Derby, and that I had the chance of doing so at the first attempt is almost too much to chew over. However—who knows? I'm not dead yet!

XIX

Flying Fox and Caiman

The Tragedy of Sibola — Beaten by "Temper"

FLYING FOX SHOWED in the Two Thousand Guineas what a horse Caiman was. Of course I knew long time before that Lord William and Huggins had hopes of Caiman proving a top-sawyer, but I've said already that I never held any view about him except that he was a good class selling plater. Still, he was backed by the American division and, in the race, I did do all I could to get a surprise run away from the big horse. In the event, Morny won as he liked. He wasn't going to be slipped as he was in the Middle Park Plate the year before.

Caiman and Flying Fox were to meet again in the St. Leger. We ran two, Disguise II being the other. Lord William had never lost confidence in Caiman, and I got "Skeets" Martin to take the mount on the second string. He demurred a bit at first at the idea of riding the one who was to do the donkey work, but in the end it was arranged. Then I went to Lord William and asked him to give me permission to ride any way I chose and to let me tell Martin what he was to do. Huggins was averse from leaving it all to me, but eventually Lord William talked him over. To hear Huggins speak about Caiman, anyone would have thought that he had already beaten Flying Fox. Of course *I* knew that it would be by the biggest bit of luck if he did. The Duke of Westminister's colt had improved enormously. He had broadened and was stronger — looking beyond the usual development when I saw him in the Two Thousand, and I knew he had gone on in the right way up to Doncaster.

There was only one thing for it, to try and devise some plan that should do in the favourite — of course, I mean something within the rules of racing. I arranged with Martin to stay with me the night before the race so that I might tell him what I thought. My plan, to which he listened very carefully, was for Disguise to lay alongside of Flying Fox to the turn for home. Martin was to "cluck" to his horse very frequently, not to shake him up, but just to keep him going by making a noise with the tongue against the roof of the mouth as loud as he could. "Keep him head and head, Skeets," I said, "and after the turn if I holler out to you 'Go on,' then pull out to the right and let me through on Caiman; but if I shout to you, 'Pull out,' you'll know I'm beaten and you must do what you can."

We had a very good start and Martin on Disguise II did exactly what had been arranged. You could have heard his "clucking" yards away. Every time he let out the sound Flying Fox would jump yards, pulling Morny's arms out of their sockets. I can tell you he was furious during the race and he didn't forget to tell Martin so after it was all over. Well, we got near the turn and rounded it with Caiman going easily. As I arranged, I shouted, "Go on, Skeets!" But Martin was an actor who had forgotten his cue. Instead of pulling out he kept on, and I was on his heels instead of getting the opening to keep Cannon on the rails. Of course any chance of pulling off the unexpected was at an end. I had to go on the outside, and, although I just headed the big horse two hundred yards from home, he then went away from me as easily as possible.

There was just a possibility that if Martin had done as we had arranged, I might have stolen the race; for with one sharp run from the turn through a clear space, I might have got a lead of Morny which he couldn't have made up in the time. Still, as I have said, far and away the best horse won the race and neither Lord William nor Huggins disapproved of my tactics. They didn't come off, that's all, but Morny I fancy will never forget the way the winner fought him every time Skeets "clucked." I laughed then, and I can laugh now, at the way he pitched into Martin. In that last burst of speed of Flying Fox's, it wasn't so much that Morny called to him, but that directly he *saw* Caiman the horse all about it and raced away from him altogether on his own. I believe that if we hadn't run two strings in that race Caiman wouldn't have been in the first three even, and that is emphatic enough. I rousted Skeets but he answered, "You called 'Go on!' and I went on"—and what was the good of arguing!

In the Spring I had ridden Sibola home a winner in the One Thousand; she was not a high-class mare but a nice-ish sort. I was riding with such confidence that I believe that there must have been a certain amount of it transferred to the mounts I had. The successes I had were certainly remarkable. Musa ran third in the One Thousand and was destined to just beat me in the Oaks, but I shall always put it down to my own fault and temper that I lost that race at Epsom. I ought to have won it with a good margin in hand. As it was, many think that Sibola did win—but the judge didn't. She was a 7 to 4 on favourite and when I went down to the paddock before the race, Lord Charles Beresford was standing with Lord William.

He said to me:

"I never bet, but I've come down here to see Sibola win and to put five pounds on her." Then he looked me straight in the eye.

"I'll win all right, my lord," I replied.

"Mind you do," he snapped, and gave me another glance.

Lord William was rather amused when I added: "And you can have a bit more on too, if you like."

We got to the post and there were three or four false breaks. I must admit that I was trying to beat the starter and he didn't half give it to me for what I was doing. At last he let them go with me not ready and left standing. I was mad with rage, and in my furious temper, I did what I had always told young boys never to attempt. It was the worst race I ever rode in my life and never shall I forgive myself for allowing my vexation to overcome my better judgment. *I made up all the lost ground going up the hill*, and when I got to the top, Sibola was a tired mare. I ought to have allowed a

In King Edward's Colours
Autumn, 1899

mile to recover the distance I had lost at the post; then we couldn't have lost. Certainly I got steadier at her a little time afterwards, and Madden on Musa and I rode a desperate finish.

After we passed the post and got down to the paddock to turn back to scale, Madden said to me, "I think you won it, Tod," and I was sure I had. We were both surprised when Musa's number was seen in the frame. There seemed a fate against me that day—at least the mood I was in made me think so. First the starter and then the judge. However, one mustn't think too much of the ideas formed at a time like that. Anyhow, I am telling this story all against myself, making no excuses at all.

Lord Charles altered towards me after that. It wasn't the loss of five pounds, but what I suppose annoyed him was that I had been so cocky about my certainty of winning. I saw him several times afterwards, but he never relaxed. Even once in Chicago, when I called on him when he was passing through, he was as cold as can be. I deserved it I suppose, and I wonder Lord William took it so well. The whole cause of my losing that race is summarised in one word, TEMPER.

* * *

Morny Cannon was having a rare good time that year, for besides winning three classic races he had taken the Great Yorkshire Handicap on Calveley, the City and Suburban with Newhaven II, and a lot more. His score for that season was a hundred and twenty wins. For a long time we got on very well together. But the new style of riding passed him by, for he could never be induced to adopt the forward seat. He need not have ridden very short to have accomplished this. I would repeat that it was quite a false idea that I rode very short: that was left to those who followed me.

Fred Rickaby, first-class rider, used to come out and take pointers from me; what I mean to say is he was not above doing so, just as I would have done had it been to my advantage. Sam Loates was quick to take to anything too, and Madden was a hustling rider who I always had to look out for. In fact, Madden took as much shaking off as any of those I rode against in 1899. He topped the list with one hundred and thirty wins.

Lord William Beresford on the Road to Epsom
Before Sibola's defeat in the Oaks

XX

Jockeys and Jockeyship

Johnny Reiff's Start — Sam and Tom Loates — Thrifty Jockeys

I HAVE OFTEN BEEN ASKED who in my opinion were the best jockeys I ever saw, and I have no hesitation whatever in saying that of the old school, Harry Griffin, the American jockey (I have explained I took a tip from him when inventing my own style), was never approached. He was the division between the old order of things and the new. It isn't that I was more easily impressed then, but going back years, I am confident that he was far and away the greatest.

The next to Griffin and of the present school was Lester Reiff, and his was really an extraordinary career. In California, he was actually put aside for incompetency, and, with many others, I could only agree with the action of the Stewards, for he couldn't do anything right. He was a good stableman, and Wishard believed in him so much that he brought him over to England with his younger brother, Johnny. Lester was quite a failure on English courses to begin with, but then suddenly he began to develop an entirely new style, and when he adopted this the difference was astounding. He was the best rider of his time I ever rode against; in fact, he was simply wonderful, as his record in England shows so unmistakably. He had no trouble in topping the list in 1900, and deserved every bit of his success. He made fewer mistakes than any of us, and was alert, would take chances, and, for his years, was a rare good judge of form. It was a great pity when he quit race riding.

Johnny Reiff was quite a little kid when he came over with his brother. He couldn't have weighed more than 4 st. 6 lbs., being then about thirteen years old. He was such an infant that some of the jockeys used to complain about his being allowed to ride; they were afraid of hurting him. Nevertheless he kept on, and with the mounts he got, rode twenty-seven winners in 1899 and one hundred and twenty-four in 1900 — making him third to Lester Reiff and Sam Loates.

Soon after he arrived in England, I went out to see him at Wishard's place near Newmarket, and found him in his knickerbockers by the porch of the house playing with some kittens. He seemed such a baby, and I watched him before I took one or two of them from him, for I share with him the immense love for cats. Johnny liked to hear me talk and used to ask me different things, which I told him freely, but the kid had already any number of ideas of his own, was a born rider and had developed it with his own intelligence. What I mean to say by "born" is not going against what I have said previously about heredity, but Johnny had the instinct for jockeyship, and from every gallop and race he rode in he seemed to learn something. Wishard was very proud of him. He was proud of Lester too,

Jockeys and Jockeyship 93

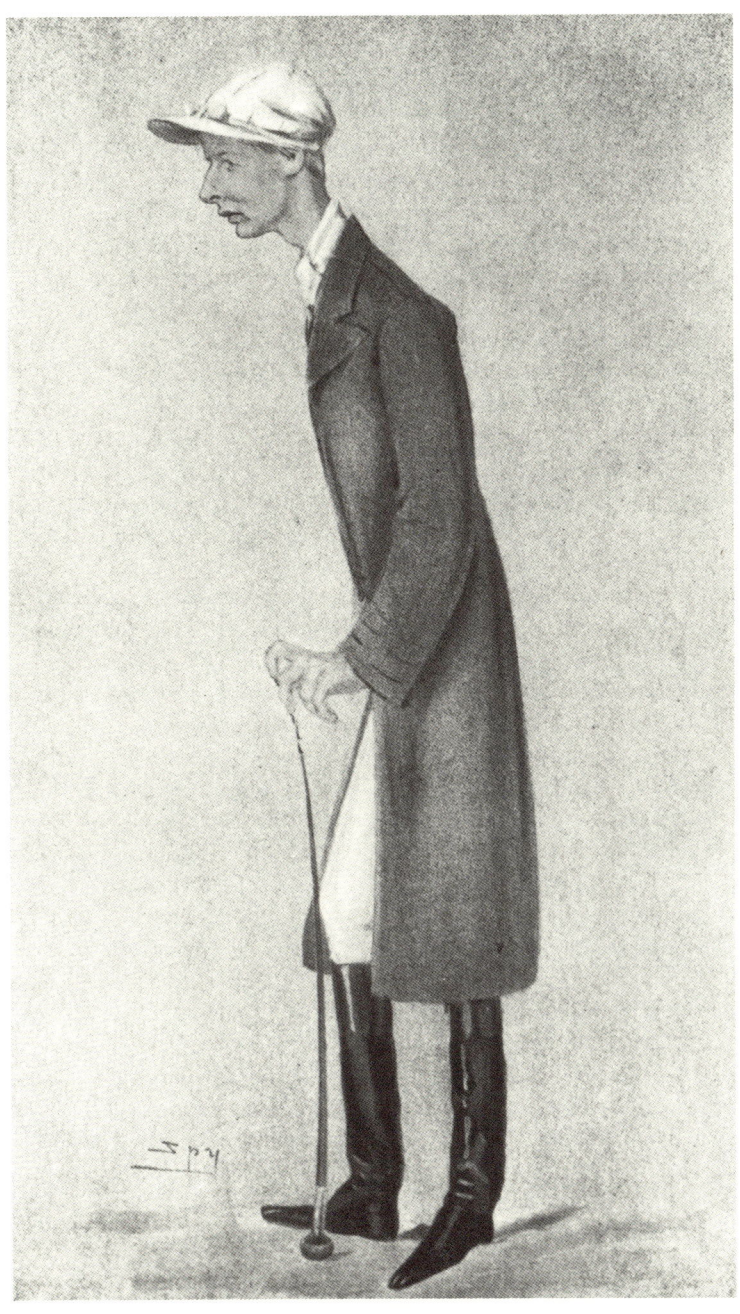

Lester Reiff
From Spy's caricature in "Vanity Fair," 1900

especially when the latter began to show what he could do. Of course Johnny moulded himself a little on what his brother had changed to. Yes indeed, Lester was without an equal during those two or three years.

It was in 1899 that I cabled over to J.H. Martin to come to England. I told "Skeets" I thought he would do very well as he had ridden for me over there, and he wasn't very happy through various causes in America at the time. He arrived, but didn't seem to shake down in his new surroundings very quickly. He got mounts, however, and when I was reported by Mr. Arthur Coventry for alleged disobedience at Sandown Park, and the local stewards sent the case to the Stewards of the Jockey Club, Martin got another chance, for with two small boys I was put on foot for three weeks. He rode a nice few winners; my suspension was his blessing. Martin was about a year older than me, and had plenty of experience. He is a fine curler, and keeping himself fit in the winter in that way has enabled him to keep going up to the present day. He was light too. By the way, that was the real cause of some of Johnny Reiff's successes too, for they were able to use dead weight and to put it in the proper place. I know that it is going against old accepted ideas to say that dead weight is better than live, but it is beyond question that it is, for it remains stationary and doesn't wobble about like poor jockeys who resemble jellyfish and seem to be trying to do a *danse de ventre* all the time on a horse's back.

One of the best American jockeys who ever came to Europe was Lucien Lyne, who never had a proper chance in England or he would have got right there. Lucien went to Belgium and has been very successful, for he is a first-class rider, but I suppose the public has to see results to appreciate a man.

One of the most powerful finishers I have seen was Willie Pratt, now trainer at Chantilly. More than one Grand Prix has been won by his strength in the last furlong. I have heard him likened in style to Fred Archer, but can only take this as the opinion of others. I know that, with several friends of mine, I packed up a big parcel after I had quit riding when Pratt had won the Grand Prix on Kizil Kourgan. He won four altogether.

If I were asked who was the best all-round rider of the past dozen years, I should undoubtedly answer George Stern. He is a hustler, and he never minds what sort of course it is—great or small, right-handed or left-handed, whether it is round or straight—all come the same to him. He is so fearless too, and takes chances, and he seldom, if ever, loses his head. One knows that he can get out of tight places, and it would take any of the others all their time to outgeneral him, for he has forgotten more than many of them will ever know. His great rivals now in this year of 1915 are Frank O'Neill and Johnny Reiff and sometimes I should be inclined to put them all three on the same mark with regard to ability.

I always thought the ex-amateur Randall was a good rider. I watched him very carefully on occasions. William Halsey too, who was not slow in adopting the forward seat, was a man of great ability, and a great horseman through his experience on jumpers.

It was an asset to me not having to "waste" like many of them. Lester Reiff had to keep himself in condition and had a good deal of trouble to ride reasonable weights; that was where Johnny Reiff got a good many chances.

I used to be called to task for not appreciating in the way the public did the ability of the late Tom Loates, but I could never see him in the same street as his brother Sam.

There was frequently a bit of bother owing to my rivalry with Tom Loates. I remember once at Epsom, one of his chief employers came to me to the jockeys' room and barred my way into it while he said: "You interfered with my horse," referring to an animal Tom had been riding and which had much disappointed the stable.

"I never even saw your horse, Mr. — —," I replied.

His answer was:

"I'll report you to the Stewards for interference."

The only thing I could retort was that he had no right to stop me. I knew the rules of racing, and his jockey had never laid any complaint against me. Nothing more came of it. My opponent had always been reckoned as the "great" Tommy Loates, and judged by the number of his successes, I suppose he was great. It was when he began to lose more than usual that the little troubles used to arise, and it was I who was blamed.

It must not be thought that I am prejudiced in saying what I have for I had no friends to speak of among jockeys, and I don't remember ever having dinner or luncheon—I mean "parties" of course—with any other jockeys in my own or any other country.

"Pittsburgh Phil" had a good many things to say about riders. Some of the brightest have been handed down. Here are a few:

> A good jockey, a good horse, a good bet. A poor jockey, a good horse, a moderate bet. A good horse, a moderate jockey, a moderate bet.
>
> Special knowledge is not a talent; a man must acquire it.
>
> The majority of the riders and horses are game and will fight for victory no matter where they are placed.
>
> Some jockeys excel on heavy tracks; a good mud rider will frequently bring a bad horse home.
>
> A jockey should not be overloaded with instructions. Honest horses ridden by honest boys are sometimes beaten by honest trainers. Instructions are given to the riders which mean sure defeat, intended for the best though they are.

"Pittsburgh Phil" must have had Lester Reiff and one or two others I have named in his mind when he said that "jockeys make a great difference in the running of horses. An intelligent jockey has a great value, for he profits by the mistakes of others." He used to add that "seventy-five per cent of the inconsistency in horse racing, which is generally put down to criminality, is nothing more or less than lack of intelligence on the part of the jockey."

Just a little more about jockeys riding in my time. There are rich men to-day and there are men of very moderate means for all their hard work and savings. I should say that George Stern is the richest professional I ever rode against, and all the time he has lived well so there is all the more credit for making the fortune. It was easy for some of them to get money together when they had plenty of riding. You can believe the story of a well-off jockey who retired from the saddle some years ago and recently died. He used to set out from Newmarket with £3 and always make up his mind that we would come back with at least £7 after having paid his expenses and not drawing anything for his rides.

In 1899, I was building up a fine fortune myself, for I had £37,000 in one bank, besides some good investments in New York and California. I should say that for the length of his career Frank Wootton made as much or more than anyone. He retired earlier than Dillon did, and for a young boy the latter certainly did well in savings during the years he was riding successfully. Madden, Halsey and Sam Loates were a trio who never had to worry about what they were going to do when they quit the saddle; however, perhaps the financial status of jockeys need not be further referred to. Expenses are great, and as for myself, I would repeat that I never charged anything for travelling nor for riding gallops. I scarcely ever rode our own at work; in fact, I can say I was nine times out of ten engaged in outside gallops for which I was never paid and never expected to be.

XXI
The Big Plunger

*100-Dollar Bills for the "Girls" — Riley Grannan's End —
Romano Hospitality*

IN THE AUTUMN OF 1900 I was again to ride the winner of the Middle Park Plate, being up on Democrat, who beat Diamond Jubilee and Goblet; these placings being repeated in the Dewhurst Plate two weeks later. Diamond Jubilee hadn't shown much at the time, but turned out altogether better than Democrat, who was really not a good horse, although of better class than Caiman. In the Middle Park they took evens about the winner, with Diamond Jubilee at 100 to 7, and in the Dewhurst they laid 5 to 2 on mine with 4 to 1 about Diamond Jubilee.

The stable always thought a great deal more of Democrat than they were justified doing. Another in the stable, Blacksmith, was in my opinion a much better horse, and I won five races off the reel on him. He was a very hard puller and ran away with me the first time I was on him, and he would give trouble all the time.

Betting on my mounts in 1899 was Charles Riley Grannan, one of the heaviest plungers when he had the money or credit that racing in modern years has seen. He might not in his day have bet so much in one sum as John W. Gates, but he would have wagered and gambled much more than Gates, if he had possessed them. He had a very big win on Democrat when I won the Middle Park. On another occasion, Riley Grannan just missed taking more money out of the Ring in one afternoon than any plunger for years before or afterwards. I can recall having ridden the first two winners and then I had the mount on Democrat against O'Donovan Rossa. Grannan had wagered £16,000, having won a very big packet over the first two events. I shall always be certain that I beat O'Donovan Rossa by half a length. There could be no mistake for the two of us were locked together and not wide apart. There was consternation on the part of many when my number didn't go up. Grannan was mad and some of the "boys" tried to console him by having bottles of wine, which he didn't take much of usually. He simply went crazy with annoyance about it, and, being in that state, came into the Ring and put £20,000 at evens on Desmond, who hadn't been out that year. I know that the first bet was £13,000 from Pickersgill.

Desmond was never seen in the race!

If Riley had drawn over Democrat, it is certain that he would have netted £70,000 that afternoon. But it was said that he would never have got away with the ready money part of it; too many of the "boys" were after him. They shadowed him and were all ready to take him to town that night.

At other times Grannan was a perfect lunatic bettor. Sometimes it came off. He was a tall thin cadaverous-looking man with nervous actions, although he was one of the quickest gamblers imaginable, either at poker, bridge, or faro. Originally he was a bell boy, or page, at an hotel in Lexington, but started playing the races and got on until he ran into money. I do not suppose that at any time he was worth more than £60,000 or £70,000, and even so he was quite liable to be broke a few days afterwards. I remember he lost 50,000 dollars one week and had nothing left. That was in New York. He was staying with me at my hotel on one occasion two or three weeks after that loss and came to me one morning when there were races at Belmont Park. I was going to drive my wife with a friend of hers out in a car, and Grannan said he would come too. He asked me if I had any money and I told him not a nickel. He showed me 10 dollars he had to begin betting with, and I knew that was about the strength of his bank roll. At all events I got a box at Belmont Park and he went down and began. He backed the first winner and then the second and the third. He had run into money by this time and had 6000 dollars on the fourth race which went down. At all events before the end of the day he had well over 5000 dollars left and brought the girls a clean 100-dollar note each and we were all right.

At another time I knew he had put 6000 dollars, all he had, on a horse for an event in the future, and he came to a mutual friend of ours and asked him for a loan of 500 dollars.

"Are you broke already?" said the man. "Why, I know you have thousands on the next race; can't you wait for that?"

"No, I can't: I want to put some more on; he can't lose, I tell you, and you *must* give it to me. I wish I had fifty thousand to put on him."

He would never hesitate for a second when he had made up his mind, and when he had a real fancy would empty himself of ready money and get all the credit he could cajole.

In 1900, Grannan came over for half the year to England but I didn't see so much of him. He had begun to bet on Lester Reiff and was going very strong, as were two other Charlies—Charles Quinn and Charles Dwyer. It was a case of up and down, one day a small fortune with Grannan and the next hardly knowing how he was to go to a meeting. Sometimes it was a bit of a scrape up to settle, for by this time he had worked himself into a lot of credit and the Ring would stand him for big sums until, of course, one Monday arrived with too big a balance against him. Still, he never lost hope nor neglected to keep in touch with the form.

One night he said to me, "If I'd been racing to-day I should have won a fortune but I've given it a rest."

I was putting him up at the time at the Lexington in New York. "There's a game of bridge to-night, Tod," he went on, "and you know that I am a good player; lend me fifty dollars and I'll make something."

He told me where the game was to be, and it cleared me out to lend him the fifty.

I didn't see him till the next evening; I thought he might have had an all-night sitting and I wasn't racing myself the next day. Just before dinner, I came across him looking down his nose over a cocktail and asked him how he got on at the bridge game, for I was looking for the fifty back and a little interest if he had had any luck.

"I didn't play no bridge," he said. "I put the fifty on a horse to-day and it went down."

He was like some old horses and was getting cunning, so eventually I helped him to get out to California, where he said he would be all right. He evidently got some money somewhere for he wrote to me cheerfully.

I heard one good story of him out there. He was up in a friend's apartment, very tired, and was taking a rest on the sofa sleeping peacefully while a dollar game of poker was going on. Hour after hour passed and still Riley never stirred. The boys had got a bit more lively in the game, and at last one of them called out "I'll raise you ten dollars." This had an electric effect on Riley, who hopped up, took a chair and said, "Give me a stack of those chips. I'm in this business." In half-an-hour he had skinned the lot of them, and was owed quite a decent sum.

It was soon after this that he went down to Reno and beat the bank out more than they could pay him. There was only one thing to do for the quick-witted Riley, to tell them that he'd have a share in the establishment and he became partners in the house. A few weeks after, however, he died, a comparatively young man—I don't think he was more than forty. At his funeral in February, 1909, there was a great oration delivered by one of those connected with the faro bank they ran. The speaker at the graveside at that mining camp had been a minister at some remote time and I have heard that it was one of the finest send-offs a dead man ever had. I saw a copy of it once, but, unhappily, cannot reproduce it. There was a quaintness about the whole proceedings which was quite pathetic. It was like one of Bret Harte's stories.

Yes, he was great value, Charles Riley Grannan, a man who seldom smiled although he possessed a dry humour that was real wit.

Betting at the same time on English tracks was Charlie Dwyer, who was then about twenty-five years old, a great plunger just like Grannan—that is, when he had it. He was the son of Mike Dwyer of the celebrated Dwyer Brothers, who have already been mentioned as successful race-horse owners, and whose horses were first hit upon by Pittsburgh Phil as worth following. The partnership between Mike and Phil Dwyer lasted years. They were originally butchers in Brooklyn, but got into the racing business and eventually gave that up for something more profitable. Mike was the plunger of the two and was known as "Plunger" Dwyer as distinct from his brother who was dubbed "Piker" Dwyer. Mike would readily have 25,000 dollars on a horse while at the same time perhaps Phil was putting 5 dollars on. However, in the end Mike left nothing, while Phil is worth away up into the millions to-day. I rode a great deal for them.

When the partnership was dissolved they tossed to determine who should have the right of the original colours, red jacket and blue cap; Phil won, and he had the honour of keeping on the jacket and cap in which such great animals as Hanover, Miss Woodford and some of the greatest horses we had in America have raced. Mike adopted all white and was very successful for many years. It was he who induced Phil to come into the racing business when he was about twenty-five years old. This led to the amassing of an enormous fortune, which however, was not kept by Mike. He was a splendid loser, for I can remember when he was in his declining years and declining luck I was riding a mare named Lady Inez. I was in great form, and apparently the mare was too, for they laid 3 to 1 on her. Mike Dwyer had laid 25,000 dollars on her, but soon after the start she broke a blood vessel, and, of course, I had to pull up. I was covered with blood on returning, and caught sight of Mike Dwyer sitting quietly as if nothing had happened. In fact one couldn't say from his face whether he had had a bet or not. I went up to him and said, "It's too bad." He replied quietly, "It can't be helped; we must hope for better luck next time."

That was the spirit he lived and died in. Phil's son died years ago. He was an only child. I believe Mike had brought Charlie up with a college education, but he was very wild and up to all sorts of pranks, and he had some escapade with a racehorse of his own in the college grounds. Eventually, he took to racing with the capital of about a dollar and ran into money, owning some good horses in his time, one, Africander, being quite first class and winning plenty of races. When in England, he was always very level-headed, and would gamble on favourites, whereas Grannan always liked horses with a price against them. Charlie had wonderful nerve and ability for his age.

Another who was betting pretty freely was Charlie Quinn. He had a handsome and most gentlemanly appearance, being all the time most popular, but he was somewhat reserved and he kept his own counsel. All three of them lived at the Savoy or the Cecil, and there were great gatherings on occasions, but one would seldom follow the lead of another in racing, adopting his own views before anything. Of course I saw something of them, but not a great deal. We all kept not exactly aloof but distinct, for they were not following me in particular, but working out their own ideas.

Recalling those times at the Cecil, I made a little error in saying that I was never entertained—at "parties" I mean. I remember that the late Mr. Romano showed hospitality to me by keeping his lights up long after the time they should by regulation have been turned out, and, with a party of friends who are all living, and whose names are well known in *certain circles*, had a little game of Nap for my amusement. I said I had never played it, but Romano said that was ridiculous and that anyone with my intelligence and with the card mind could pick it up in five minutes if he watched it. Well, I *did* watch it and dropped £350 ready money in half-an-hour. It was so silly of Mr. Romano's friends to rush the game so quickly, for had there been some encouragement, I suppose that I would just as easily have dropped in the long run (I mean at many sittings) £3500. I didn't tumble to it a bit at the moment, but when I got up from the table and they wanted to give me my revenge at some other game the graft was as clear as daylight. Some of the gentlemen who worked the West End and Continental cities, and who are alive and well, may like to know that they missed that day the smallest in size, yet perhaps one of the biggest mugs about at that time. I only stopped short at thinking I quite knew everything.

XXII

A Visit to America

A Missed Bargain – No Record of Bets – Handicapping Americans

WHEN I WAS SUSPENDED for three weeks after the Eclipse Meeting at Sandown Park in July, I had, of course, nothing to do, so I took a run over to America, spending part of my time there in New York and four days at Saratoga. I was asked to ride but I refused, as I considered that, as I was suspended in England, there might be some objection.

Of course I was asked any amount of questions as to how the suspension came about, and the papers had something to say as well, the principal statement being that I must have been at my old tricks – trying to beat the starter. As a matter of fact, Mr. Coventry had told Lord Marcus Beresford that he was not altogether pleased at the sentence.

At Saratoga, I gambled each day and won over 10,000 dollars, so it was a profitable trip. By the way, the suspension I have just alluded to was the only one I suffered in England, except when I was put down for the remainder of the meeting (one day) at Doncaster after I had beaten Eager on Lucknow.

Returning to England, I was certain that the rest had done me no end of good, and I began riding about the first of September. That Autumn I had my first opportunity of riding on a French race-course. Baron Schickler sent over for me to ride a horse in a Plate for him, and I won it. The jockeys riding in France then, with the exception of one or two, were a joke – as many Anglo-French trainers can vouch. On the grey, I just beat Dodd a head: he said he was kidding me and could have won if he had liked. The truth was that he really didn't think anything of me, as he has told me since. At all events my horse had his head in front at the end of the race, I had £200 for my expenses in going over, and I always received this sum when engaged on subsequent occasions. The £200 fee could have been maintained at that, but a certain American jockey with a successful record quite unnecessarily cut it down to £50. I didn't want to go anyway, even for £200; crossing the Channel and so on and missing the Sunday rest took the gilt off the gingerbread. Things are a great deal more stringent in France now than they were sixteen years ago, for I was never asked to show my licence and I might, apart from my colour, have been Jack Johnson instead of Tod Sloan.

It was in Paris that I first formed the idea of the negligent way horses were kept, about which I have written previously, but I liked the trip and looked forward to others afterwards. The American invasion had not begun in France, but was getting in full blast in England, and a good deal was being said of the number of races won by certain jockeys and trainers, and all sorts of statements made. The number of bettors who came over was one of the worst things for the riders, and it was natural that the in-and-out career of some of the gamblers should rather scandalise old-fashioned people in England. It was not that the Americans knew any more how to wager and make a good bargain with the bookmakers than Englishmen did, but there were so many suggestions that they stood in with the jockeys that things became most uncomfortable all round, and the Jockey Club may have become uneasy through the many innuendoes put about. Some of the backers, failing to settle, made things worse than ever, and there were wholesale charges of doping.

When in America on the visit just mentioned, I again asked "Pittsburgh Phil" whether he intended to take a holiday in Europe for a time, and sometimes he thought he would, and then he changed his mind; but the more he thought of it, he said, the more he preferred to stay where he was. By the way, I have just read some statements attributed to "Phil" about part of his career which I should like to give a different version of, especially for those sporting men in America who read this.

One of these refers to a horse named Previous who belonged to Mike Dwyer. It is stated that he was a very sulky horse who would not get away at the post for many jockeys, in fact, not extend himself at all. He was never a sulker but he liked certain conditions of going better than others. When I beat Hamburg on him it was another case of Caiman and Flying Fox. I kidded Taral who rode Hamburg and just headed him.

It was curious that when Previous was a two-year-old, Mike Dwyer said to me that he was going to sell him and had received an offer of 900 dollars and he should let him go. "Don't do that," I said. "If you want to part with him, I'll give you 900 dollars, but keep him and you'll win races." But it took a lot of persuasion to bring it about. I spoke to Charlie Dwyer and begged him to induce his father not to part with the animal. It was then arranged that I was to ride him in a Plate, which I won; shortly afterwards he took another event as well. Later on, he was put in a much more important race and he won again. By this time he was reckoned as being worth 5000 dollars; and after one or two more successes, and the beating of Hamburg, he was thought one of the best horses in America. He was nothing of the kind.

Another statement which Pittsburgh Phil was supposed to have made was that Skeets Martin was and is a good mud rider and it was this knowledge that caused him to put Skeets up on Howard Mann who won the Brooklyn Handicap, beating his other two entries, Belmar and The Winner. "Tod Sloan was riding for me then"—I quote Pittsburgh Phil's words—"and he knew that Howard Mann could beat good horses in the mud, but he did not think he could outstep Belmar. I believed that Howard Mann could beat Belmar under certain conditions and told Martin so. I thought Martin was better than Sloan in the mud, and when Sloan chose the mount on Belmar I was secretly pleased. The only orders I gave in in the race were to Martin to get up on Howard Mann, get off, and go about his business. I added in a joking way that if Tod were within hearing distance of him at the head of the stretch to tell him to hurry home or he would be too late. Whether Skeets ever said it I do not know, but if he did, Tod never heard him. Howard Mann was halfway home before Belmar hit the quarter pole."

The real facts of the case are that Phil only had Belmar and Howard Mann in the race and Fred Taral was to be put on Belmar who had no chance, but I was so fond of the horse and had won on him so frequently that I didn't want to see him perhaps knocked about by a rider who didn't understand him; so I got Skeets for Howard Mann since Phil was determined to run the two. There was no question of Skeets being such a great star in the mud. In fact, a reference to a previous chapter will show that "Skeets" was not very anxious about riding Proclamation in the mud, and handed me that winning mount in the Manchester November Handicap. Phil was certainly right when he said a good mud rider will frequently bring a bad horse home, because the riders of the good horses are not always as game as they might be. Weak boys are always handicapped on a heavy track. In such conditions, a horse needs help to keep him from sprawling and from wasting the energy that will be useful later. I am sure Skeets will not take the above amiss, for his standing has always been admitted, but he never put himself up as a specialist on a sulking horse.

When I was at Saratoga during that holiday, I noticed that Phil was just as careless about not jotting down bets as he always had been. I have seen him have a wager of 10,000 or 15,000 dollars altogether, perhaps split up between three men. After the race, if he won it, he would sometimes but not always write it down, and if he lost, would occasionally not bother a bit until the end of the day. It was not to be wondered at that he was not a hard man to convince that he had left out a record of a bet when he was claimed for something he hadn't paid. His friends often asked him why he didn't make notes. He would smile and answer that he had trusted to his memory for so long and that he couldn't be bothered. I never heard of his having a secretary, as it has been stated he had. A secretary wasn't at all in his line of country, although he had plenty of men working for him with the bookmakers.

Two other big bettors, John Drake, who came to England in 1899, and John W. Gates, who made such a stir in 1900 and 1901, were very exact in their records of wagers; the former in particular, whether the bets were made by himself or through a commissioner. Gates was the bigger gambler on the racecourse of the two and would often prefer to go along the rails himself to make his bets, because some of the layers he could call down—in fact, buffalo them. Of course, the way these men bet made a sensation. One day in America, by the way, Gates was betting so high that he might have lost a million dollars. The bookmakers saw to it that he didn't. It wasn't that they were afraid of his not settling, but they didn't want him to lose too much in one day. He had lost a vast sum before the last race—I think it was at Sheepshead Bay—and wanted to put 200,000 dollars on a 3 to 1 on chance in the last race. But he was a bit late and they told him they wouldn't have it and turned him down. He was furious at the moment, but that hot favourite was just beaten!—and he did a war dance at his own escape and at what they had missed.

Mr. Drake was a managing director of a big hotel company in Chicago, where it is well known Gates also lived. In England, Duke and Wishard, the trainers, were in partnership, or rather there was a syndicate of which Drake wasn't a member. There was a talk of Duke going away, so there would have been a case of dissolved partnership. But from whatever cause, Duke did not go and bought Wishard out, or at all events Wishard went from the concern rather against his will. In consultation with Drake, Wishard said, "Well, Duke has all the horses, which we have so carefully got together; it's a bit awkward, but at all events I have the two boys, Lester and Johnny Reiff."

Mr. Drake has told me (and he confirmed it only the other day) that he went to his bank and made all arrangements and told Wishard to go ahead and get a stable together. They bought the first animal, Escurio, out of a selling race and put him in a handicap. He was given top weight, which of course came as a big surprise. It was a question of handicapping the owner, trainer, and the jockey—Lester Reiff. The English officials were mad about the dope question at the time, yet Escurio, despite his top weight, started at 7 to 4 on in a good field and won it. It has been stated so many times that Drake and Gates won £100,000 over Royal Flush in the Stewards' Cup that I was glad to have an opportunity in this year of 1915 of asking Mr. Drake about it. He said that a hundred thousand represented about the exact figure. There was a great purchase for you, Royal Flush, if you like! They bought him privately for £400 and his record in 1900 was a real good one, showing the wonderful improvement which could be made in a horse by up-to-date methods. Let me add that when Eager won the celebrated match against Royal Flush Drake and Gates did not have a penny on their horse, for he was absolutely no good in the going.

XXIII

The Ascot Incident

Yachting Suit at Ascot — Lord William's Action — The "Cop" pitches the Tale

WHAT HAD BEEN DESCRIBED as "the Ascot incident in Tod Sloan's career" has been scandalously discussed for years, and I should say that quite ten thousand people have alleged that they saw the whole business! I was supposed to have made a murderous assault on a waiter with a champagne bottle. The occurrences of that afternoon at Ascot never seem to have been forgotten.

Now I have promised to put my heart on the table with regard to nearly every incident of my life: sometimes it may be in excuse, at others in apology, but above all I want to clear up certain reports which have been exaggerated or even maliciously invented. It seems strange that such a small man as myself, a jockey simply trying to win and treading in the heels of so few with whom he came in contact, should have been the object of such antagonism. Whatever my private life was, it was for the most part with friends, and whatever others thought, I did not bother them with my opinions. I always tried to be aggressive as little as possible, never getting into arguments unless there was a "butt-in" on someone else's part — which there frequently was.

Before describing that Ascot business, it is only justice perhaps to say that the morning after it occurred, I went to the stewards and made a full explanation. They accepted it freely, saying it was unfortunate, but that they had nothing against me for it. Furthermore, they allowed me to ride during the rest of the meeting and all that season and during the year afterwards, 1900.

Here are the facts. After I had finished my work that bright summer's day at Ascot, I went with George Chaloner, for whom I was riding, and another man — who had been engaged by Lord William to see me through any little incident which might arise and to show me the way about — to the lawn behind the stands, and we sat down at a table. It was very hot and there was a small bottle of champagne ordered, of which I took very little, not having had a drink the whole day. After a time, George Chaloner got up, saying:

"I have to see about my horses, but don't you leave till I come back." He was particular in repeating that I wasn't to go away, but I never exactly knew whether he had any idea of "rough house" being played or not; anyhow he was very emphatic. I had a cottage near the course and, as it was very warm, I had changed into a white yachting suit with white braid and a peaked yachting cap, which I had worn in America when on my boat. Of course it was a curious get-up on Ascot Heath, but the racing was just over and that white suit was very comfortable in the warmth of the June sun.

Well Chaloner left and the big fellow who had been appointed by Lord William as a sort of minder for me sat down with me at my table. There was only one waiter about. Two tables away from me there was a man sitting who kept on glaring at me and presently he called the waiter over and they had a loud whispered conversation, part of which, I got the idea, was to the effect that the man sitting down would give the waiter five shillings if he would upset the table and the champagne over me — and my suit! I could not make out then, nor have I been able to since, whether he was annoyed with me personally or that my "costume" got up and hit him. Do you understand? I thought the whole thing was maliciously done. Shortly, an accident did happen; our table was upset, and I caught the bottle before it had got to the ground. Having it in my right hand as the waiter lurched towards me, I made a light jab at him with the neck of it, meaning just to give him a reminder. The bottle never left my hand, but where I touched him on the lip he was cut, not a bit badly, but enough to bring a little blood. He went away then and was talking to the proprietor for a while. A few got wind of the fact that there had been a bit of a shindy and came around. I had just left the place, without waiting any longer on Chaloner, when Bill Goode came to me and said:

"That waiter has got a cut in the mouth. Now you don't want any fuss about it; you don't know that place like I do and it would be as well to square him."

I protested against doing anything of the kind. However, he kept on at me and at last I gave way to his advice and handed him five pounds — five pounds in gold mind you. Goode came back and told me that the man wasn't hurt and was not only satisfied with the fiver, but I could have another go at him for the same price!

The whole thing, at the time, seemed a simple annoyance and dinner almost made me forget all about it. However, in the evening another man, a fellow-employee of the injured waiter, asked for me and handed me a blood-stained five-pound note, saying that his friend could not be bribed for the severe injury which I had caused him. . . .

And then the papers took the matter up and there was a new version every day. The majority stated that I had "heaved" the bottle at the man, that I was drunk — everything in fact was said that wasn't true!

Still the talk went on and I wanted to take proceedings, but Lord William said: "Little man, let sleeping dogs lie." It was the first time in my life I had heard the expression; I know I ought to have known it before, but it seemed so appropriate that I never forgot it afterwards.

The incident was still being discussed and was, I should think, being worn threadbare. Then one day Lord William came to me and said he had hushed up the whole business and had paid several hundred pounds. He added:

"Don't let's think anything more about it; keep your mind on your riding. I've paid the money so that's all right; I want nothing from you." But I went over the affair again, trying to convince him that the whole thing had started in the beastly attempt to bully me by the waiter and his associate.

Then Lord William used all his charm of manner to persuade me to keep quiet and to say nothing more.

"The stewards exonerated you; that's the chief thing, little man; and don't let's argue any more about it," he said.

But I kept on, although in a respectful way.

"As you have paid, my lord," I declared at last, "it can't be helped." But naturally I insisted on standing the expense myself: it was deducted from my retainer at my repeated urgent requests, although for a long time Lord William would not consent.

There is the story in as much detail as it is wise to indulge in of how I thought I had been made the victim of an assault and of how I replied to it. I still think I should have been justified in doing something a bit stronger. I would ask fair judgment on this, for I have stated the case without the slightest exaggeration and without excusing myself. Those who read this can ask themselves what they would do in similar circumstances. I am not a giant and didn't know exactly how far those two intended to go. There had been one or two instances before when I had been hustled rather badly on railway platforms; at one time indeed, I was nearly going down under the engine. There are other things, too, which happened which it is needless to bring up after so many years. That warning of George Chaloner's, however, was significant.

As I have said, every other person who discussed the incident had his own version. About four years afterwards, I was down at Maidenhead at a cottage occupied by the late Major "Jim" Hill. There were one or two other men there too. A knock came at the door, and a police officer came in, saying he was in a bit of trouble because a present of coal and wood and one or two other little things which Major (then Capt.) Hill had given him had been found out, and he was likely to be called over the coals (no pun intended). Jim Hill said that the present was no bribe; it had just been a little gift to the man's wife and children, for he took an interest in the latter.

The officer was then asked to have a drink, and the men began to draw him out about different little things and got on to the topic of racing. The "Cop" had scarcely noticed me; in any case he didn't know who I was. He spoke about Morny Cannon, Maher, Martin and others and then Jim said:

"What about that chap Sloan? Did you ever see him?"

The man's face broadened into a smile: "Well I should say so. Wasn't I at Ascot when he slung that magnum at the waiter and split his skull. Hot stuff I tell you, my lords—I mean Colonel" (he called them all sorts of things that evening). Resuming, he said: "Well, Captain, it is very nice of you and their lordships to ask me to have another drink; I never take more than one, but as I'm off duty I *will* have another spot. Yes, that there Sloan is mustard. What he don't know, isn't worth picking up; but he *can* ride—I'll give him his due. But that Ascot affair— I was on duty just by, and Sloan wasn't charged. I went up to him and asked him for an explanation, but kept my eye open to see if another bottle was coming at me. I tell you, my lords and gentlemen, he's a fire eater, that there Sloan. He's a wonderful fellow with a horse; they say he talks to 'em but—wot oh! mustard and cress!"

He wasn't told that I was there; he may have got to know later on, but I don't think so. I tell the story because it is amusing, and also to make clearer the fact that so many thousands pretended they were there, whereas there were not more than seven in the vicinity altogether.

XXIV

Merman's Gold Cup

Merman's Gold Cup—Engaged for Roughside—"The Whole Truth"

AFTER THE SEASON of 1899 I went over to America, riding in California, and returning, as in the previous year, in time for Lincoln. It was not apparent at first, but as the season progressed there were black clouds appearing; some of them were very small certainly, but there were indications of a coming storm. The Americans were secretly and openly discussed, and it was well-known that certain inquiries were pending, chiefly on the charge of dope. Successes were almost entirely attributed to the use of drugs, and of course this was rumoured against trainers. All those connected with American stables were dragged into the talk; in fact, there was an uncomfortable atmosphere about everything.

Lester and Johnny Reiff were doing very well, although Morny had started off by winning the Lincoln Great Metropolitan, and City and Suburban. I scored in the Chester Cup on Roughside, finished third in the Derby on Disguise II, was third in the Oaks on Lady Schomberg, and second in the Manchester Cup on Joe Chamberlain. Then Johnny Reiff won the Hunt Cup and Stewards' Cup on Royal Flush.

Merman carried me home a 100 to 7 winner in the Ascot Gold Cup; Skeets Martin won the Northumberland Plate on Joe Chamberlain, and Johnny Reiff the Goodwood Plate and Great Ebor on Jiffy II. After winning the Middle Park Plate twice I finished second on Orchid and was second on Codoman in the Cambridgeshire. I was not riding the last three weeks of the season, having ninety-two winners out of 310 mounts, making a tie with Morny, who, however, had had one hundred and sixty-six mounts more than I. Lester was first and Johnny third.

The successes of the two Reiffs had naturally not called off the attention from the great topic of the American invasion and its consequences. There were plenty who were ready to say anything that could be suggested about horses who had run curiously well or unaccountably badly. All the same, for jockeys who always rode to win, there could not be serious thoughts of any disaster, and nothing was further from our thoughts; certainly nothing was further from mine. Looking back now at that time, I find that everything stands out sharp and clear and that details and impressions have stayed in my memory. How indeed could it be otherwise, when my career as a jockey was to come to an end for so many years. Before coming to the climax—which was reached in the Autumn over Codoman's second in the Cambridgeshire—I should like to say a few words about some of the earlier races and especially about Merman.

Returning to Scale after Merman's Gold Cup

It was Gold Cup day at Ascot. Mrs. Langtry's horse had been brought there, but the reason why was not very clear, for Robinson was against running him in the Cup, saying that he was short of two or three gallops. I pointed out that this was not necessarily against him: at all events he was a fresh horse and had not been overtrained as I heard one or two of the others had been. Robinson said he couldn't do anything until he saw the owner. Earlier in the afternoon I had met Mrs. Langtry and she told me the same thing—that she had to listen to what Robinson said, and couldn't move in the matter until she had consulted him. In fact, each of them was running about looking for the other. Then I saw Mrs. Langtry again and said frankly to her:

"You always told me you'd be a good friend to me; now here I am without a mount and in the Gold Cup too. One thing I promise you: I'll bring your horse back to the paddock after the race as good as he went out. He sha'n't be knocked about at all; he can win in his own way. After all it's the Gold Cup and Merman *is* a good horse."

All the jockeys had weighed out and the time was almost up when at last Mrs. Langtry and Robinson finished their talk and decided to run Merman. Robinson said to me, "It isn't quite fair to run him but they are doing so to please you, I suppose."

I was late at scale and I didn't get half a scolding from Mr. Manning. Anyhow out we went. I was told that in the Ring they were laying 33 to 1 against Merman. I know that some of my followers got 25's. They laid odds on Perth III who had been sent over from France and was ridden by the late Tommy Lane.

Merman was such a nice horse to ride. I could do anything with him. In the race things broke just as I anticipated; I tacked on behind and had the wind break for over a mile and a half, and, as the race was run, really a worse horse might have won it. Round we went and I could feel Merman was full of running, and when he felt like going along I let him out and won from Scintillant and The Grafter with the favourite nowhere. I had an idea that Robinson wasn't altogether pleased, for of course they had missed a golden opportunity of backing a good-priced one. Mrs. Langtry had won a rich stake and the Gold Cup, and she congratulated me on winning. I got the usual five-guinea fee and that's what the Ascot Gold Cup was worth to me that year. The Stewards blame jockeys for betting! Merman was an old horse at the time; it will be remembered he won the Cesarewitch in 1897 when a five-year-old.

Another interesting experience was over Roughside in the Chester Cup. I didn't know much about him but I had read up his performances and I had a sort of presentiment that I ought to ride him. I told George Chaloner who said:

"Why have you got such a fancy to ride that horse? Why, he has been hurdling and he won at the game too."

That made me keener than ever to get the mount if possible, but I took no action at all to do so, for I didn't know the owner. But one day somebody came to me at Sandown Park where Roughside was in a jumping race and said, "Will you ride Roughside for Mr. Atherton Brown? He is ill now but I am told to ask you." And without hesitation he added, "You're on a monkey if you win."

Of course I accepted the mount and I looked forward to the race for I had got a peculiar fancy that I should win it; in fact, without being familiar with the horse's capacity I knew that from the work he had done on the race-course hurdling he was as hard as nails, and might easily be capable of going from end to end.

It was just as I thought. Slipping away at the start I made my own pace — waiting in front. When they came near me I would increase the pace a bit, and when I slowed, they did. I lost no more ground than a champion cycle rider. I remembered what the owner's friend had said about my five hundred pounds and I slipped round that soup-plate course and I won it right enough.

But I never saw that five hundred pounds. Mr. Atherton Brown sent me a silver cigarette-case, and I daresay he never heard of his friend's promise to me, and certainly never authorised it.

I didn't bet on that race; in fact, I had given up betting. It's all very well — and I'm not saying this to kick against the rules — but a jockey has to live, and I would repeat at the risk of boring the reader that I never charged any expenses, any valets' fares, nor a shilling for riding gallops. Winning and losing fees sometimes do not amount to enough to pay all the cost of travelling at racing prices. I don't know what I should have got over Roughside if he had dead heated. Some of my readers may work that out for themselves.

On Disguise II in the Derby, I had no chance although he was third, for the simple reason that he had no pretension to stay a mile and a half. Joe Chamberlain, which finished second with me in the Manchester Cup, was hardly a racehorse at all and he was up against a good boy, the Oaks winner La Roche.

In the Middle Park Plate in the autumn, Orchid was a great horse for pace but had no idea of staying; he was a rattle-brained animal and one had to fight him all the time to place him. He turned out a good sprint afterwards, but that's all I ever thought he would do.

All these events led up to the time in the autumn when Codoman and I became acquainted. The association with this horse brought about so much trouble that it is with some feeling I approach the story concerning him. I cannot but think that the incidents surrounding everything in the race, the betting part of it all, the public talk concerning him, what I was supposed to have done and what I didn't do — I think they must all be told at length. Looking back, I see plainly that there are plenty of things to blame myself for. I will tell the truth anyway, and then after all this lapse of years, the public and the heads of the Turf can consider the whole affair in a calm spirit. Many of the actors in it are still alive, and jockeys and others can disprove many of the allegations which were made against me at the time — after the race was over.

XXV

Codoman

Changing Codoman's Plates – Santoi as Trial Horse – Long Delay at Post

IN THE MIDDLE OF THE WEEK, about the 30th of September or 1st October, I received from Paris a telegram from M. Maurice Ephrussi asking me whether I would ride Codoman in the Prix du Conseil Municipal, and, if I would, how much I should want. A reply was immediately sent saying, "Yes, and two hundred pounds as the fee to cover everything." Then promptly came another wire instructing me to be there on Sunday morning. I knew nothing about the horse and the few I asked could not throw any light on his chance except that he had run well in the spring, but had been unplaced in the French Derby, and another important race.

I can't say I was extra keen about making the trip, but at all events, it was a big race and the prospect of winning did give a little excitement to the journey. After a slight rest at my hotel I went to M. Ephrussi's house for luncheon where I was to receive more information. I had taken over with me a set of light American plates, but the difficulty began when I tried to persuade M. Ephrussi to use them. He said that his trainer, old Mr. Carter, would be against it, and that he would have to consider him in the matter. He also thought it would be perhaps better to let the horse run in the shoes he was used to. But keeping at him, I saw that he was coming round to the arguments I used. He told me he thought Codoman had a real good chance. "Then if he has," I asked, "why not make it more of a certainty?"

Finally it was left that he would try and talk it over with Carter when we got out to the course. There was some difficulty in this and perhaps it was only natural that an old and experienced trainer like Carter should resent a boy butting in and suggesting what should be done. I saw that he was ill-pleased and not at all inclined to be content, but at last he did yield and the plates were changed.

The plates made all the difference and some people told me they had never seen Codoman travel as well before. I was lying first or second all the way and shouted to the boy who was alongside me that I was not going to make my run until the top of the hill. He didn't answer and I suppose he thought that I might be kidding him; at all events he took no notice. Just as announced I slipped the horse along exactly where I had indicated, and all those who remember that event in 1900 will know that he won comfortably. M. Ephrussi was very pleased but I had no congratulations from Mr. Carter, who, however, let me say at once, has been very pleasant to me in recent years.

There was at the time no serious idea of Codoman running in the Cambridgeshire. Anyhow, the race in Paris had been a good one for me and several of my friends. The question of any present was not touched upon at the time, but of course, I received the five thousand francs for going over. I was pleased with the horse and began to think that although he had incurred a 10-lb. penalty for the Cambridgeshire, which brought his weight up to 8-10, he might nevertheless have a chance. There had, however, been some talk about my riding one or two others in the race. M. Ephrussi came over to Newmarket for Cesarewitch week and on the Wednesday, after the big race, which beyond doubt Berrill should have won—and in my opinion could have done so easily—I decided not to pursue the chance of riding Berrill.

M. Ephrussi, I believe, had consulted someone as to what would be an adequate present to give me for winning the French race. He had packed up a big parcel of money over that event. During the afternoon he handed me a cheque for seven hundred pounds, for which I was grateful. I thought him extremely liberal and there and then I said, "I want you, M. Ephrussi, to send Codoman over for the Cambridgeshire and I'll win it for you provided you let me have the charge of the horse for a week before the race. Let the head lad bring him over and instruct him that I am to have absolute responsibility for him. I will take him to George Chaloner's place and will get a real good horse to gallop him with. You can bet what you like on his chance."

He discussed it all, and after a bit wrote a telegram to Mr. Carter with the instructions I so much desired, and the horse was expected to arrive on the following Monday or Tuesday.

Then I began to think over the chances of all the others in the race, and I confess that I was terribly afraid of Berrill, who only had to give his proper running to be a great danger; in fact, I had an idea then and afterwards that he might have won the double penalty and all, but he was fiddled about by curious riding in the Cesarewitch and I thought it just possible that he might turn cunning in consequence.

Before Codoman arrived, I had persuaded Mr. George Edwardes to let me have Santoi, then a three-year-old, who had not shown to any great advantage up to then. I wanted him at Chaloner's place, and I begged Mr. Edwardes to let me take charge of him for the week before he was due to run in an engagement on the first day.

The week before the Cambridgeshire was practically devoted to looking after the pair of them. They had easy work for a day or two, and then one morning they were given a rough up. I was on Codoman and a lad on Santoi. I let the two horses kid each other that one could beat the other; as a matter of fact, they were about as level as two horses could be; but Codoman finished in front. I had a great opinion of Santoi—in fact, a much greater liking than Mr. Edwardes had. I told my friends too what I thought of Codoman's chance win and place, and there were packets of money put on him each way; in fact, nearly every wager was on those lines.

The day of the race approached, Santoi was in the Select Stakes at Newmarket, and after a little persuasion, Mr. Edwardes agreed to run him, but at first

WALTER DAVIS
The Trainer of Santoi

declined to back him. He said: "According to you it was a sort of fake gallop, not a trial, and Codoman was just as good; that isn't much of a test to risk a lot of money on."

I told him what a good horse Codoman was, and at that moment I was convinced Santoi could win, for I had begun to have an enormous opinion of him. I have referred to him in a former chapter of the book as being one of the two best I have ever ridden in my life. At last I induced Mr. Edwardes to have a big bet, and I was not going to be a loser myself.

The whole thing was nearly coming undone at the post; Santoi was impossible. He fiddled me about, and when the starter sent us off, he stood right still. The others were a hundred yards away before I could entice him to get a move on. There was nothing for it but to be patient and canter after them. He made up none of the leeway in the first furlongs, but after that things seemed brighter. I would take a pull at him and then he would pull away from me and I let the reins slip through my fingers as if he had beaten me. I played nonsense with him, and he was tickled to death. Then he caught hold of his bit and began to run. He looked ahead of him and moved as if he would show me what he could do. I didn't need to bother him after that, for he thought he had me beaten and would teach me. We had made up about fifty yards and there never was a horse to move as he did rising out of the dip. All those who had backed him thought he was beaten anyhow, when they saw him left out. In the end he came along like a steam engine, passed everything in the last hundred and fifty yards, and won anyhow. It was one of the most extraordinary races imaginable, as anyone who saw it may remember.

The Cambridgeshire looked so much better for Codoman after that, with the pile of money heaped on him that night. In addition to everything which had gone on before, it was a wonder that such a good price as 100 to 7 was procurable on the day of the race. I had thought of Berrill a few days before, but on the day of the race I was not afraid of any other of the runners.

Mr. Luckman has told me a lot about the talk which was supposed to have taken place in the jockeys' room before and after the race, but what I have stated to him in conversation I should like to repeat to everyone who reads this. At no period of that afternoon did I speak to anyone except Maher, who said to me after the race: "I wish mine had won; I had a promise of five thousand dollars if he had."

I answered him: "You can put mine in pounds and a great deal more than five thousand." As a matter of fact I should have been rich for life.

But to deal with the race: we went down to the post and it will be remembered there was a fifty-minutes' delay, during which of course Codoman was carrying 8-10 continuously, whereas Berrill, a four-year-old, had only 7-9. When we got off at last, after that weary time with my chance getting less and less, I could see that Berrill had the lot of us easily beaten; in fact, he had only to win in anyway he liked. However, he went all over the course. He could have won by twenty lengths, instead of the four which, if I remember rightly, the judge placed him in front of me. There was a no question of hard luck in the incidents of the race; Berrill was an absolute certainty as it proved. I have no hesitation in repeating that he could have won the Cesarewitch easily. Codoman had run a good horse but we couldn't reckon on one like the winner. As it was, I was not at all a loser over the race, for like a great many I had netted a good sum on balance through getting 8 to 1, 7 to 1 and other odds to big mounts for a place, which was something to be grateful for.

I am told that after the race I abused Thompson who rode Berrill. I had never seen him before, and I have never done so since; but I can state with all due regard to truth that I never uttered a word to him in my life. The good thing hadn't come off; that's all. Well there was the usual talk about having my done this, that and the other, but apart from natural disappointment at not winning an important event, I looked upon it quite as an ordinary race in the natural excitement of others which were to follow in the next two racing days at Newmarket. There had been twenty-four runners and M. Ephrussi, I am sure, thought that everything possible had been done with his horse but he had met another much better at the weights. Berrill was receiving a year and 13 lb., and has proved at the stud that he was a horse of class. His owner had a dead certainty in him and the wonder is that he was ever allowed to start at 20 to 1. Many of us could have kicked ourselves afterwards that he was allowed to run loose without a saving investment.

After the Cambridgeshire the clouds began to get a little darker, and there were little rumours about which I was to be asked certain questions by the Stewards; but I did not pay a great amount of heed at the time to the talk which was going round. What was the use of worrying before it was necessary? I had already determined to finish the season with Newmarket. I had not been in very good health, and I was convinced that a rest would do me all the good in the world. I did in fact cease riding for the season after the Friday.

XXVI

Dark Clouds

The Black Outlook — Riding Gallops — Losing £20,000 — Sale of Mauvezin — Lord Harewood's Advice — Throes of Unrest

ON THURSDAY, the day after the Cambridgeshire was run, the Stewards sent for me. I guessed what was coming. They told me that it had come to their knowledge that I had some big bets on Codoman, and also that I had been promised a present by a certain gentleman if the horse won. I acknowledged both things at once, and then they asked:

"Don't you know it's against the rules for a boy to bet?"

I explained that I thought it was all right — as it was in America — for a jockey to back what he rode himself but that it was all wrong if he backed any other animal. I also admitted that Mr. Frank Gardner had promised me a handsome present, running into four figures of money, in the event of my winning.

They reprimanded me, and I went out to ride as usual, finishing up the week with the win on Encombe, whom, as I have said, I advised King Edward — then Prince of Wales — to back.

Returning at once to London I let myself loose on a life of pleasure and I thoroughly enjoyed the change, although naturally in a very few days I was physically unfit. It didn't seem to matter though, as I had announced — and it had been stated in the sporting papers — that I was not to be in the saddle any more that year.

But one morning, two days before the Liverpool Cup, Lord Derby, then Lord Stanley, sent a letter to me saying that he wanted me to ride a mare of his in that race. She had a nice light weight, and they fancied her chance. Here was a dilemma! I replied most respectfully that I had finished my year's riding at Newmarket, that I had been playing cards until very late at night; that I had been drinking whiskeys and sodas, and that I should neither do myself justice nor would it be right in his own interests for me to accept the mount, for the race might easily be thrown away on account of my being quite out of training. I expressed my deep regret and thanked his lordship very much for the offer. I am afraid that that letter of mine gave rise to considerable misunderstanding. The mare ran with a boy on her back and only lost by a head, so (although I say it myself) it could be assumed that had I been at my best and riding she would have been first instead of second. This is another explanation to add to what I have already said to Lord Derby.

At the regular dinner at Newmarket when the topic of Codoman was mentioned, the late Captain Machell told Mr. George Lambton that he had already backed Codoman: "Sloan has put me on 33 fifties."

Of course this got about, even before the race. As a matter of fact, a lot of my money went on at 33 to 1, and I had obliged the Captain with a share. I may as well say here that the sum I should have cleaned up had Codoman beaten Berrill was about sixty-six thousand pounds.

There was another incident which happened that year and which I fear prejudiced me. A member of the Jockey Club came up and spoke to me as I was going out to the paddock. He told me that he wanted me to ride a horse of his the next day, and I answered—I hope quite respectfully—that if he would wait I would look at my book when I got back to the jockeys' room. Of course I meant my engagement diary. He said to me as he turned away, "I wait for no jockey; you won't have the chance again." Several times after that I tried to get an opportunity of explaining to him that it wouldn't have been right for me to accept the engagement without making sure that I hadn't promised to ride another horse. He would never listen; in fact, he would not even allow me to speak to him.

All these things began to be talked about and thought about too, and when I went to say good-bye to Lord William Beresford at Carlton House Terrace he said to me:

"Things look pretty black, little man, but we must hope for the best." I answered that I would not be discouraged: I couldn't believe that after the severe reprimand they had given me, the Stewards would actually withhold my next year's licence. Still what Lord William said naturally made me think.

I went over to America after three weeks in London and rode in California, and on my way from the East and stopping at Chicago I first got news of serious trouble. I read in the papers there that it was announced that the English Jockey Club had intimated to J.T. Sloan that it was advisable for him not to apply for his licence during that season of 1901.

There was a crusher! All the same it did not imply in any way that my number was up for many years to come. I believed that if I lived quietly it would be all right in the following year.

On getting back to England I was able to see some of the comments made at the time by some of the newspapers. One writer in the leading sporting paper said, "Sloan is so valuable as a jockey that his absence will be felt. That Sloan only followed the custom of the English jockeys in making the heavy bets which formed one reason for his exclusion is apparent. With those going to and fro from the racecourse it came to be a recognised thing that Sloan betted habitually, and at times heavily. It would no doubt have been difficult for a private person to have justified this opinion by chapter and verse, but the Stewards of the Jockey Club have means at their command for getting at the truth of things; in short they found that Sloan has betted, also that he had accepted the offer of a large present from Mr. Frank Gardner in the event of his winning the Cambridgeshire on Codoman; and with proof of these two offences before them they acted as described. That many of our jockeys bet and not always in half sovereigns, there is reason for believing; and of all practices against the letter of the law, this is one which we can least afford to tolerate. It is not as if a jockey always backed the horse he is riding, that would imply an assurance that he would do his best to win, but unfortunately the money is at times on some other horse or against his own mounts, which is the simplest form of making winning sure. Proof is not always so easy as it appears to have been in Sloan's case, and the firmness displayed by the Stewards will engender caution."

I can swear that I never bet on anything but my own mounts. I did not make a parade of it for obvious reasons, but what I told the Stewards was absolutely correct; that I did not think the rules of English racing were against a jockey supporting anything he rode himself. Neither did I attempt in any way to deny what they said to me about Mr. Frank Gardner.

Another paper remarked that "So many excellent people are convinced that the American contingent were playing an underhand game that an exhaustive inquiry is as necessary as welcome."

The following was fair comment perhaps, but didn't do me any good: "I do not see anything objectionable in a jockey betting on his mounts so long as he backs a horse to win; but Sloan deserves a punishment which has been inflicted on him for apparently advising Mr. F. Gardner to back Codoman for the Cambridgeshire and accepting the offer of a large sum from that gentleman if the tip came off. This kind of interference with another man's horse is highly objectionable, and the Stewards are very properly resolved to stop such transactions. Jockeys will not, in the future, be disposed to accept gifts from outsiders; even though, at one time, such presents were daily offered and accepted, and fashionable riders did not disdain to receive them from notorious sharps. The possibility of Sloan's return to official favour in England is recognised in the following extract: 'He had better apply himself to the correction and reformation of his manners and excesses, and possibly he may get another licence in 1902, if he conducts himself discreetly during the next year.'"

The best thing to do was a difficult thing to make up one's mind about. I was torn two ways: I had money and had inclination towards a long holiday; yet I went to Newmarket, rode gallops (which I was allowed to do) and generally kept myself to myself, in the hope that the Stewards would relent, if not in that season of 1901, at all events when the applications came up for the following year.

I contracted the craze for motoring and in the summer went over to France and was a good deal about with Henri Fournier, who it will be remembered had been a champion driver, winning among other prizes the Paris-Bordeaux race, the Paris-Berlin, and the Paris-Vienna. We had several quite long runs, and then we paid a visit to Deauville, where of course there was gambling at the club—I had always been used to playing, as previous chapters will show, and I did not see any reason why I shouldn't continue. Neither did I see why they wouldn't let me shoot pigeons at Deauville, but there was some objection raised on the ground that I didn't belong to any regular club, which apparently was necessary to get me among those at the traps.

I had several little set-backs of this kind which made life a little bit dull at times. I used to debate with myself whether to go back to England or not, but decided eventually that France was better for the moment. There I should not annoy anybody, and I was not doing any harm in being adviser to an owner, for I was allowed to ride and work in a stable but *not* on race-course—that is to say, I was forbidden to race in colours. I met various people that summer and early autumn, and Lord Carnarvon was good enough to consult me several times with regard to French horses. This led to the purchase of a few horses, including Mauvezin, and the engagement of "Boots" Durnell already mentioned. Things were going fairly well and I was keeping my form. M. Charron was very interested in learning race riding, so that he could figure with other amateur jockeys. He too had been a crack automobilist, having won the Gordon-Bennett Cup, but nothing would content him until he learned how to ride with the forward seat, in fact in my own style. I began to show him what to do and he was a very apt pupil.

It was at Deauville that I formed the idea of going to America and taking Fournier with me, with the intention of starting a big automobile business. We sailed about the middle of August, taking with us two big Mors racers, one of which cost me fifty-five thousand francs. There were also three other cars, one a small one, which had won the Paris-Bordeaux run. At the time I possessed sixty-two thousand pounds in ready money, in addition to the investments I had made in real estate in America, so it was a serious proposition, this automobile idea. The plan was to get a company together and I was prepared to invest a great part of my own money. Altogether, to begin with, there were fifty thousand dollars invested in cars, which were to be used as models in starting the factory.

That trip was destined to be a disaster. In less than a month, I lost altogether about one hundred thousand dollars or twenty thousand pounds. For a commencement, there was forty-five per cent duty to be paid on the cars, and then Fournier was fined heavily, a sum of seven thousand dollars (which I paid), for undervaluating one of the cars with the customs. They said that if one car cost fifty-five thousand francs, why didn't its fellow? But the latter was sold to Fournier at a big discount because he had already driven it. It actually cost only thirty-five thousand. It was a good start-off.

Then I went racing and managed to lose thirty-one thousand dollars in one day, and I also lost a packet at cards.

The few horses at Maisons Laffitte had been left in the charge of "Boots" Durnell, whose great idea was that he could ride, whereas he couldn't. He was a great man in the stable for all that.

One evening I actually refused ten thousand dollars which was definitely offered for one of the cars. I would have sold it but Fournier dissuaded me: "What's the good of parting with it? We shall only have to send to France for another as a model to work from."

There alone was lost two thousand pounds which might have come to me out of the wreck. Ultimately it was pawned and I never saw a dollar of its value.

To make a long story short, I never, for one cause or another, enjoyed so much as a wheel of those automobiles. For instance, one was smashed up by Fournier who was showing a party of newspaper men how he could race a locomotive and who got it on a level-crossing. The car and the train met. Fortunately, no one was killed.

The cause of my going back to Europe was that one morning I got a cable from Mr. Felix Oppenheim: "Come at once. Durnell warned off." I took ship immediately and discovered on arrival that Durnell, insisting on riding when I had repeatedly told him not to, had actually been put on foot for incompetency. He had been left at the post or something and the Stewards took a serious view of it. I am quite sure he meant nothing wrong and it was only his vanity in thinking he was a jockey which brought it all about. The results had to be put up with though and I had to see about looking after the horses for their autumn engagements. They belonged to Charron, Baron Leonino, Felix Oppenheim, Lord Carnarvon and Mr. Debsay. We had only paid eleven thousand francs for Mauvezin; Charron and I going halves in him. I wrote to Lord Carnarvon telling him I had a good horse and he had better come and see him. When we bought him, we were told he couldn't stay more than five furlongs, but the improvement made in him was wonderful. Lord Carnarvon said he would take him off our hands if we would let him, and wrote a cheque there and then for eleven thousand francs. That was about two months before, when I had first brought over Durnell to France. We won six straight races with him, winning a big handicap at Maisons Laffitte, the horse carrying top weight. I may as well finish about Mauvezin here. When he had got to the top of the handicap he was no longer much use in France, so he went over to R.C. Dawson's place at Whatcombe.

I shall always think we ought to have won the Lincolnshire Handicap, but he didn't get away too well and nearly fell at the crossing when half-way home.

It was curious how several of us missed winning a packet over the horse when he took the Stewards' Cup. I had miscalculated the day, and was at the Hotel Cecil about half-past twelve on the Tuesday with Mr. Murray Griffith, who had always been a good friend to me. I told him of the chance of Mauvezin and that I was going down to Goodwood to put a lot of money on him. He looked up at the clock:

"You will have to hurry up to be there even three hours after the race is run; they'll be off in about two hours."

There was nothing for it but to grin and bear it, but we got busy with the starting price offices and managed one way and the other to get on one hundred and fifty pounds, which wasn't so bad under the circumstances, for he started at 10 to 1. I was glad that Lord Carnarvon won a big stake over the success. I don't suppose anyone ever had such a bargain for four hundred and forty pounds.

Another horse Lord Carnarvon bought in France was Londres, a great big animal over seventeen hands high, who was addicted to breaking blood vessels; but he never did so after he came with us, and scored over and over again. He ought to have won the Grand Prix de Nice, but somehow MacIntyre, who rode him, was not in happy mood that day. He led all the way until the post. He was just caught by a good horse, Retz, ridden by George Stern. Another nice horse was Misadventure, for whom we paid five thousand francs and sold for twenty thousand francs. Londres was also a great bargain at seven thousand francs.

I must not forget that there was some compensation for the disappointment over Goodwood. A Frenchman had come over with me, a man well known in Paris, who couldn't speak a word of English. Perched on the top of his head was the smallest Panama hat ever worn by a grown-up man. He was the success on the Wednesday afternoon at Goodwood. Society people and others forgot their manners and came to paddock to see the sight. It was great value.

Of course, in that Autumn of 1901, I had seriously to consider what was to be done after the big losses I had made in America; but acquiring these bargains in horses and winning money over them too, brought me to the conclusion that sticking to my own business—horses—was perhaps far and away the best thing to do. We had Max Lebaudy's old house at Maisons Laffitte, and there used to be great consultations about probable purchases and how they should be placed to win. Several of my friends suggested that I should go on with ownership and superintend training, and certainly I knew in riding gallops that I hadn't lost a bit of form.

Not a word had been said about my not getting a licence for the following year, so I stuck on full of hope that the Stewards would not keep the bar up forever. After the season finished in France I went to Egypt with "Skeets" Martin and had the usual tourist's holiday. I suppose my impressions about Egypt are not worth anything, but I am going to say that to me the place was the greatest disappointment—but perhaps that was my own want of appreciation. I often wished what we had chosen Switzerland or Monte Carlo, in fact anywhere else.

In the month of February no official intimation had reached me, but I heard indirectly that there was a grave doubt about the licence; this was when I went to England in the early spring. One day in the paddock at Newmarket, Lord Harewood said to me: "Sloan, what do you want to bother about riding for? You've got plenty of money. Why don't you settle down to a gentleman's life? Buy a stable of horses and run them. That's far and away the best thing you can do."

Of course I thought it over, but still I couldn't bring myself to believe that they would keep me out all the season. If I had known then what I learnt in after years, that my indiscretions were to be reckoned against me for half some people's lifetime, the whole course of my life and investments would have been different. With sixty thousand pounds odd and other property, I might have done really well, but frankly I felt that other sources of income would be open to me very shortly so I was careless about that useful amount. How I cursed that trip to America!

At Newmarket in the spring of 1902 I had rooms near the station. They were very handy for going out and riding gallops. Most of these I did for Robert Sherwood of St. Gatien House, and I never felt better in my life. Then I began to notice that a few Newmarket trainers had developed a rather cool manner toward me. They did not seem to know whether they were in order if they put me up in a trial or rough up. As a matter of fact, as I have explained, there was nothing against my taking part in anything of the kind, for the Stewards had said that I could do so.

Well, I went on trying my best by every possible means to reinstate myself in favour and, at that time, I had become more accustomed to Newmarket than at any previous period.

Several times I was inclined to take the friendly tip given me by Lord Harewood and definitely give up any idea of riding again and to settle down as an owner. Possibly I should have got a licence to train my own animals. But I was only about twenty-seven years old and was sure that I could ride as well or better than ever, and the money to be made as a jockey was far in excess of anything it was possible to make with any stable I could set up. Then too, I was occasionally possessed by the spirit of roving or travel. Should I go away again? I had been here, there and everywhere. It was not pleasant, however, to give up racing under the stigma that I had to retire without a jockey licence. If a licence had only been procurable, I do believe on looking back that I should have been quite willing to give an undertaking not to avail myself of it!

The majority of my friends stuck to me through all this and that cheered me more than can be said. But those were not really happy days. The more inquiries were made as to the possibility getting my ticket back again, the more undecided seemed the situation. It was sickening business too, when in London, having to reply to all sorts of people—some of whom I had scarcely ever met—as to what I was going to do. The truth was, I didn't know, and I felt rather inclined to give rough answers when quite strangers, especially Americans, became too inquisitive. Some presumed on a casual chat to ask me to tell the whole story over again. To begin with I couldn't have done so, for it was a whole combination of circumstances, as I have explained, which led up to the action the Stewards took.

The number of nights which were spent trying to make up my mind I can't count, but plans made when lying awake were quite upset by a few words of encouragement the next day given by serious friends who knew I supposed what they were talking about.

I do not know whether this is all sufficiently clear, but the only way I can describe it is that, what with hope and fear, in 1902 I was going through H-E-L-L.

XXVII
Nabot

The Late King Leopold – All from Five Francs – Off to Shoot Pigeons

AFTER PASSING THROUGH several weeks of the spring of 1902 in England, I could see no reason for staying on there, and I went back to France and spent my time giving advice and helping in the running of horses owned by Charron. But there was no money in it, and losses over betting accumulated until I really had some cause for worry. Nevertheless, a good day would put me in heart again, and during the important weeks in England I had a few really profitable days and my banking account was by no means exhausted. In July I bought a big 90-horse power Panhard for two thousand pounds, and also a smaller Mors car of 15 h.p. Pinson, who had been the mechanic during the Paris-Vienna race which this big power car had won, was my chauffeur although I usually drove the bigger car myself. I took both cars to Deauville and Dieppe for their seasons in August.

The expenses were very heavy, for at the Hotel de Paris at Trouville—which little town, of course, everyone knows adjoins Deauville—nothing else would do for me but the best suite in the house. There were "others" to pay for, including a valet, the chauffeur and other servants. The expenses totted up to a very big amount. However, I suppose when we are gambling we do not pay much attention to a little matter like daily expenses. I have been to a good many places, however, and not spent so much money.

This reminds me of when I was once at the Grand Union Hotel at Saratoga for the races. I had got my apartment before the season began. Mr. August Belmont arrived and made a little fuss about paying twenty-five dollars a day for his room or rooms, but the manager, much to my disgust as I didn't want to be too much in the limelight, said: "Oh no, sir, I assure you I am not asking too much, especially to a gentleman of your position; for Mr. Tod Sloan is paying more than twenty-five dollars a day."

It was at Trouville that I had the honour of being spoken to several times by the late King Leopold of the Belgians. He had the next table to ours and would speak across to me about various topics. He never said much, but it was all in a kindly way, and he never failed to recognise me, whomever he was with. There was another stupid story put in circulation at Trouville which found its way over to the American papers. It was pure invention but it told, unintentionally perhaps, to my discredit. Beyond question, I had one of the best tables in the big restaurant at the Hotel de Paris and some American journalist told a yarn that King Leopold had gone to the hotel manager requesting that a certain table, meaning mine, should be reserved for him. The manager was made to reply: "I am very sorry, your Majesty, and I hope you will in your kindness accept my apology, but I let that table that you want to Mr. Tod Sloan and I cannot turn him out."

It was a stupid story to invent, but many people who did not like me began to repeat it, making me out what I really wasn't. I should like to see any hotel manager refusing the request of such a guest as King Leopold! Besides I was not quite so far gone that I would not have given up any table to even a less distinguished personage.

Well, Trouville had its joys and sorrows, the former being the social part of it. There were bad runs at the races and in the "bank" at the club of the Casino. The gambling habit I could not cure myself of: in fact, frustration of this kind became almost a necessity to me for the fact of being without any licence was telling more and more heavily on me. It seemed so terrible that, although I had just as much confidence in myself as ever, I was debarred from making my living at the one thing I was good at. Motoring about the country was pleasant enough and I made new friends, but was all rather aimless and it was a welcome break to go away to Dieppe for a week or ten days there. We all motored, of course.

It was at Dieppe that I had rather wonderful experience of good and bad luck. One evening with about eighteen thousand francs in my pocket, I joined in a baccarat bank with Mr. "Solly" Joel and Mr. Henning. In about an hour and a half, we cleared over one thousand pounds each. When we had cut it up, Mr. Joel and Mr. Henning went off to the *Doris*, the former's yacht, but like a fool I stayed on and, not content with my winnings, of course, I had to join in the bank again. I lost every cent both of the one thousand pounds and of the seven hundred pounds odd with which, as I have explained, I began the evening. I get up from the table feeling pretty sick and went and had a drink. Feeling in my pocket, I found I had exactly seven francs. One franc paid for the brandy I was drinking; a franc I put aside for the cloakroom attendant. I was determined to go home without a sou, so I put the remaining five-franc piece on the gaming-table as I went out, intending to throw it away and not to think anything more of it. As a matter of fact, I didn't see the first coup, but on looking round saw that there were two "cartwheels" where I had only thrown one. I determined to leave them and the stake went on doubling up until there were eight louis or one hundred and sixty francs. Of these I left five, taking off three for odd expenses. Again I won, and yet again, but the second time at another table. Then of course, I had enough to join in a small bank again. In another hour I had cashed in twenty-seven thousand francs, which left me again a good winner on the evening. It was a remarkable performance and rivals many of the yarns one hears about gamblers' luck, for it all came from that five francs. If, when I was having my brandy, I had met a friend or two, I dare say I should have offered them drinks and my five francs would have gone. But such was my luck that I was left to drink alone!

It was in the autumn of that year that I had a great deal to do with the preparation of the Count de Bresson's grey horse, Nabot. He was in the

Cambridgeshire with 7 stone. Nabot was then a three-year old and one of the fastest I had ever come across. It had not been discovered whether he could stay well enough, but one morning I gave him a fast gallop over a mile, in which he came out well. It was therefore determined that Nabot should be sent to Newmarket. He was at a real good price. In fact, he started at 20 to 1 owing to the run on the eventual winner, Ballantrae. Although the latter won comfortably, I have hesitation in saying that Nabot should have done so. His jockey, an American boy named Thompson, riding in France, didn't know the course well enough. In consequence, the grey could only finish third. We backed him to win a fortune but, as luck would have it, some of us quit good winners by having as much on for a place as to win. So it was not altogether a failure.

It is curious what a fateful race the Cambridgeshire has been to me. First St. Cloud II; then I was left on Nunsuch; the Codoman trouble; and then just missing first place with Nabot when it was so important to me. I have no doubt what I have said about the French horse may be quarreled with by many English critics, but personally I was never so sure about anything as winning. I am not excusing myself in the matter for I didn't ride him. However, it's no use thinking too much about it. It is so long ago.

As may be remembered Nabot was bought for two thousand guineas, if I remember rightly, by Sir John Blundell Maple. Sir John came to me in the paddock in Newmarket and asked whether I thought him a nice horse to buy. Of course I said yes. He also asked whether the horse had been doped, and I answered to the best of my knowledge that horse had never been given anything in his racing career. There were a good many stories about at the time as to doping, and I believe poor Alec Waugh, who managed Sir J.B. Maple's horses, was firmly convinced that Nabot had been, and thought his owner had a very dear bargain.

I should like to say another word about Thompson. He was a very good rider in France but he never seemed to give his best performances in England. Certainly he won the City and Suburban in 1903 on Brambilla, but I think Robert Denman, who trained Mr. Edmond Blanc's Vinicius (second to Rock Sand in 1903), was one of the most disappointed men at Epsom that day. Still, full credit should be given to the jockey for his French performances.

I hung on in France to the end of the racing, but then I went down to Monte Carlo, chiefly on account of the pigeon-shooting.

XXVIII

At the Traps

Cleaning up 100,000 Francs—Laying and Backing—Various Good Shots

I HAD THE TASTE FOR FIREARMS even when a very young boy. I used to fire off a gun, a small single-barrelled muzzle-loader, when I was about ten years old; and then proceeding by easy stages, shooting at rabbits, squirrels, and birds, until when I was about thirteen, I managed to get hold of a great purchase, a very tiny double-barrelled breech-loader which nevertheless did quite good work. My eye became trained and I began to think that eventually something much greater could be done. But I knew little or nothing about pigeon-shooting, never even having seen a picture of it.

Going along from year to year there was always plenty of sport to be had especially during the winters out in California, but it wasn't until the winter of 1900 that I had my first go at the traps. All things considered the result was quite good, and I acquired the taste. It has never been shaken off since. I had other chances of practice but my big pigeon-shooting season was to be in those early days of 1903 in that trip to Monte Carlo. I won the Grand Prix du Littoral of ten thousand francs, and a big gold medal, killing thirteen birds out of thirteen.

It was rather curious how I got into that prize. I went down to make my entry and things having gone badly at the tables, I discovered I hadn't got twenty francs in my pocket. I met Crittenden Robinson—the great shot—and said to him: "Got any money?"

He gave me his pocket-book saying: "Help yourself," but I only took the two hundred francs that I wanted to pay for the entries. Coming off the ground I met George Cooper, who was making a book on the event. I took 50 to 1 from him to ten louis about myself.

Before going into the story of how I won, I should like to say that fortune never comes singlehanded, for with a little money I went to the rooms that evening and, starting off with three straight roulette bets, went back to the Hermitage Hotel that night and locked up with the cashier a hundred thousand francs. Every word of this is literally correct. I had no money at all before—nothing but jewelry.

The runners up to me in the Prix du Littoral were Count Filippi and M. Brasseur with twelve out of thirteen. There were sixty-three guns altogether. When I had shot my tenth bird overtures were made to me to divide, one French shooter saying that I could have half the pool but that one of their division would have to take the medal. Several Englishmen present who knew about this came to me and said: "You're the only English-speaking one left in the event, go right through with

"The Flying Bird" and Tod Sloan
The Chatham Cup, Nice. A caricature by Mich

it. Don't give them a chance of thinking they can beat you!" And go through with it I did, with the result already known. There were many little expenses in connection with that prize. For instance, fifty francs to the man who picked up the last bird I had shot, and a bill that night of one thousand four hundred francs for dinner. They seemed to have a bottle of champagne to each person with each course, and the out-of-season things some of them asked for and managed to get surprised even those who knew Monte Carlo pretty well. Of course too, there were little presents to "others." Two ladies claimed the wings of that last pigeon between them, and each wing had to be mounted on a hat to suit the wearers—but that was a trifle.

On going into the Rooms the night of winning the Prix du Littoral, I was given a message to go over to the Trente et Quarante game to cut the cards for "an eminent personage." I said I wouldn't go unless I knew who it was.

"You had better come, monsieur: it's the Grand Duke Michael."

"Who?" I asked, not hearing very well, and then he repeated the name and, of course, I went at once. The Grand Duke received me very graciously and said some nice things to which I hope I replied with proper modesty. Here was another Royal or rather Imperial personality for me to meet.

I shall always think it rather bad luck that I missed a "place" in the Grand Prix du Casino that was decided a few weeks before. There was a bit of a wangle over the ninth bird by Baron de Lossy. (He is dead now, God bless him!) He called me down for calling "No bird." But I was quite right and Lord Sevile came to my rescue by declaring: "Whatever is said, he'll have another bird at all events." All this trouble, which was quite unjustifiable, as very many who shot in the event can testify to-day, made me very nervous, for before it occurred I had absolute confidence in myself and was shooting in great form. When I had my tenth bird, it was not unnatural that I was a bit shaky, but I just dragged it down. There were very few left in and I killed the eleventh bird in clean style. Then came the twelfth. I had recovered my nerve by this time and was almost certain that I had notched another point, but it just fell on to the top of the rail and into the sea instead of dropping on the right side. I had killed eleven out of twelve, and with any ordinary luck I should have had the twelfth. It may be remembered that the winner was Pellier Johnston with nineteen birds straight, Mackintosh being second with eighteen out of nineteen, two others tying for the third place with seventeen out of eighteen; then several of us were level with eleven out of twelve.

I was shooting with a gun I had bought for two hundred pounds in Bond Street, London, and my success spoke well for the cartridges made by the Coopal Company of Belgium.

There were other bits of money picked up that season by shooting at Monte Carlo. Thiebaux was the biggest layer, and I suppose George Cooper of the English division made some of the biggest bets. Charlie Hannam mixed it, some days laying and other days backing. I should like to have all the money which he has lost over pigeon-shooting in one way and the other; still, it is all part of his winter holiday, so I suppose he doesn't mind!

Various little things annoyed me that winter, but it was very likely because I was over-sensitive after what occurred in England.

Certainly the English lot were very nice and sympathetic, but many of the Frenchmen and Italians seemed to go on the lines that I hadn't received my licence from the English Jockey Club; and although they were outwardly polite, they were inclined to be snubby. If I had the money to go in, it wasn't their business of course. For by this time, I wasn't a jockey but a private citizen with a certain reserve of assets. In any case, I was not a professional pigeon-shot as many of those were to whom the French and Italians were civil. Still it didn't matter much. I had my own bunch to talk to and was having a good time anyway.

I was continually impressed with the different personalities shooting at Monte Carlo. I should say that the majority who read this book will know of Mackintosh, the Australian, and Crittenden Robinson, the Californian; the former was, I suppose, the more brilliant shot, but Robinson had that extra stamina which would last him out in a tough battle, and he was an older man too. He used to give me many tips. That season Mackintosh shot eight hundred and forty-six pigeons out of nine hundred and ninety, while Robinson had a score of eight hundred and eighty-five out of one thousand and sixty-four. The winner of the Grand Prix du Casino, Pellier Johnston, was not shooting much and scored thirty-five out of thirty-nine. I only had four hundred and thirty birds with three hundred and fourteen kills.

I shall always think that Harry Roberts is one of the grandest shots I ever saw, and perhaps he can take the honours among the Englishmen. I have always heard from real good judges that perhaps the greatest man who ever shot pigeons was a Captain Brewer, but I never saw him. Crosby, who came from somewhere in Iowa and was known as "Tobacco Bill," was a marvelous man with a gun. He had a peculiar habit of squirting a big mouthful of tobacco which he had in his cheek, at the very moment of crying "pull" to the man at the traps. Perhaps when this book is reviewed, and some of the critics are as kind as they can be to it, they may be able to supplement by suggestions with additional information about those I wrote of.

By the way, one of the most remarkable shots, especially among young men, was a Californian who came over to Europe when he was only twenty years of age, perhaps even less. His name was Clarence Norman. I am told by many who should know that he was very likely the best pigeon-shot who ever lived. I know that Crittenden Robinson thought Norman was in a class absolutely by himself, and this coming from such a great shot as Robinson was acknowledged to be an opinion worth remembering.

It has always struck me that while there might be an age limit for other sports, there is no age limit for pigeon-shots.

Take Harry Roberts for instance. He has kept his form in the most extraordinary way. Another remarkable instance was that of Baron de Dordolot. Several men of over fifty who were shooting at Monte Carlo used to call the Baron "Pop," signifying that he was a generation older than themselves. This wonder among

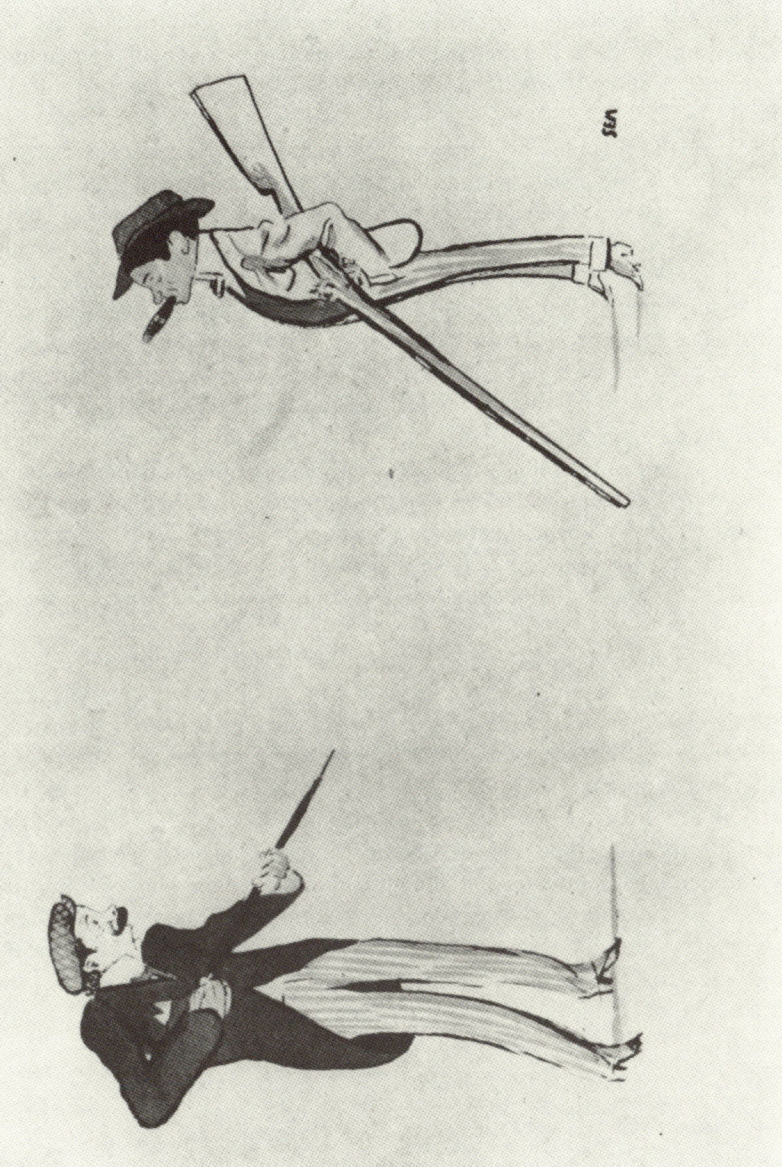

PRINCE PONIATOWSKI AND TOD SLOAN AT THE TRAPS
A caricature by Sem

veterans, in his limited shooting in the season I have been writing about, killed one hundred and ninety-two out of two hundred and forty-two birds. Prince Poniatowski, another veteran, could shoot well. "Sem" the French caricaturist drew a remarkable picture of the Prince, who was a very tall thin man, carrying a very small gun, while he depicted me with a weapon as long as a rifle carried in any old warfare. "Sem" said himself that this drawing was one of the happiest things he ever did.

Perhaps the shooter who impressed me more than any other was Baron de Montpellier. He had a good record that season, winning six first prizes and two seconds. But that was not so much the point. He was such a picturesque and stylish shot; he could put in the most wonderful finger work on his gun. Everyone would be all attention when he walked out to shoot. The two shots would be as near as possible simultaneous; you would see one puff follow the other in a flash and would hardly realise what space of a second there was between the first and second. Yet there were two separate aims calculated in a way that would have made him a prize gunner on any warship. He was an impressive figure and my recollection of him is as fresh to-day as it was then.

Mention of Prince Poniatowski reminds me that his son in California showed me the greatest kindness when I was out there in January 1901. There was a lot of talk to the effect that I hadn't yet got back my licence in England, but he paid little attention to it: "I am president of the Ingleside track and Sloan can ride here—that's all." And I did, but I did not ride in Oaklands, also in California, that season nor afterwards.

I have mentioned in an earlier chapter that Buffalo Bill had spoken to me when I was a little child. I met him frequently in after years and he would always encourage any ambition of mine in the way of shooting, recommending me to take up trick shooting. But, to me, there never seemed any money in that kind of work, at all events at my age. Colonel Cody can be ranked as one of the greatest trick shots who ever lived. I never met nor saw the great Captain Bogardus, who was remarkable in his time, and there were plenty of others I did not come across either. A lot of men have sprung up in the pigeon-shooting world who were in reality professionals, boosters for powder companies who paid all their expenses. There was no status of the amateur about them. But shooting has been a semi-profession with so many that it is not advisable to go too deeply into the matter. I do not want to offend anyone.

XXIX
"Sloan's Chance Hopeless"

To try Rose de Mai — Maître Labori — "Mr. Mean" — No Friendship in Racing

AFTER LEAVING MONTE CARLO in that spring of 1903, I still had the hope that my licence would be forthcoming—but it wasn't of course. A little time before, my spirits had been raised by some encouragement I had had to the effect that the French Société might give me a licence to ride in France. Mr. George Edwardes told me to call on a certain distinguished authoress and playwright. We met in her home in the Avenue du Bois de Boulogne; she spoke English well and was very sympathetic in offering her assistance on my behalf with certain distinguished people. From time to time, I heard how things were going; they seemed to spell success for the efforts that were being made. Week followed week and still everything looked promising. One day I received a message that a certain friend of hers—a man—was to meet two men of importance at a minor race meeting, that it was expected that the matter would be settled then, and that a telegram should be sent off that very afternoon. It arrived with the fateful words

"Sloan's chance hopeless. Eugene Leigh has won five races!"

That finished it.

All stories as to my efforts in 1900 to get a licence for Leigh to train at Newmarket were raked up in the end by backbiters and slanderers. The Americans were in bad enough odour and I was supposed to be allied with Leigh from the moment he came to Europe. It will be remembered that he trained in the country in England. At that time, a trainer had only to have a licence when he wanted to follow his calling at Newmarket. It was he and one or two others who were the cause of a new rule being passed by the English Jockey Club which makes it compulsory for all trainers, whether at Newmarket or elsewhere, to receive a Jockey Club licence. So Leigh changed from England to France. While now he is recognised everywhere as an individual and a good trainer, there was a tremendous amount of "chat" in those days, and for some mysterious reason whatever chance I had of getting my "ticket" was all done in because of his success that afternoon. It all seemed so trivial.

When in Monte Carlo I met Mr. Raphael, well known on the English Turf as an owner and breeder. He won the Derby in 1912 with Tagalie. He told me that he wanted me to ride a horse of his in the Derby, for he had no doubt at that time my licence would be given back to me. Such, in fact, was the general opinion. Mr.

Raphael told me: "There are many in favour of giving you back what you so long missed." However, I was gradually driven to the realisation that there was, for the present at least, nothing doing.

I began to turn my attention to motor-racing and was going to drive in the Paris-Madrid race, but somehow or other my car proved too heavy and my stake money was sent back. I went down the road and had a good look at it at various stages. It will be remembered that there were a number of casualties and the authorities would not let them go farther than Bordeaux. Two lost their lives in this race, including that charming man, Loraine Barrow, who was well known both to the editor of this book and to me; he had his home at Biarritz where he was generally liked. I had breakfast with him the day before he was killed by the accident to his car. Charron took a party with him, including two ladies, in an ordinary touring car and finished well up in the race. But then he was a superb driver and had nerves of steel. He offered to take me, but I preferred to see them all go by at different places.

It was my friendship for Charron which led to my trouble with the Société d'Encouragement. Charron had no trainer but prepared various horses for himself and others at Chantilly. The day before the Prix du Diane he came to me in great trouble saying that Rose de Mai had been suffering from a cold and begged me to come down to have a look at her. Later in the day, the owner, who was a member of the Jockey Club, told me in his curious English, how good it was of me.

"Mr. Charron has told me," he continued, "and I cannot thank you in sufficient way. Ah, but it is terrible, and you are a good man to be so kind."

I shall never forget the journey down to Chantilly in the car for I had to give up the front seat to a lady and I was frozen sitting at the back. Indeed, I began to think what an idiot I had been in coming, for there wasn't a shilling in it for me. The visit did lead to all sorts of trouble as the sequel will show. We stayed at the Condé for the night, and were up early. I had a good look at the mare, a very handsome animal. She coughed once or twice and slobbed at the nose. However, I got up on her and Charron rode Limonade, who was her constant companion at exercise. There was no intention to gallop them, of course, and we trotted to get into the open having to cross the "Aigles"—a particular gallop at Chantilly. There was nothing done on this gallop at all; in fact, it was more a walk out than anything. But we were seen in the distance by several jockeys and trainers and it got about that we had been on ground prohibited on Sunday. However, of that, later.

On getting back, I advised Charron and the owner to let her take her chance, and gave Ransch, who was to ride her, his instructions. He was not to knock her about in any way, but to let her slip along if she felt like it. He was by no means to force her in any way at all. Further I recommended Charron, who leaned on my judgment, if she seemed any worse after the race, to let her have a very long ease up. We heard a little bit of talk during the morning as to having been on the "Aigles"; it appeared they had recognised my seat on the mare, and the "horrible" story had been repeated from one to the other.

M. Charron's First Lesson in Riding at Chantilly

The result of the race was that Rose de Mai won easily. She had opened to 2 to 1 and gone out to 14 to 1 before the start. I never thought it worth having anything on her, for I didn't know then how moderate the opposition was. I think Charron put on ten louis for me or something in the "mutuel," but I can't recollect exactly.

After the race M. Caillault, who was second, lodged an objection on the score that I was the trainer of the mare. The Stewards held a big pow-wow over it, but didn't disqualify. However, for being on the "Aigles" on a Sunday and in answer, I suppose, to the objection, they fined Charron a thousand francs, and warned me off the saddling enclosure and jockeys' room — permanently. It was indeed a body blow. I couldn't afford to have even the smallest thing against me at that time, for it would all tell in the matter of my getting a licence in France or any other country. Unfortunately, at that time, I had no one to give me sound advice or I might have taken a different course. Perhaps it doesn't much matter now, but I had more anxiety at the time than I care to remember.

In a hot-headed way, I rushed in to clear myself and brought an action against the Société d'Encouragement and claimed damages. I managed to retain the great pleader, Maître Labori. One of the most charming men I ever met in my life, he spoke to me in English all the time. He told me I might win but I should get nothing, and the case was bound to do me harm. But I determined to go ahead and the records will show that I got the verdict, but with no damages. The Société, on the other hand, had to pay all the costs. When I went off to America some time afterwards, they appealed and I didn't know anything about it; but Maître Labori took up the case and won the appeal — again with costs. Thus the warning off from that enclosure didn't hold.

The case cost me from start to finish about fifteen thousand francs or six hundred pounds. The money wanted a bit of finding at the time, and one morning when it was absolutely necessary for me to put up several thousand francs on account of costs I ran into a well-known private bank in Paris with my available jewelry, among which were seventeen tie pins, most of them given me by owners. Among them was a large pear-shaped pearl of perfect quality and colour presented to me by Mr. "Solly" Joel. It must have cost him at least five hundred pounds. The whole lot was worth one hundred thousand francs. I asked the bank to let me have ten thousand francs and I would pay twelve thousand to get them back. Pawnbroking in France being a monopoly of the State — the Mont de Piété — it was impossible to "lend"; they had to buy the lot from me for ten thousand francs and agree to sell it back for twelve thousand. But there was no written contract to this effect. I hadn't the money for some time and, going to America in the meantime, I returned to discover to my horror that they had sold everything. I do not know who got Mr. Joel's pearl, but I am inclined to think that it decorates the scarf of a certain champagne magnate; some of the other things were acquired by jockeys and trainers. Very few of the lot was I able to get hold of, for financial reverses do not come singly. It was a terrible loss to me, and one which can never be replaced.

Just another reference to Rose de Mai. There was a certain owner who was always nosing round, who sidled up to me on the day of that race just before the horses went to post, and asked: "Has she any chance?"

Now I wanted to get one back at him and the only way was through his pocket, so I replied, "She'll walk in," and was tickled to death at the idea that he might go and lose ten thousand francs. He put his money on in a very clever way and scarcely reduced the price at all. He must have won a tremendous packet. Of course, I was glad for Charron's sake that she won, but all the same I kicked myself for putting the owner on. He never suspected the truth and even said "Thank you" — but that was all! He knew I smoked cigars, but I suppose he forgot it when he banked his money.

This reminds me of an absolutely true story about a friend of mine who used to race in America but now lives in Europe. He was in the habit of giving a man, quite an amateur, tips from time to time, and the fellow, who was in business and travelled about selling his goods, made thousands of dollars in consequence. Now in private life, he would never dip down into his pocket for anything. He would smoke his friend's cigars, let him pay for theatre tickets, would bring a girl or two with him and would let the giver of the tips pay for the meals; in fact, in every way he would accept everything and give nothing. He even liked his street-car fares to be paid for him. To sum him up, he was the meanest fellow possible, in spite of the fact that he had a good and regular commercial income and was under obligation for thousands of dollars won through my friend's tips. It was that unwillingness even to pay his street-car fare that goaded my friend to frenzy, and at last he determined to get even with him.

He went to "Mr. Mean" one day and said: "How much would you bet if I gave you a real good thing, a big outsider who might start at perhaps 50 or 100 to 1?"

The reply was three hundred dollars.

"That's no good," said my friend: "you'll have to put much more than that on; mind you, I don't want any of it."

"Mr. Mean" thought for a moment and answered he would put on five hundred and perhaps more. So it was agreed that they were to go racing next afternoon. Quite early my friend went to a certain big bookmaker and asked him to run down the card and pick out something without a ghost of a chance. Looking down the list the bookmaker said: "I'll bet you five dollars that this one will be absolutely last. Is that good enough for you? What's more she'll be at 100 to 200 to 1." My friend bet him the five dollars, being quite content at the knowledge that he was sure to lose. Then he gave the name of the horse to the mean man who showed hundred-dollar bills to the extent of fifteen hundred dollars in all. He had plucked up courage and was going to put the lot on. He took advice, however, and ultimately split it up into smaller bills so that he should not alarm the bookmakers and reduce the price from 100 to 1 at which the horse opened when the betting began.

Chuckling to himself the giver of the tip went up on the stand to see the fun. The start was rather ragged and something happened to the favourite. That outsider won by half-a-length, and the pile "Mr. Mean" won I believe made him

Rose de Mai

give up racing! My friend netted the five dollars the bookmaker laid him. He tried to ring it in that "Mr. Mean" should hand over a thousand dollars to "give to the jockey," but—not a cent. Of course, I needn't tell you where the thousand dollars would have gone, or the best part of it.

Tommy Griffin, who owned and trained in America, may remember that incident, although he had nothing to do with the tip. I fancy he trained the horse though, and that he was the most surprised man on the course that day. Mention of Griffin, who retired from the saddle to train and own horses, and for whom I always rode when he wanted me to, reminds me of the way in which he was thoroughly soured against owners great and small. He was running a favourite little horse of his at a selling race and hated to part with him, but they ran him up after he had won and he had to let his treasure go. Ever after that it didn't matter who it was whether it was Mr. August Belmont or Mr. W.C. Whitney or anyone, if he fancied a horse he would stick at it till he had bought him. Even with me, one of his greatest friends, he was just the same. He gave me fair warning of what he intended to do, and would stick at no friendship nor respect anyone's feelings in the matter of buying out of selling races. I had a horse named Rubicon for whom I paid seventeen hundred dollars. He ran in "Pittsburgh Phil's" name and colours, and I won five straight races on him, eventually putting him in a high-class selling race worth five thousand dollars. I rode and won. Griffin plugged away at the bidding and eventually had Rubicon knocked down to him for four thousand five hundred dollars. Of course I never dreamed he would go on, nor could I realise that anyone would pay so much for a plater. I don't think I ever came quite so near crying over anything in my life, but I remembered then all that Griffin had said to me previously. All he added now was: "I'm sorry, Tod; I'm your friend and I'm also a friend of Phil's, but I always told you what I'd do." Nothing would shake him. He wouldn't sell me the horse back. "Racing is a business," he answered when I asked him. "I had my bit of grief the day I lost that favourite horse of mine. It's no good talking; you mustn't keep up a grudge against me, for I'd sooner be a friend than otherwise, but I'd do exactly the same thing tomorrow if you had something else in a race which I wanted."

Of course the big fellows used to get a bit mad with him at times, but Griffin was fearless and didn't pay the slightest heed when it was whispered to him that he had better be careful. He always relied on his stock saying that business was business, and he refused to be talked out of his new method. Many others have had a similar experience. Of course, in cases where horses are bought or claimed, it has often been a matter of private grievances coming out, but Griffin never bore the slightest animosity against anybody: all names were the same to him.

XXX

Dope

Long Priced Rides — Never saw Fred Archer — At New Orleans

I FOUND, during the following year, that many visitors to Paris were curious enough to ask me all sorts of questions about certain incidents which had happened during my racing career which had been cut off so suddenly. I can remember especially being asked what long shots had been steered home by me, and some of the answers which were given may be useful to add to those which have already appeared. In England, in my first season, I brought off successfully several 25 to 1 and 33 to 1 chances.

Among the longer shots in America that I can remember was an animal belonging to the late Louis Ezell. There were plenty of 100 to 1 bets taken about him that afternoon in Chicago. Remember that it was way back when it was thought I couldn't ride—in fact, I was just at my worst! If memory serves it was in 1893. Ezell said to me: "Do the best you can. I don't think he's a got chance; at all events I'll leave the colt to you." For all I know he had looked about for a boy who couldn't possibly win, for as I said in a previous chapter, that was the kind of reputation I had at the time. I happened to get fairly well away and certainly I was dead keen on winning. I let the colt slip along, making every post a winning one. During the race, there was time to think it over. I had received no instructions about "pulling him in behind," and if I had I would not have followed them—I shouldn't even have listened. I think my friends and those who have criticised me can say with perfect certainty that nothing would ever satisfy me but to *win*. I looked round in that race in Chicago and could see nothing near me. Still I shook my mount up, and I won pulling up. My brother Cash rode in the same race and told me afterwards that he was never so surprised in his life. It was like his cheek! By the way, although he was always known as "Cash," his proper name was Cassius Braynand Sloan, the second name being after my Uncle Braynand.

After the race just alluded to, Ezell was not pleased—no, not at all! He said: "What did you go and win for? I wanted to bet on this one when I thought he had a chance. You ought to have known that it was the first time I had him out."

I didn't figure it up but I came to the conclusion that it was a question of his wanting me to "qualify" him. However, surely he knew I was too inexperienced for that. It wasn't worth while answering, for I was so tickled to death at winning a race. Ezell thought me a fool and left it at that.

There were several long priced winners in England, Sea Fog for instance, whom I rode for Sir R. Waldie Griffith. If I remember rightly, this horse started at

33 to 1. It was before the American invasion and before anyone had started betting blindly on anything. I had the good or bad luck to ride. Sea Fog brought me in a nice little bit of spending money for I had a standing bet of ten pounds each way on each of my mounts.

Another question I may as well answer here is as to what horse I have personally found the most consistent. In answering I should certainly include Belmar already referred to, while the best two-year-old I ever rode was a colt named Jean Beraud owned by Dave Gideon, the uncle of Melville Gideon, so well known as the composer and singer of rag-time. I do not know whether the latter remembers the young horse in question, for Melville is some years my junior. Among the many musicians I have met in my life, I put him down as one of the greatest in his own line. I was once a bit of a tenor myself; in fact, I had always a keen appreciation and a certain amount of knowledge of music of all kinds. Melville Gideon was quite a wonder as a boy, and afterwards studied music in Germany. He is versatile to a degree and has only to stick to it to be able to do anything. Anyhow, he has amused a great public in all parts of the world, while his melodies seem destined to last as long as "The Swanee River."

Another topic I have been frequently interviewed about—by French journalists in particular—is the question of "dope." It would be silly to say that the meaning of the term was not known to me; but I can say frankly, without any fear of being hauled up, that I never handled dope of any kind nor lent myself to its use. One of the first questions put to me in this connection was always as to whether drugs were liable to injure a horse permanently, and my intelligent reply could only be that a real stimulant would perhaps help an animal who was a little faint-hearted or had a weakness in temperament, much as a man could be "assisted" by whisky or brandy properly applied. I do not know, having been out of racing for so long, whether the old-fashioned English stimulants of port wine or old ale, which I have read have been given to horses for generations, are still permitted; but I have been told by many old-time racing men in England that they were very effective on occasions. I have never, to my knowledge, seen or ridden a horse having this kind of homely dope, but it is quite possible to maintain that no permanent harm could be done by swallowing either. I have also read and heard about whisky being used, but I should keep an open mind about its possibility.

Dope is given to horses to stop them. This I am almost certain of. Surely a poisonous drug might injure a horse's racing career for all time. Good gracious me! Think of the effect on an athlete: his stomach and nervous system might be ruined forever from the effect of swallowing the kind of poison which beyond question has been given to race-horses. We Americans were all supposed to be absolute experts in dope, but don't believe half you hear on the subject; three-quarters of it is absurd. Modern training methods and riding in new styles made so much difference that critics could not understand altered form and attributed it to little bits of "You know what, mixed as we know how."

One of the greatest regrets of my life was that I never saw Fred Archer ride. I

LORD CARNARVON AND TOD SLOAN AT LONGCHAMPS
A caricature by Sem

have stood several times by his graveside in the cemetery at Newmarket and tried to picture him from his photograph doing those wonderful records which I had read so much of. Americans in my early days were always discussing the merits of Archer compared with those of boys like McLoughlin and Garrison. I was continually told that Archer had ridden two thousand seven hundred and forty-eight winners during his career of nineteen years. There is sufficient in this to make him the greatest living jockey of all time. Doesn't it seem a terrible thing for any man to be cut off from trying to equal that record? Perhaps it might not have been possible, but, with the average I earned in several years, that of about thirty-three per cent of winners in some seasons, and thirty-eight per cent in California, I feel that if I had lasted out physically the past fifteen years might have brought up the number of winning mounts to nearly the figures obtained by the immortal horseman who had a jockey's career less long than mine would have been.

I made many attempts during the year which followed to find out what chance I had of getting my licence again, but despite having good friends, I had no encouragement at all. In fact, the prospect became more and more dismal. I went over to America in the spring of 1904 and should have returned beyond question in the fall of the year, had there been any bright outlook. I had many powerful friends in New York who tried to do everything possible for me, but it all proved hopeless. In the East, they would not give me a licence on the score that they might offend the English Jockey Club, with which reasoning I have no kind of quarrel. Ed Corrigan, who was opening a new race-track at New Orleans, wired to me to go out to see him at Los Angeles. He offered to give me ten thousand dollars for the season if I would ride on his course. Naturally I was to be the star turn or advertisement for the new track. Over three thousand pounds for a season was not to be sneezed at. I consulted my friends to see what they thought about it all. I had been keeping myself pretty fit riding at exercise, and I may say that I never had any difficulty in getting round into condition after a slack time. I had natural confidence and I never put on flesh, so it was easier for me than for others. There were many friends to leave in New York, and a certain amount of hesitancy was inevitable. Neither did I quite like the idea of riding on a track which, although not exactly "outlawed," was liable to be barred. Such were the conditions of affairs in New Orleans; and I did not think for a moment that they would allow me to get in the saddle at the rival track whose dates were about the same as where I was to figure. It turned out just as I had anticipated, and I had no heart at all in the work which was before me.

It proved a terrible place: the horses were up to their bellies in mud, and their temperament changed just as my own had done. I felt exiled and I never took any interest in the work at all. I played bridge at night and was so disgruntled that I lost heart in the whole business. I won five races out of fourteen mounts, but that was no good to anyone and I gave it up.

XXXI
My Marriage

My Monologue — My Engagement — What a "Buck" is

I WAS RATHER DISGUSTED after that New Orleans trip, and I settled down in New York again, buying a new car and going racing with varying luck. My courtship of Miss Julia Sanderson had lasted a long time, and eventually I was married to my "first and only wife" on 21st August 1907. I had taken a flat in 45th Street and furnished it. The real happiness which followed was the best solace possible for disappointments, and all those pleasant days, months and years helped me to think that after all there was a great deal left in life. My wife remained on the stage after we were married, while I had started a big billiard-room containing eighteen tables with John McGraw, the great baseball player, and at the time of writing, manager of the "Giants" team. This business occupied a great deal of time, as I was sometimes up looking after the show for half the night. Still it was a good place and the profits were steady.

Soon after my billiard enterprise, an offer came to me to appear on the vaudeville stage in a monologue entertainment. The inducement was great: fifteen hundred dollars a week. Certain facts were related to the dramatic author and manager, George M. Cohan, and he put together something which I learnt by heart. There was no question of stage fright in advance, but as the time for my first appearance came round I had necessarily a certain amount of nervousness as to whether I should make good or not. The first engagement was at Hammerstein's. The question of what I should wear was debated, and at last it was decided that evening clothes would be the most suitable. It went all right and business was excellent, I used to get a good number of laughs—more, I suppose, on account of Cohan's witty lines; at all events the credit must be left to him. It is a pity that I cannot now remember the whole of the monologue. Stories about England were told, not altogether to boost the country I had ridden in. Little yarns about some of the antiquated customs of the old country nearly always go down to a mixed audience at a vaudeville show in America. There was one story about the English national game of cricket. I had to describe how a man went to the wicket with his bat when he was a boy, and stayed there until his whiskers began to grow, and on and on year after year until he became grey and was succeeded by his son. It was a gibe against the slowness of the game as compared with the thrilling quickness of baseball. I shall always think that with a few more demonstrations of baseball the taste for it in England would have been started. Everything is crowded into about three hours, and some day even Englishmen will refuse to be entertained by a struggle which is not decided for three days—and then sometimes not finished.

Another story I told concerned my advice to the great James Rowe about a horse race. I was supposed to say to him: "You had better have a bet on my mount to-day," and he refused, telling me that I had told him to back the same animal a few days before and he had lost five hundred dollars. Then I brought down the house by telling how I ultimately convinced him with the argument: "*I am putting five hundred dollars on him to-day!*" An audience always likes stories told against oneself.

Then I rung in another story about America's great jockey Snapper Garrison. I recounted how I had met him on the race-track and said: "Why don't you go on the stage the same as I am and earn fifteen hundred dollars a week? You have only to go before an audience and tell them what you did when you were riding."

He was supposed to reply: "Tell them what I *did*? Why, I wouldn't do that for ten thousand a week!" It doesn't, perhaps, look so funny in cold print but I got across with it—again thanks to Mr. George Cohan. By the way, Mr. Cohan is one of the best friends possible to those he likes or who are in need of a helping hand. The little charities he has done are numberless. One day he walked into a saloon kept by a man he had known in happier circumstances. He had heard that this particular saloon-keeper had not been going very strong and had been struggling to overcome misfortune. He also knew for certain that the place was absolutely the man's own property. Calling for a couple of drinks, he threw down a thousand-dollar note and told the barman to "ring it up in the machine" (the check till). It was a graceful way of doing something without making a fuss about his bounty.

My wife went from one show to another in musical comedy and paid two visits to London—much to my regret—that need not be alluded to. There was one incident, however, which I shall never forget, that being when I raced across the Atlantic to see her, cabling her beforehand not to sail until after my arrival. Somehow the cable miscarried: whose fault it was doesn't matter, but when I arrived she had sailed twelve hours before! We must have passed each other somewhere off the coast of Ireland. It is no use reviving that memory, but there are times in one's life when we can be in a state of what I would call the hopelessness of despair. Talk about anything which had occurred before in my life, the trouble about the licence, losing thousands of pounds, in fact anything which can be remembered: they were as nothing compared with my feelings when I reached England and found that she had gone. Still, the personal note in connection with the girl who was gracious enough to take my name can be dismissed.

The following, which was published at the time, may be interesting (it was just before our marriage):—

"JOCKEY HAS BEEN DEVOTED

"There's a pretty definite rumour in circulation that names Julia Sanderson of the 'Fantana' forces as the prospective bride of J. Todhunter Sloan, the noted jockey. And although Miss Sanderson has taken occasion, in the way of mild

Miss Julia Sanderson

rebuke, to receive the story in the spirit of jest, the report, to use the well-known phrase appropriate at such times, will not down.

"Until Sloan was summoned to New Orleans to resume his seat in the saddle at Ed. Corrigan's City Park race-track, he and Miss Sanderson had been observed frequently in each other's company, and the diminutive jockey played the gallant so devotedly that the report of an engagement was the principal topic in the 'Fantana' company.

"Just before Sloan started for the South, he and Miss Sanderson occupied a box at a Sunday night concert in a New York theatre. During the intermission several mutual friends took occasion to congratulate them on the reported engagement. Sloan tried to blush and said nothing. Miss Sanderson smiled feebly and remarked that it wasn't wise to believe all reports.

"Miss Sanderson's rise on the musical stage has been meteoric. She was an unknown chorus girl in *Winsome Winnie* when Paula Edwardes, the star, was suddenly called away by the death of her brother. Without previous rehearsal Miss Sanderson sang the title rôle and made a hit. She was subsequently assigned to a rôle of importance in *A Chinese Honeymoon*, and after Madge Lessing retired from *Wang* received the part of Mataya."

From Hammerstein's my engagement extended to Brooklyn and elsewhere, but the strain of two shows a day became too great; it was all right looking forward to the evening only, but I didn't feel equal to the afternoon too, and perhaps rather foolishly made no more bookings. It must be remembered that naturally the big billiard hall could not be looked after quite so well, and there was enough in this to give us a good living. That particular trip to America, where I only intended to go for a few months in 1904, extended up to 1908. It can be put down here that despite my having no licence to ride, and my repeated failures to get one, old friends stuck to me and that I made new ones. Year succeeds year very quickly when we get over a certain age and those happy three years after my marriage seemed to fly. Of course, there were little ups and downs of fortune which are inseparable from the experiences of those who go racing, but somehow, when there is racing, money seems to circulate more freely and there were always a certain number of "bucks" in my pocket. For those who are ignorant as to what a "buck" is, it might be explained that this is slang for a dollar, and here is a story about an old-time prize-fighter who used to be a frequenter of my billiard-room.

This man would sit watching a game for hours, interfering with no one. Occasionally somebody would slip him something to help him along. I heard a fine little bit of comedy one afternoon when an old gentleman was shaking hands and bidding him good-bye. The old pugilist said:

"I beg your pardon, but could you lend me a buck before you go? I want to buy some food."

"Certainly," was the ready response, as he took out his pocket-book, "but tell me how much a 'buck' is, I have never heard of it." Without the slightest hesitation the old fighter said with a smile of innocent childhood: "Two dollars."

Another time he met an old friend down in the billiard-room and they talked for over an hour. Suddenly, the occasional visitor got up to go.

"You're not going to leave me like that," said the ex-boxer, "without even a car fare?"

"Oh, I'll give you that, all right," said the "financier", as he opened his wallet. "I'll give you a car fare. Where do you want to go?"

"To Kansas City!" said the bright boy. They both laughed; and at all events enough was forthcoming for a half-way journey for where the pug. *didn't* want to go.

He was an excellent story-teller himself, and I can remember that one day he came in mopping his forehead, saying that he had never been for such a long walk for weeks. It appears that a young fellow who had squandered one or two fortunes had been put on a close allowance by his family. He was put to live in a big hotel down town where he could have everything in that house: meals, cigars, drinks, in fact all he wanted within reason; but not a penny of ready money was given him. The fighter met him and wanted a good drink and cigar. "Come to my place," said the young fellow, but neither had the money for the car fare and they had to tramp it over two miles with the thermometer nearly 100° in the shade.

"Never again," said the old man; "although I must say I did have four glasses of whisky and smoked four cigars, and he gave me these two to bring away with me."

Certainly it was an extraordinary way for a family to try and keep a boy in order.

I am reminded by this of just another yarn concerning an owner in America. He had two sons who hated the idea of work. The father had tried them several times, but they were such absolute slackers that he gave it up as a bad job. He let them stay at home, where they had everything they wanted, and their allowance for pocket money was five dollars a day. If the father did not see them in the morning the sum was left with the greatest punctuality in an envelope on the hall table and in no circumstances did he increase the allowance nor let them anticipate it. He paid for their clothes, too, up to a certain sum every year, and when they went away for the summer vacation the money was doled out in precisely the same fashion.

XXXII
Hope Deferred

Ruined through Winning — Acquiring Abelard II — "The Knock"

THROUGHOUT THIS BOOK I am afraid that I may have said too much of my perpetual hopes and fears about getting a licence. At all events, at the beginning of 1909 I was led to believe there was yet another chance, but—the usual result.

I went back to France therefore, and then on to Ostend. Here one day I was introduced to Lord Torrington: we seemed to have a lot of interests in common straight away. The friendship struck up there lasted for a long time. We saw out the remainder of the season at Ostend, having determined to go on to Brussels immediately afterwards. Lord Torrington proved a splendid sportsman and was on for any enterprise which the means at our disposal could exploit. We learned to know each other better and better, and we had no hesitation about embarking on a little deal together at the opening of the Autumn season. I saw an animal walking round the paddock which I mistook for a colt, but which proved, to my surprise, to be a filly. Getting closer to her, her good looks impressed me very much; in fact, she looked all over a winner, and of much better class than the others. I told "T" what I thought of her and we had a nice bet about her on the off chance, and we arranged that if she did win we would try to buy her.

Everything turned out successfully: she won, and we secured her for three thousand francs. That was the start of the stable. The filly was Campenoise, who afterwards won many races. We put her in the charge of Adament Douliere, who trained at Mons for the President of the Jockey Club, M. Coppée. He was one of the nicest men I ever met in Belgium and would take any amount of trouble with horses. Campenoise never ran in a Selling Plate after that. The first time we ran her, in Lord Torrington's colours of course, she won, and we had already made a nice profit on our investment. All we touched seemed to turn into money for a time, until the end of the season came. Lord Torrington went off for a trip to the West Indies and I decided to spend a week in Paris. It was at the time of the floods. Paris was lighter and gayer than at any time during the first war winter of 1914-1915. There was plenty of excitement, too, when the water was reported to be rising so many inches a day. But at the hotels and restaurants no one was upset. It was just something to look at and wonder about.

In the spring of the year Mr. George Edwardes sent over for me to ride a trial for him at Ogbourne and I went. It was my first meeting with his trainer, Pat Hartigan.

After several rides Mr. Edwardes asked: "Well how's the stable getting on in Belgium; do you want one or two?"

There was an old horse I had seen who had first been leading the two-year-olds, been switched on afterwards to some older horses, and even then had not finished. Then my eye caught a black, but I was told I couldn't have him. Then I suggested I would like the old horse, who proved to be Abelard II.

"Oh, choose anything else but him," said Pat Hartigan. "Don't take him; he's too useful." Mr. Edwardes laughed: "Oh, you want them all, Pat! You take him, Tod; you can have him with pleasure." He practically gave him to me.

I had heard that the old 'un had let Mr. Edwardes down once or twice, and perhaps for this reason he wasn't so sorry to see the back of him, so that he should not lose any more money. At all events, I was very proud of our new property and he was duly sent over to Belgium.

It must be mentioned that at this time I had been promised a trainer's licence in Belgium, and there was every reason to think it would be handed to me in a few days. At last it seemed that my luck was changing and that I was to start off with a real good chance of making good. Several of my friends congratulated me in advance on my good fortune, and some of them went as far as to say that they would support me. I had made my plans and was counting the hours to the time when it should be announced to those I respected in England and America that at last I had a "ticket" to do something at my legitimate game.

But destiny again interfered. There arrived another minor tragedy of a life in which there had been so many ups and downs. Abelard II was put in a hurdle race. I had no idea that he could stay and this race was lost entirely through carelessness. Abelard wouldn't go with Jimmy Hare waiting behind on him and the race was lost. A few days later he was engaged in the Grand Steeplechase, and in this from flag fall Abelard raced away on his own, Jimmy Hare being quite unable to stop him. At one time he was quite two hundred and fifty yards in front, and at no part of the race less than two hundred yards to the good. He won in a trot, and no one was more surprised than myself.

After the race Baron Gernier said to Mr. Harry Van der Poole, "Sloan wants his licence, doesn't he?" and took it out of his pocket. There it was in black and white and Harry Van der Poole reached out for it, but the Baron proceeded to tear it up into small pieces, saying as he did so: "Oh yes; Sloan can have it; here it is."

I can hardly speak of the incident, and every time I thought of it for a year or two afterwards, a lump would come into my throat at the thought of what I had missed. Nothing would satisfy them but that there had been something queer about the first race. However, I can solemnly state that no one has ever been more innocent than myself or anyone connected with the horse. Simply we didn't know him the first time and Abelard insisted on us knowing him when he ran in that Steeplechase. He won all sorts of races on the flat and over jumps, and the last event he ran in Belgium he actually carried 11-4 and won.

That last race was just a little while before the Cambridgeshire. It will be remembered that in that race he had the light weight of 6-9. He was sent over to Newmarket, to a stable where the trainer owning the establishment did his very best, giving him one of the finest boxes in the place; but Abelard was a horse of peculiar temperament and character. He loved solitude, and at home I would always have him in the quietest part of the yard. As it happened, at Newmarket, although his quarters were so good, there was a noise outside his box with the lads coming and going, rattling buckets and so on. Nothing was better calculated to upset this sensitive horse. When I arrived in Newmarket on the day of the race two or three of us went out to see him, and I was rather shocked at his appearance, for he had lost nearly fifty pounds in weight. His chance didn't look so rosy. Lord Torrington had backed him to win a very large sum at long prices and there was still a chance considering how light a weight he had to carry. Mr. Edwardes never had the slightest idea of his winning; in fact, he ridiculed me — but he hadn't seen the way Abelard had won his races in Belgium. Admitted that the class there is below that of England and France, still, when a horse gives stones away on the flat to quite useful horses it must be taken some notice of. He never showed at all in the Cambridgeshire. I think his rider thought that the horse was going to run away with him or something. However, one mustn't blame him. It was a disappointment, nevertheless. If Abelard could have appeared on Newmarket Heath that Wednesday in the same fettle as he was in on many days in Belgium, he would have made a different showing; but for all that, Christmas Daisy would have wanted beating by anything in training.

George Parfrement had ridden in the Steeplechase in Belgium when Abelard had won, and was determined in the Prix des Drags at Auteuil not to let our horse get so far away from him. I thought he was sure to fall if George kept to this tack of lying on his heels. At the stone wall Abelard pecked and his rider was shot out of the saddle but the horse did not fall.

After the Cambridgeshire, it will be remembered that Abelard won on the flat and his performances after over hurdles in England can be remembered.

* * *

After the incident of the tearing up of the licence, all hope seemed at an end about obtaining anything. It seemed to me almost persecution, for a full explanation could have been given, but of course I had no status in regard to the horse, and was not given a chance. I was not the only sufferer, however.

About this time there was an Englishman in Belgium, a young trainer, well educated, a good fellow and a veterinary surgeon, although he did not practise. For some reason or other, he could not obtain a licence in France and came to Belgium to try his luck there. But he met with all sorts of rebuffs and the endeavour seemed hopeless. What was it? There was a whisper that he understood too much about "dope" — a disgraceful allegation. The bar was up in France; it seemed that he would find it up perpetually in France, and it seemed that he would find it up perpetually in Belgium, too. Time went on with apparently no relaxing on the part of the Stewards. At last, through very strong inside influence, that of a big shareholder I think at one of the race-tracks, the Englishman obtained permission. The trouble then was to obtain a horse or two. Eventually, he got hold of one—a very bad actor and not an enviable animal to make a start with. He took any amount of trouble, however, with this "one and only" and won the first five races the horse ran in! Then followed more persecution: after each of these five races there was an objection lodged and *all of them overruled*. Can you beat it? In some cases it was a charge of "dope" and in others something trivial. However, he had shown what he could do, and a few more horses came to him; while in the following season, he had more offered to him than he could train, having a grand string and winning any amount of races.

That man is George Newton, who now is private trainer in France for Mr. Stern. He has the confidence of his owner and all those he comes in touch with. Good luck to him for the pluck he had in fighting on and on and—beating 'em.

An Englishman or an American soon gets used to life abroad, but when so many things can occur in private "talks" among the ruling body, and all sorts of things are listened to which there is no chance of denying, I ask you, what can be done?

After that Abelard incident, as fast as I wanted to explain and felt convinced I could, all the time a lot of backbiters, who would abuse the friendship of anyone, gave me "the knock." Some of them had not seen either race! Jimmy Hare, now training in England, will say what he knows and how unjustifiable it all was.

At the Carlton Hotel, Nice
1913

XXXIII
The Theodore Myers Stable

Kaufmann's Methods — Mr. Myers' Success — In April 1915

SURELY THERE NEVER WAS a more preposterous system established than that of the Société d'Encouragement in France, when they engaged Professor Kaufmann. The Austrian Jockey Club had been the first to start the business of examining the saliva of race-horses after a race in the search for traces of drugs which might have been administered to a horse. Kaufmann came to Paris with his theories and his assistants, and was engaged straight away and went about his work. There was not great inquiry as to whether his system was infallible; he was just launched on his policeman work. Just fancy an Austrian squad, able to make full inquiries about everything going on in France, going to all the race meetings, including some adjoining important fortified places. This is no charge that he or any of his assistants were spying. But what a change between then and now. What a hoist an Austrian would get at the time of writing (early in 1915) if he tried to nose into everything in France, both on and off a race-course! Things have certainly altered. They would have kissed them then; they might lynch him now.

It will be scarcely believable to those who do not know that after the appointment of Professor Kaufmann, all the examinations were at first in secret. Eventually, after many complaints, the trainer was allowed to be present. But to start off, there might as well have been no owner and no trainer, for all connected with a horse were kept outside. What an outrage! Many a good horse, too, has been ruined while standing there sweating after a race without a rub-down or being rugged up until the wonderful professor or his crew arrived from the weighing enclosure or buffet. When the swabbing out was done the horse was turned over to his lad.

Small wonder that some trainers went almost crazy with rage at the treatment their horses received, and at the time mentioned, when such as Denman, the Carters, the Cunningtons, in fact all trainers, had to cool their heels while their horses cooled and got chilled — well, it was unspeakable.

Was Kaufmann right in what he was supposed to find out? Who can say? He had to do something to justify himself, and the blame is not so much his as those who countenanced such proceedings. And what ridiculous happenings there were, too!

Take the case of Bonbon Rose. The pari-mutuel paid out over the race — over Bonbon Rose of course — but when the result of the "test" was known, the horse was disqualified and the stake given to the second. M. de Monbel very rightly brought an action to recover the stake. Now in all countries bets follow stakes, so the backers of the second should have been able to "touch." It seems too absurd that there should have been heavy winners over an animal which never got the race.

Again, why weren't the second and third also examined by the Specialist? The manner employed was to pick any horse out promiscuously and make a test: no trainer knew when his would be up for it.

To administer drugs to a horse is "doping." For the sake of argument, however, let it be considered whether leaving a certain number of kola nuts about on the grass for a horse to pick up if he liked is "administering dope" or not. Some horses would pick them up readily enough, while others would not touch them. If a horse gets what he likes, therefore, and that which stimulates or sustains him — is that doping him? Athletes nibble a piece of kola nut and are encouraged to extra exertion. What is good for a man cannot be harmful to a horse. Mind, I am only putting a case for argument. Some horses like dandelions and others don't. I am not sure but that dandelions might give a result on analysis which might suggest that something beyond "real grub" had been given to a horse. I hope those who read this will chew it all over.

*   *   *

My first venture in having any connection in horses with Mr. Theodore Myers, Ex-Controller of New York, was one day at Auteuil. It was a horse I wanted to buy and found I had only about three thousand francs, the price being about six thousand francs. I asked Mr. Myers if he had any money on him to make up the sum. He told me that he would put up the other half and go in partnership over him, but that horse must run in his name and colours. That was all right, in fact just as it should be. It was the beginning of a very pleasant association, and from first to last a good number of horses passed through our hands. At one time we had nearly thirty horses in the stable near Brussels and Ross Adams was the resident trainer. Mr. Myers became very fond of the horses, indeed of the whole business, and was tireless in asking questions about each of them. What could they do? Where and when were they likely to run? What sort of chance did they possess? Of course there were the many disappointments inseparable from a racing stable. Of those now remaining Mr. Myers' property are two mares, Chester and Jonquille. With more careful training, the latter, a grey, might have turned out anything: she was a perfect beauty as a two-year-old when we bought her.

There was one race which she won at Maisons Laffitte over which I am afraid both Mr. Myers and myself made some bad friends. The going was not exactly in her favour and she was so badly drawn — in fact, in a position on the other side of the course, from which very few, if any, win. How could either of us therefore give one point of encouragement to inquiring friends!

It seemed any odds against. I fancy someone put on a hundred francs for me, but I would not waste a shilling of my own over her — in the circumstances. Mr.

Myers had a few hundred francs on her. She was his animal and he was a rich man, so he had a right to indulge in a hobby. She won a big price, Johnny Reiff just getting the filly home. Then started the "rat-tats." "Why hadn't we told them?" I never heard the end of it that afternoon, nor the next day either; it was always coming at me from one and another. It was no use telling the truth, for I was disbelieved, and in fact charged with misleading inquirers, these including many old friends, some of whom gave me the cold shoulder ever afterwards, and some of whom I cut out for being so surly about it. This may not be so interesting to English readers, but the case is of the kind that many others have experienced on a race-course. It would have been madness to encourage them to back the mare; in fact I was on a hiding to nothing whatever happened.

It is a most difficult thing, too, to give an owner the right idea when to bet and when not to, especially when that man has not been racing all of his life. Half a suggestion by a trainer to an experienced owner is enough sometimes; the latter will take the responsibility on himself and kick afterwards. So many owners and trainers have fallen out over this, some being too hopeful while others hate to have any hand in making a suggestion. If the owner is a betting man, there is frequently a better time afterwards when advising a failure than when a man of non-speculation has an occasional small flutter and it goes down.

I am afraid Mr. Myers thought I was over-confident sometimes and he would say so on occasions—after a race—but always cheerfully. Archie MacIntyre, now in Roumania, rode a good deal for us; also others; and there was frequently a race thrown away through not following orders. I don't believe in hampering a boy with too many instructions, but in the case of horses of peculiar temperaments—well, I studied this more than many did.

Taking them all round, they were a cheap lot of horses Mr. Myers had, but they could win all the same. By degrees, however, Mr. Myers got tired of racing and weeded out the stable, selling some and giving away others until finally he gave it all up, only keeping the two mentioned for breeding purposes.

When all those pleasant days in Brussels are remembered, it is a terrible thing to think of all the places we went to and spent such a happy time in being swept away and gone for a long time, so far as racing is concerned. In its way, Belgium was a paradise for a small owner: he could have a chance with moderate-priced horses and back them at fair odds, too, thus helping him to make it pay. Whether racing will be revived again is one of those puzzles we in the spring of 1915 cannot solve.

A few lucky owners managed to get away with a few of their horses to England, and to win races, too. The Belgian-bred stock were improving every year there is no doubt, and racing was going quite the right way. Of course, expensive sires could not be purchased, but good results can be obtained without extravagance. It is not necessary to specify horses, but one of the first things all true lovers of racing will wish for is that racing be restored. This sounds empty as it is written but—who knows! It will be curious in future years to read what was written in April 1915!

XXXIV
Some Minor Successes

A Doctor's Advice – Rehearsing an Operation – Great Night at Ostend – What Hanlon Did for Me

ONE OF THOSE CHARMING FRIENDS who had helped in every possible way in Brussels in all I tried to do and who looked after my health was Dr. Bouhlle. He was one of the best friends I had in that country. He would give me such excellent advice regarding my health, and some excellent "man of the world" pointers as to what I should do. He was medical officer to the Jockey Club there and had naturally a certain amount of influence. I cannot thank him enough for his dozens of acts of friendship. I have always made friends with medical men.

At the Cecil in London in 1899 I was suffering, as I thought, from nervous breakdown, and I was sure of the insomnia, for sleep was next to impossible. The Prince of Wales was told of it, and suggested to Lord William Beresford to send me to Sir Francis Laking; the latter was told that I was coming to consult him. He thoroughly examined me, and certainly I had fallen away, not weighing an ounce more than 6-7. Sir Francis was most amiable to me, asked me a lot of questions about myself, and was quite a delightful man to talk to. His verdict was that I was in bad case and must rest up for at least two months. I ought to go away, he said, and be looked after by a trained nurse. He told me also that he would leave the choice of a sanatorium to me. I listened very attentively to him, but eventually struck in with: "I have to ride in the Derby next week. I *must*; I have the chance of a good mount."

Sir Francis expostulated with me on the madness of it, and told me that he would not be responsible for anything which might happen. He was very emphatic.

Of course I rode in the Derby. It shows what one can do in a fanciful mood. I know that when I have been broke I *have* had no hallucinations—is that the right word?—about being ill, but on a big earning capacity and with a full bank I often found myself nervous about my heart, my lungs, my—well, especially the former. It was very delightful of the Prince of Wales to mention to Lord William that there was just the odd interest taken by him in my health. It was just on a par with all he did for those he took any passing or permanent interest in. I must add, too, that Lord William used to say to me: "Little man, you *must* look after yourself"—and this wasn't because he wanted me to do nothing but ride for him; it was something altogether above that—a great good man's interest. Would to God he had lived! And I will go further—I cannot think but that had he lived, some greater consideration—if only in a spirit of clemency—would have been extended to me. God! it is a terrible thing to be barred for life. What can be the reason of it all?

Surely someone must realise the fierce difficulties of living without a licence to follow one's calling.

Going back to doctors and surgeons, I must here put down my heartfelt thanks to all of them, for I do not suppose that the fees I have had to pay have amounted to more than one hundred pounds in my life—and I was a bit of an "inquirer" on the "ailment stakes." Dr. Bull and Dr. Jannaway of New York were very kind when I thought that I had an affection of the heart, but they both at different times gave me a clean bill of health.

Dr. A.C. Bernays of St. Louis was perhaps one of the greatest personalities among surgeons whom I ever met. I was privileged to become a great friend of his and had the opportunity of studying one of the cleverest surgeons in America. It is far more interesting to state some facts about the man than to remember any small or great thing which he ever did for me. A.C. Bernays, I believe, performed the most marvelous feats in surgery that the scientific world has ever known. He had the wonderful case in his charge of the woman who had been shot three times through the brain by her husband—who was condemned and executed, by the way.

The woman lasted four days by the most wonderful feat of surgical jugglery—forgive the word—and Dr. Bernays actually had her talking for a few minutes on the third day; but, of course, she was doomed, and in the ordinary course of life should have died on the same night as she was shot, but—A.C. Bernays ruled otherwise. In connection with this case, the surgeon's claim against the estate of the deceased man and woman was disputed. It was a question of fifty thousand dollars. The administrators were against it, but eventually "Doc" Bernays made good his right. He had sat up with the wife watching her unceasingly for four days and nights, and this was taken into consideration. He had ruined his health, but had achieved a triumph for surgery. The whole details of what he had done were given in the scientific journals.

When a great congress of medical men was held—I think in Berlin—Dr. Bernays performed a most wonderful operation on the spot which was reported everywhere and staggered those present by its skill and originality. It may seem strange that I could take so much interest in it all, but I knew the man and what he could do.

I had an extra knowledge of him from my repeated conversations with him: he would find a ready and willing listener in me at all times. He would sometimes say: "Tod, I have an operation to do tomorrow morning which I have never had before, with all my experience. I will tell you what it is, and what I am going to do." Then he would rehearse it and I would sit silent and wondering at the—what shall I call it?—the genius of the man. It was flattering to me to have his confidence, and I more than half understood what he was talking about.

What a loss to everything and everybody he was when he died! He was quite a young man, not much over fifty. Given the chances and the education, I have often thought that I should have liked to be a doctor. Fancy "Doctor Sloan" on the brass plate outside! I couldn't have stood the "old ladies' physician" stunt, but real

THE FIRST TIME AN AEROPLANE CARRIED FOUR PEOPLE
I am astride the gasoline tank, and with me are M. Leganieux, the aviator, and M. Martinez

practical surgery, lunacy cases or something exciting, I feel I should have made a mark at. But what's the use of thinking—I was only a jockey and now am ex-jockey, a would-be trainer, a would-be at many things! As a child, I learned an old saying about "making your bed and lying on it"—but, in all honesty, others tucked in those hard sheets I had to make acquaintance with. I'm not wailing nor snivelling; but that I should have to go through life without that chance I have prayed and longed for seems too terrible.

* * *

In a previous chapter I have mentioned Sir Thelwell Thomas of Liverpool, who kindly attended me at the request of Lord Derby, then Lord Stanley. His lordship kindly gave me a carriage to take me to the Adelphi Hotel, Liverpool. It was after the accident when riding Maluma. My ear was nearly off, and I was in great pain. I was put in a cot in my bedroom and the great surgeon came to me. He refused to perform the operation without chloroform; in fact, he said he couldn't with success or justice to himself. He had a medical man with him to administer it, but when I had the first whiff I showed fight and threatened all sorts of things if it were gone on with. I was such a fresh kid! I was in agony, however.

Sir Thelwell then began putting in the stitches one after the other until I counted ten. "Can I speak to you?" I asked. "If you want to make me happy, you'll leave off at that and not put a single one more in."

"Perhaps that's enough," he answered. "At all events we'll make it do."

Looking back, I can remember all the details exactly, and my suffering. I think if he had gone on another minute my heart would have given out. As it was, when I got up off the cot, my knees collapsed and the surgeon and a friend who was with me had to lift me up—I was down and out.

I hope these little personal incidents will not annoy a public, who perhaps wants to hear some more exciting details of other people, but this is, after all, "Tod Sloan," and must be told if only as an appreciation of what others have done for me. In very truth, the greatest possible kindnesses have been received from the greatest in their profession.

* * *

I have been wandering from Belgium, but several other Belgian incidents must be mentioned. A few seasons back I arrived in Ostend without a sou. Something had to be done, and with a horse or two I managed to rake a few thousand francs together to make things go easier. There was racing and a little bit of baccarat and chemin de fer, but the bulk of a "young" bank roll came in from the course. It grew and grew until one night I went into the Casino with, I suppose, about fifteen thousand francs. A few odd bets and it swelled up to nearly twenty thousand. Mr. Gaston Dreyfus, the French owner, was in the bank and I called him "banco" for eighteen thousand francs. He looked at me for a few seconds and then "passed" the bank. It was handed round the table until I took it at the eighteen thousand and had a pass of three! My winnings that night were about one hundred thousand francs. A night or two after I called a thirty-two-thousand-franc "banco" when M. Brodsky was in the bank, and he passed it. I took it and had a pass of three. That was another great evening! I lived on the best and did what I could for those less fortunate. It shows you what luck is, for in that time I accumulated a packet, and then, in the last three nights, I lost one hundred and fifty thousand francs. All the same, after paying up everything, I had a nice wad of ninety thousand francs to take back to Paris for the autumn racing.

The first thing to do was to get a flat, and I took a furnished *appartement* at 1 Rue de Messine at one thousand francs, or forty pounds, a month, paying three months in advance. It was just as well that I did. I bought a brand-new Gobron car for eighteen thousand francs. There was the chauffeur to pay and two servants and — other details. I entertained and loved it all, but could I keep the money? Not a bit of it. I was broke in three weeks and had to "look around."

When the racing was over in Paris I wanted to go to St. Moritz, Switzerland calling us that winter. The car was sold and small debts paid up. After all what *did* it matter! there was always the chance. So tickets were taken for St. Moritz for a friend, a valet and my dog — the west of Scotland white terrier which will be seen in various pictures. I had only about fifty pounds in my pocket, but the idea of a holiday was everything.

We lived the outdoor life and played bridge in the evening. Things ran well for me and I won on that trip about eight hundred pounds — at bridge only. It shows you that, despite a drop of over ninety thousand francs to about one thousand francs, one should never despair. There's nothing like getting used to the ups and downs. Those who gamble can always hope.

Of all the games of cards I have played in my life, there has never been a game that appealed to me so much as bridge. We used to play the old game in London and elsewhere — but the comparatively new Auction Bridge: surely there was never anything like it! Its fascination beats that of all the other games of chance and skill which have ever been devised. American billiards always fascinated me, and then came my learning of the English game, at which my Editor tells me I play pretty well. At all events I can beat him readily enough — or so he says! "Solo" had its fascinations, poker its late hours and unsatisfactory endings, with sometimes no one satisfied; but give me the thrills of bridge with a satisfactory partner! Carrying a "dud," however, and having to lift him out of trouble time after time isn't funny.

In writing all this I am afraid I have wandered a good deal from the story of my life, but the various topics have to be taken up as thought of or suggested, and the distraction of cards and dominoes can help us to keep our sanity on occasions. I do not intend to suggest that there has ever been a suspicion of anything in the way of "Pots" or "Bug-house" in our family, but anyone who has a big nervous strain is liable to want something to take the attention off more serious topics.

AFTER THE ST. MORITZ ANNUAL BILLIARD TOURNAMENT
Mr. Heathorn, the Referee, is on the extreme left

I have met many great players at bridge, have watched their peculiarities and have studied how they played the game. A man can so easily start off with the best possible ideas about prudence and then be spurred to risk. On the other hand, there are "pikers" at the game who have no audacity and will see opponents win a game where a little courage would get them out of a hole. There are books and theories, but there is nothing like practice and encouragement.

Speaking of the latter—encouragement—perhaps I should have never gone on with race riding many years ago but for the comforting words of Charles Hanlon. It is almost entirely due to him that I persevered with the forward seat. It was he who dissuaded me from going on the stage and made me stick to riding. He encouraged others, too, and America has a lot to thank him for in the way he could discriminate between what would be for the benefit of the Turf and what would not. He combined intelligence with a manner and a way of speaking which anyone had to listen to. His picture will give some idea of the kind of man he was.

XXXV

My Dog Piper

"Has anyone seen Piper?"—Piper and the German—All I was Fit for

I CANNOT THINK how I have resisted so long the temptation to talk about my dog Piper. More than one photograph of him appears in the book. Some dogs are merely dogs, but Piper was Piper—an individual, an inseparable companion, my pal! Mind you, sometimes it happens that dogs can be "general"—that is, have too many friends, and in this Piper somewhat erred. I never knew exactly when to expect him back when he disappeared, and on occasions he never gave me the slightest indication when he was going. When he broke away on his own "jag" he would come around after and begin his hunt for me; why, I wonder, did he start all round the bar-rooms of Paris on the off-chance of finding me? He knew my haunts, I suppose. And he would go mad when at last he ran me to earth. Still, he was such a casual fellow that I would never make too much fuss of him when he found me, pretending to be rather offended when he picked me up—offended at his being so offhanded during the previous day or two. He "twigged" it all right and would try and ingratiate himself by every dog sign of affection and "playing up."

With all his sagacity and devotion, Piper was a "dam-fool" dog if it comes to that, for he was crazy on automobiling, and would take the chance of being kidnapped for an odd ride. That is how the grievous end came. One day I was going to the American Express office and saw Piper fooling about with some of his own countrymen, Highland officers, standing alongside their cars by the Grand Hotel. I didn't take any notice, thinking he would follow me. He wasn't there when I came back, so I thought he had gone home, or at all events that he was somewhere on his "rounds." There was no necessity to bother about him, for he had frequently disappeared for a couple of days at a time. On this occasion, however, I waited and waited without any news of him. All the police stations were notified and every effort was made to find him, but without success, and a friend of three and a half years was lost to me. I can only suppose that he jumped in one of the cars which was going off and the Highlanders must have thought that they had a mascot which could not be turned out without risk to their luck.

If this should happen to be seen in print by any of them, and Piper is in the land of the living, I am quite sure that he would be restored to me in Paris, for it is almost a certainty that he is in France.

The history of the dog is that he may have been stolen in England long before I got hold of him. The tale of the man who first made the sale was that he had won the gold medal in Cardiff, beating sixteen other West Highland terriers. Even-

Shooting Clay Pigeons at St. Moritz

tually, he found his way to France. Whether he swam or hid himself on a boat is not known; at all events, Captain Langford of the Travellers' Club gave him to Lucien Lyne, who asked me to look after him for a few days. The following week Lyne asked me: "How's the dog behaving?"

I made a face and answered:

"I've seen some ill-behaved dogs in my time, but this one is the limit."

"Then you keep the dam dog," answered Lucien—and I did. Of course I had been kidding Lucien, who, however, never rapped me about it afterwards.

Piper was perhaps the best-known dog on the Continent, being able to find his way all over Nice, Monte Carlo, St. Moritz, Paris, Brussels and Ostend. I am certain that he knew one place from another, and he knew very well where I stayed in each place. He was a wonderful traveller, too. When we boarded a train he would go under the seat straight away, either in a compartment or a sleeping-car, and would never be seen until we arrived at our destination, when he would stretch himself and trot out on the platform and wait for me.

Talking about "stretching," I could make him yawn whenever I wanted to. I needed only to gape and pretend to yawn to make him open his mouth, all the time making a most fearsome noise; it was funny.*

Piper never cared much for women; they could scarcely ever induce him to go to them; and he would *never* make friends with young children; at some time or other some child must have earned his contempt. Many of my friends, however, were just as fond of him as I was, and I was asked for him by many. I wish now that I had given him to Henry Tepé ("Henry") in the Rue Volney, for he was so fond of that dog and so was Piper of him.

I was approached once by a certain Count in Belgium as to how much I would demand for Piper's stud fee, the Crown Princess Stephanie having some prize bitches. I said they were welcome to Piper for a time, and I was promised half one litter. But it proved to be like many other promises I have had: I never saw one pup even, although I heard there were six grand youngsters in the first lot.

I never had a licence for him nor did he ever wear a collar. He would go in and out of my apartment just like a man and I am sure would often try to talk. He endeavoured to say something quite civilly to a big German once at St. Moritz, and the hulking pig kicked him. Piper looked to me to take up the quarrel, and I did. The German was three times my size, and it must looked funny when I faced that "Boche."

"What did you want to kick my dog for?" I asked him.

He smiled at first, then he must have seen my dangerous "bantam" look, for he turned green and—apologised. I think Piper was disappointed that there was no scrap; he might have been useful round the German's calves.

It may seem odd to some people that I have given so much space to just a dog, but apart from liking all dogs, Piper was out by himself in intelligence; we

* You should see and hear Tod's imitation of it.—EDITOR.

My Dog Piper 169

WITH MY DOG, PIPER, AT ST. MORITZ

understood each other just like two men talking. I miss him still and have never had the heart to get another. There are some living creatures in the world who cannot be replaced, and Piper was one—of two.

* * *

In the first chapter of this book I mentioned my first dog—Tony. One of the lasting memories of my life is when I assassinated a dog to save Tony's life. Yet I was almost as fond of the dog I murdered as I was of Tony. It was a question of the oldest friend having to be protected. It was when I was working at the oil wells. I used to have to take a can every morning to Pat Grace's cottage for milk. Pat also worked at the wells. He had a big bull-dog known as "Pat Grace's bull-dog." This dog and I would play together, rollick in the grass, pretend to bite each other and spar like two kids.

One morning I had forgotten that Tony had come with me to Pat Grace's for the milk, and before I knew anything, the bull had grabbed him by the neck through the fence, and was shaking the stuffing out of my dog. Then the two bounded through the fence on the railway track and Grace's bull had a new hold on Tony. My dog weighed about 26 lb., while his attacker was heavier than I was— about 56 lb. There was my lovely dog being chewed to death in front of my eyes! What was to be done! If the bull had turned on me he would have done for me. I had a big clasp-knife in my pocket, and it was the work of a minute to whip it out and give the first stab at that hulking brute—I felt that way about him then, although he was my pal in peace-times. In a second another deep jab followed up to the hilt of the knife, and then—it closed on me and cut my fingers open to the bone. Tony was gasping and whimpering. Myself, I let that bull have a one-two, a half-blade stab and one which put him out. Tony had got away and was licking his wounds.

I don't know how I got away myself, but I did, delivered the milk, had a look at Tony, and—went back to work. The first thing I did was to go up to Pat Grace, who was sitting around after his breakfast.

"Pat, I've killed your dog," I began. "He tried to kill mine and I stabbed him to death."

There was a pause, and his face turned deathly white. He half got up, then mastered himself, and replied: "Then you better go and bury him, Tod." And he turned away and never spoke to me again in his life.

I tramped back, crying over the bull which I was so fond of. It was a bit of a task to drag that 56 or 58 lb. dog to a pit I had ready for him, but I did. I cursed the fate of things that made it necessary for dogs to chew up each other, for, with Tony out of the way, I could have been just as fond of the other fellow. However, the last look was given him and I felt happier when he was out of sight.

Of course there was a lot of talk about it all in our district. I was mentioned as "only being fit for a School of Correction," and altogether put down as hopeless. What a lot of chat can take place in a little community! I wasn't altogether pleased with myself, all the same.

XXXVI
A Little Fighting

Dal Hawkins v. my Valet — Results Tell — Silencing a Whistler

IN MENTIONING FIGHTERS, I have referred to my friendship with Jim Corbett. I had also a cordial acquaintance with Bob Fitzsimmons, Kid M'Coy and others at various times. I shall always look on Corbett as the greatest fighter of our time. He proved it over and over again, especially when going twenty rounds with Jim Jeffries, then a much younger man — in fact at his prime, and seven years younger than Jim. Neither of these men I have mentioned had much to do with the race-course, paying only occasional visits. Corbett, from being a bank clerk, became a pugilist, and made his great name by beating John L. Sullivan in the twenty-first round. He followed that up by beating Charlie Mitchell very easily, and being beaten himself by Fitzsimmons at Carson City. Of course there were many minor victories.

A sort of preliminary for that great fight at Carson City was at the same place when Dal Hawkins, who weighed about 136 lbs., had nearly killed Martin Flaherty — a great fighter, too. Somehow Hawkins and I did not get on very well. I forget what led to it, but I answered him back one day by saying: "Why I've got a man who can beat you easily — my valet." I was referring to "Mac," as he was known on the race-course, his full name being MacGoolrich. He was always saying that he could fight, so one day I made a match for 200 dollars a side for my "dark one" against "Dal." He hadn't put down his stake, so I roasted him one day in the Baldwin House at San Francisco.

"I've put up ten 20-dollar gold pieces," I said. "Where's *your* money? Afraid of being whipped? Why should I leave my money down any longer?" He looked at me a bit ugly like, and then said: "Oh! I'll get it," and went out of the place to do so. He came back with 100 dollars, all he could raise for the moment, so we made the match for the reduced sum down, on the understanding that it was to be increased to 500 dollars later on. I had done the thing for a bit of a joke at first, but MacGoolrich was always so sure of what he could do, that I stuck to it. Of course, it had all started by my kidding Dal. It was to be one of several bouts put on at the Opera House, San Francisco. I remember that Pittsburgh Phil and I had the big stage box.

MacGoolrich had stage fright, I could see, but apart from that he was no class at all. If Dal had gone for him in the first round, my man would have been down and out in no time at all. But Hawkins sparred cautiously, not being sure whether I had sprung a real daisy on him. He was fogged about it all. When they came up for the second turn there was no time lost, and Mac was cut to ribbons. My! but Hawkins simply murdered him. Mac, in fact, was out for a long time. What a game they had with him when he went racing again! The boys would rattle a bucket behind, or run up quietly and then yell: "Look out, Mac, here's Dal coming."

No one left him alone at all, and his life was a misery. But he had been such a swanker before with regard to his fighting! And to think in that first round Dal thought he might be out against a ringer! Hawkins and I made it up in after years, but he had heard the full story long before that.

I had a coloured valet, Dick Keys, of whom I have spoken: he thought he could fight too, but he had no heart—or "guts," if I may use rather a vulgar expression. Fred Taral, the jockey, was a rival just then of mine, and was sore with me about several things, chief of which being the fact that I had replaced him in riding Hamburg. There was still more jealousy and enmity between Dick Keys and Taral's coloured valet. In fact, it grew worse and worse as day followed day. At all events, a match was made between the two. Willie Sims, the coloured rider, known both in France and England, asked me about my valet, and I told him that he had no real stamina and wouldn't stay. "Never mind," said Willie, "we've *got* to win; we'll win."

The two were both heavy fellows, and outwardly they looked a good match. Sims said again, when the match drew near: "We'll *have* to win."

It took place at the Coney Island Athletic Club. Willie Sims was in Keys' corner; the match was four rounds. The two boxers looked like a pair of chimpanzees when brought in; I never saw such a picture, they shaped and crouched just as if they ought to have been up a tree, or in a Zoo.

Taral's nigger led off and let Keys have some beauties, although neither of them knew anything about fighting. Wallop, wallop—how my man got it! I thought he would have been "dead" in the first round, but he scraped through, somehow. Willie Sims whispered encouragement to him and in he went for the second. What the other nig had done to him in the first was nothing to what he handed out in the second; he was sent all over the ring, and how he got up and faced more punishment was a licker; he did nothing in return. Back they went to their corners, and here something happened to my man which made him more like a monkey than ever. By mistake, they dashed some ammonia into his face out of a bottle instead of water. He sprang up with a yell and danced all over the ring. No one knew what had happened, and there was a roar of laughing. The wonderful Willie Sims soothed him somehow and got him up again, to be whipped about in much the same way as before. Willie didn't look downcast about it all, so I only looked on to enjoy the fun; yet I never thought for a moment that my man could last it out, and—even suppose he did! Sims must have mesmerised him or something, for notwithstanding Keys being down twice in the last round—once for the count of eight—he flopped back more dead than alive.

Up went the Referee's hand. "Keys wins!" That was the announcement. What yells and booing! You could have heard them miles away. Keys didn't know where he was; however, he got round—and then the side he put on! He bought a red necktie and a new suit. He could afford to: the match had been for 200 dollars a side. When they all began from that time to chip him and say: "What a decision!" or "Why, Taral's nigger could murder you!" Dick's only answer, given with a wag of his head, was "RESULTS!"—meaning, of course, "Results tell."

Just another story of a nigger. When I was out in San Francisco there was a nigger arrived there armed with a letter from George Considine of New York to me. It said merely that the nigger wanted a show, and that, according to the nigger, he "could fight till the cows came home." He was a biggish fellow, weighing about 155 lbs. We arranged a try-out for him against a local man and went to see the show. Considine's nigger, as I shall call him, came into the Ring full of confidence, showing his white teeth as his smile broadened. He was as cheerful and confident as possible, so I said to Joe Eppinger, who was just behind him: "There may be something in this feller."

"Anyhow, we'll see some fun," answered Joe.

They were to spar six rounds. When they began the nig was still laughing. Then it began to wear off as the round proceeded, and he looked astonished at the end of it, for the other fellow was handing out jabs and hooks. He went in for the second and got lifted off his feet and had it all roads. At the end of it he looked like quitting, but Joe Eppinger kidded him, saying: "Go in; you're all right; he's nearly had enough of it; that last knock down was only an accident." So up he got again.

In the third he was driven round the Ring, and it required all Joe's cleverness to get him in again. "The fight's on points," Joe said. "You've outpointed him already, and you're sure to get the decision if you go up to him."

At the end of the fourth, which was a repetition of the others, Eppinger tried to use the same old wheezes, adding: "You're sure of it now, ask Tod Sloan; he says you'll walk in."

"I don't seem to see it in the same way as you fellers do," the nig replied. However, he went in again. After more slaughter, Joe started afresh: "That was a beauty: your man's beaten. Why, he wants to quit now."

"Does he, boss; does he really? Well, send someone to the other feller and tell him let's call it a draw."

"Why, there's more dog in you than in any nigger I ever saw," calls out Joe to him. "Why, in Mr. Considine's letter to Tod Sloan, he said you could fight 'till the cows came home.' "

"That's right, but tell Mr. Sloan that I see 'em coming."

* * *

There *are* a brave lot of people about. I was riding home in a street car in San Francisco one night with a fellow called Gus Gentry, who was always talking fight. I was sitting next to an old fellow, who fidgeted about when I was whistling—I have spoken of the habit.

"Quit whistling," roared the old fellow. Gentry, who was farthest away from him, nudged me and said: "You go on whistling, Tod."

The old fellow leaned across my back, looked at Gus, and said: "*You* whistle."

Gus never made a sound, and after a minute the old fellow laughed and looked at us: "I don't hear either of you fellers whistling." He got off soon after, and when we were travelling about 200 yards farther, and the car running at about 25 miles an hour, Gus broke in: "I'm burning up; I've a good mind to jump off the car and go back and kick the stuffing out of that fellow. What right had he to stop us whistling?"

"I didn't hear *you* whistling, Gus," I answered.

"No, but I'm *not* a whistler like you, Tod. I wasn't brought up to it like; in fact, I *can't* whistle — not what they call whistling."

* * *

Just another word about Jim Corbett. Always a good fellow, he liked to sit down in a bar-room with Frank Ives, the billiard player, and myself and talk for hours. The three of us travelled about a good deal together, in America, in the nineties. Frank Ives had the billiard-room in New York before McGraw and I took it. He led an indoor life and the atmosphere he lived in affected his health; the poor fellow died of consumption. Yet in his earlier times he had been a good baseball player and an all-round good athlete.

Bob Fitzsimmons, although not such a good raconteur as Jim Corbett, who has made plenty of money at it, had a lot of anecdotes and possesses a fine dry wit. Both Jim and Bob were staunch friends to one, and have been level-headed enough to provide for themselves and their wives — to whom they have proved devoted husbands.

XXXVII
Making a Book

Raided — Charron as a Pupil — Newmarket — In the Red Cross — One and Only "Henry"

ONE OF THE GREAT MISTAKES I MADE was taking the New York Bar in the Rue Daunou, Paris. My predecessor, Milton Henry, lost a packet over it, and it was waste of time for me. However, with the war coming, all I had to do with it was finished. I had previously run a big bar, of course, in connection with my billiard-saloon in New York, and knew a good deal about the business, but — there is always so much to learn.

It has been said that I made a book in the Paris bar, but I had nothing to do with anything of the kind. Not that I have never made a book. I have — in New York. I had a rather nice flat, and some of my friends used to say to me: "Why don't you start booking at your place? There's every facility." So I started an extra telephone and Charlie Hauser, a brother of the great story-teller in Paris, was on the "piece-at-each-ear" game. There used to be a pretty collection of all nations up at my "apartment": grafters, diamond merchants, the knock-outs from the Balkan provinces, and — others. We betted ready and settled after each official result. They would have five, ten, fifteen, twenty dollars on a horse, and sometimes fifty or a hundred. There was no starting price, as understood in England, but a list of prices would be put up and they could take their choice. There was varying success, of course, but it paid for a while. I can tell you, though, that I used to look at the carpets and chairs when they had all gone. The collection of cigar stubs and remnants of bad words took some time sweeping up.

One afternoon, just before the fourth race was due, Charlie Ballard, the jockey, came in by chance. The crowd were looking down the card and thinking over what they would do. Charlie Hauser, who was at the telephone as usual, taking the commissions of Germans, Poles, Russians — and others, looked through the door, saying: "Is Charlie here? somebody's asking for him." But Charlie Ballard wasn't wanted; he never even went to the receiver.

"I'll have a bet on this race," said one. "A hundred dollars on So-and-so" — and he mentioned the name of the horse.

"Well then, put me on 20 dollars, Tod," added another. It was a 4½ to 1 chance. Then there was a short pause and a minute or two elapsed. "Champion won," called out Hauser through the door. It was what the two had backed. But I didn't tumble it and in due course paid out. The evening passed and even the next day came but I was no wiser. The guy who had stuck me for the 450 dollars had a great night, I heard, and said I was "easy." Then it began—by remarks of one or two—to leak out to me. They had coded the runners in the race. One was "Charlie," of course, another was Fred, say, yet another George, while I suppose the others were represented by Fritz, or Ivan, or Bill. At all events the strength of the result was given by "Is 'Charlie' here?" The code of "Charlie" had come off all right. I fell across the fellow who had stuck me for the 450 dollars, and he laughed, saying: "You always *were* a mug and always will be—so, why not?" It was unanswerable.

The show went on, however, until one day "Big Tim" (Senator) Sullivan gave me the glad word.

"You'd better be doing no business to-day, Tod. Just be at home as a gentleman at ease." So there was nothing doing and we smoked our cigars, just one or two of us. They came as expected, those "cops", had a look round and then asked me what I was doing there. "What d'yer think?" I replied. "This is my 'at home' day and I'm expecting the company." However, they didn't bother, and off they went, but bookmaking at that place was finished for good and all.

I had a look round and found a suite of rooms at an hotel up town, just near Fiftieth Street and Seventh Avenue. I sent word round to the clientèle, and up they came the first afternoon. We hadn't been going an hour before the cops came. They didn't come in with any kid-glove way, but simply smashed the door in and caught us all red-handed. They didn't grab the money, though; that was planted all right. The inspector came over and of course took me as the principal, with the telephone clerk and my others, too; and they put down the names and addresses of all the frequenters.

I began to parley with him. I told him the tale that it would be a terrible thing for me. I had applied for my licence, which I hoped to get, and it would be a dreadful thing if I had to go off in the Patrol Wagon. I didn't mind what it cost, the fine and all that, but if it got into the papers and I was made the main guy in it, all my prospects would be ruined. He laughed at first and then said, without any hint that I should give him any of my pocket-book, "You'll come with me alone, then." I guessed he was all right and meant me to slip him when we got outside. It turned out pretty well, as I thought. Once in Seventh Avenue he turned to me, saying: "Beat it now [Go off quick] and don't let me hear of you again." And I never did. That was the end of the bookmaking business.

The only other time that I came across the police in New York was when we were exceeding the speed limit—so they said—in an automobile coming into the city. There was a terror named Tracy in those days, who used to get scores of record-breakers into his net. He got us and rode on his bicycle all the way by our side to the police station; my two pals had been taken, too. We were run in, and they fixed the cash bail at 100 dollars for us all. We turned out our pockets, and could only find about 35 dollars among the three of us. We had another with us, but he had not been charged. We asked him how he was fixed, and he said he had 100 dollars on him, but it "didn't belong to him." We knew that story, for he was a real "hard heart," but we made him put up that 100 dollars. Of course, he wanted to pouch the 35 we had, but I put that down where it wouldn't come very quickly. We had to see the evening through after that. He kept on saying: "But *why* not give me that 35?" I explained to him that his money was all right. We should turn up in the morning and his "100" would be released. Of course it went down after a bit of a demur.

Next morning I was at the Court House before 9:30, and asking for "Battery Dan," as we knew the Police Court Judge, who was a great friend of Tim Sullivan. I asked and asked until at last I was told that he had arrived. The police officer said he'd take my name in. I wouldn't have that and said I would knock at his door and walk in myself. Doing so I came into a room before Tim Sullivan and "Battery Dan."

"In trouble again, Tod?" began "Big Tim." "We can't help you this time, I'm afraid; it's all up with you."

"How much money have you, Tod?" asked "Battery Dan." "Are you going to the race-track to-day?"

I told him I had about 15 dollars and free entry and he asked me how much it cost to pay the usual entrance. When he learned from Tim that it was 3 dollars, "Dan" told me to give him the 3 dollars and get out. That was the joke he played on me and I never heard another word about it. America can be, after all, a "free" country!

Although I have mentioned a few little details about betting, laying horses never had any real fascination for me, and, strictly speaking, when I was not riding, the big wagers made were more in emphasis of an opinion than a gamble. The proof of this is provided by the semi-refusal to support animals which I did not believe to be at the top of their form—Rose de Mai, for instance, already alluded to. By the way, when the Comte de St. Phalle left Charron as his trainer, he did nothing to speak of, although he had, in one season with Charron, won 480,000 francs in stakes.

Certainly Charron was one of the quickest pupils possible to find; he could understand straight away what he had to do, in respect of adapting himself just as well to the horse as he had done to the bicycle and automobile. He has now a nice place out at Maisons Laffitte and it is to be presumed that he will cling to horses for the remainder of his life, although he has such important interests of other kinds. The picture in the book shows him taking his first instruction in race-riding. How pleased I was with him!

While Charron and many other trainers have done well at Maisons Laffitte in turning out winners, that centre is far from ideal for training purposes, the horses there having to journey to Achères, to get tried out. The course at "Maisons" is admirable, especially that straight mile and a quarter with excellent turf all the way. It beats Chantilly in this respect, although perhaps there is no finer training place in the world than the French headquarters. The great point about choosing a suitable place to train horses is to have the gallops as near as possible to the stables. Some of the Wiltshire and other Southern English stables are much too far

In Algiers
1914

removed from where the work has to take place. Take Darling's establishment at Beckhampton, or Robinson's at Foxhill, or Ogbourne, where Mr. George Edwardes has his horses. I should consider that in some cases, a horse had done quite enough exercise when he arrived at the place where he was expected to "work"—in other words, he might be overdone with that extra bit. This is very like hacking a long way to a meet— so little is left to work on in a horse. Chantilly is splendid in this respect, and lucky is the man who has a good horse to train there. When Mr. Theodore Myers took the place in Brussels, a picture of the stable yard appearing in this book, we had only three quarters of a mile to go to begin work—the greatest of all considerations.

Of course there is only one great race-course in the world: Newmarket, nothing ever laid out or adapted from nature ever approached it. Every distance, plenty of room, splendid going in all seasons—what can equal it? Some of the spectators and visitors from abroad complain of the accommodation, but racing isn't a circus; it should first suit the horses, and all things come afterwards. What does it matter when horses have to be tried out whether the finer points of the race cannot be seen until the horses are nearing home? There has been a real test of merit. It astonished me when I first saw it, that wonderful heath, and I never slackened in enthusiasm. I wish to goodness I was riding there this afternoon—the Second Spring Meeting is in full swing. We have no turf tracks in America. At Sheepshead Bay, there is a grass inner track on which perhaps one race a day is run, but it is—nothing.

Newmarket is extraordinary, and if a jockey will keep his line, trying to get on the right strip where the brush harrow has been, there can be confidence that, if at the right time the proper effort is made, a boy can do his horse justice. Compare it with any other course in England—why, the idea is absurd. Epsom is a joke but a fine sight-seeing track. It has often been a wonder to me that so many good horses have won the Derby, but I suppose a good horse can race under any conditions. The test of stamina at Epsom, too, comes in on account of that uphill bit at the beginning of the Epsom mile and a half: many a horse has lost the race there. I have said how I threw the Oaks away on Sibola. That downhill well-worn-out grass at Epsom can be a real danger in summer: it is more providential luck than anything else that a jockey is not killed every meeting. Despite the turns at Sandown Park it is not so easy, that rise at the finish finding out far more horses than, for instance, Kempton, which ends on the dead flat with a breather at the turn. Hurst Park is severe on young horses, and so is Newmarket, when they finish at the Stands. But England is the place for racing, while there is nowhere better in the world for training than Chantilly.

* * *

It was never to be imagined in the years before 1914 that I should be living in Paris when the Germans were only twenty-five miles, or less, from it; that pre-

Mr. Theodore Myers's Training Quarters at Groenendael
Mr. Myers is on the extreme left

viously the mobilisation in France for the greatest war in the world should take place, and that I was to be in uniform driving a Red Cross wagon. The trouble, it will be remembered, was anticipated many days before, the chief indication being the scarcity of small money. It was the most difficult to get change for even a fifty-franc note, everyone hoarding up gold and silver coinage; as for foreign money, except for English sovereigns, there were all sorts of impositions in giving change. There was a curious calmness about it all, however, which spoke a lot for the courage of the French people. I wish as much could be said for some of the foreigners left in Paris. I remember one day in particular. Several people rushed to my room early in the morning. I had just gone to bed. "Get up and be off," they cried; to which I replied, "Why should I, when I have only just come to bed?" But they couldn't be stopped, and raced off, trying to get seats to skip away out of the country. This was about three weeks after the opening of the war.

Straight away, I had tried to get something to do, first, as a sharpshooter. But there were two reasons against my acceptance, one being that I was so small that I couldn't stretch out to march with ordinary soldiers, and the other that I was an American subject. Then there was the fruitless endeavour to get a job in connection with a mitrailleuse, for I had been tried out with this, and I was sure that I could make good work with it—certainly I should have been a smaller target than many others.

There was nothing for it, then, but to get into the French Red Cross and French Ambulance, but, even here, all there was to do was to drive officers about, chiefly those of the French Red Cross. It was discouraging. All applications to do something more interesting or to be sent to the front were usually met by the objection that I had been warned off the turf in England, which, to begin with was not true, and in the second place what my troubles had been with the English Jockey Club surely could have no possible bearing on my having useful work when so many were wanted. However, it was a repetition, in a way, of what had happened when I tried to get into the Automobile Club, and when I was asked to resign my membership of the Touring Club of France. I can assure you I did not give up wearing the uniform and trying my best to get near the fighting until it seemed futile. Perhaps after this is written, and with a prolonged war, my services may yet be accepted.

Of course, with the stopping of racing at the opening of the meeting at Deauville, there was a good deal of hardship to those who couldn't afford the break. Several of the Americans went away at once to the United States, others wisely kept their horses there at Deauville until they saw what was likely to happen at Chantilly and Maisons Laffitte. As a matter of fact at the French Turf headquarters German troops never occupied the place; it was only a question of a certain number of Uhlans coming in to see how the country was defended, whether the roads were open, etc. It wasn't a very pleasant experience, however, and only a very few horses were removed—chiefly those of no value, and as I have said, they were not much grieved for. What must be admired there was the quietness with which

WORKING FOR THE AMBULANCE
1914-1915

the minority took the advent of the German scouts. They had been warned before of the near approach of the enemy and many of the lads went away, but others of them stuck to their yards quite fearlessly, despite the gloomy stories which had been sent down from day to day.

With regard to the taking of good horses by the Government at a nominal price, of course war is war, but it was heart-breaking for owners to lose valuable animals. They would gladly have paid the price of ten horses. For instance, Lord Loris, who won the big steeplechase at Auteuil in 1914, was taken for sixty pounds, I think it was. Still, that wasn't the point: the horse languished away under entirely changed conditions, never doing any work at all to speak of, and died. There were others, too, which began to droop the moment they were stabled uncomfortably, had changed diet, and lost all the care which had been bestowed on them.

Speaking of steeplechasing, one of the saddest events in the early stage of the war was the death of Alec Carter. Many may remember, that from serving his two years in a cavalry regiment, he was given a commission in an infantry battalion and was killed very shortly after that. It seems almost a pity that many of the greatest in their various lines should be wiped out when they could perhaps have been used to better advantage. Several of those I have known cannot be replaced, and various sports and games must lose the benefit of such fine teachers. Still again, war is war, and although one man happens to be the best lawn-tennis player in the world he cannot be excepted, but must take the same chance as others.

During those trying times what was there to do? Where were Americans and English people to go with no amusements? Where they did congregate was at Henry's Bar in the Rue Volney. Henry Tepé is perhaps the best-known man to Americans in Europe, as for many years he has had the chance of meeting celebrities from my country. It has been quite a usual thing for one important personality to say to another in New York, "I'll meet you at Henry's Bar two weeks next Friday." Both know Henry and he knows each of them, so that a ready inquiry obtains an equally direct reply. If we had as many dollars as Henry, or as many dollars as he possesses friends, we should be all right.

Two Pirates
Milton Henry and Tod Sloan Fishing for Treasure in Algiers

"Henry"
M. Henry Tepé

XXXVIII

Suggestions

Effect of the "Mutuel"—Le Blizon and the Eclipse—Lord Durham's Speech

OF COURSE, during my riding career, and since the forced times as a spectator, I have devoted a good deal of thought to the question whether the speculative side of racing was properly conducted, and whether, by controlling bookmakers, the public could not have a better chance of coming in greater numbers to meetings. The high prices charged for admittance to the exclusive parts of English courses must deter many hundreds from attending—I mean among those who do not feel in their proper place in the cheaper enclosures. What is charged on some days at Ascot, Liverpool, Epsom, etc., is almost prohibitive, and the sovereign for other meetings could be reduced if income were sought for elsewhere. Compare this with the maximum price, sixteen shillings, in France or the three dollars which takes one everywhere in America except the club enclosure. What should be done is to attract as many influential people as possible—thus would racing obtain more friends, which is what it wants to fight those who would do away with it.

It is very unlikely, in the opinion of many, that the pari-mutuel will ever be adopted in England, and that England need not regret. Personally, I am dead against it. Certainly in France, the value of the stakes makes it possible for an owner to pay his way without any betting, or rather I should say a certain number of smaller owners can exist. The pari-mutuel, in fact, in some respects might be a curse in England as it is in France. The public has a right to know what is going on in prices, for "market" makes everything more interesting. In countries where the pari-mutuel is an institution, owners throw in their weight at the last moment, frequently when everyone is ready to look at the race. Therefore, previous prices can be entirely false. Of course, it may be said that owners have to pay their way and do not run their animals for the public benefit, but, after all, there should be a sort of bond of sympathy between those who run horses and those who, by paying their gate money, contribute to the "pool" which provides the stakes. The whole topic will always remain a bone of contention, but during many years I have had the opportunity of listening to what others have to say concerning it, and what I have said above is the combination of opinion.

Another thing: if the pari-mutuel were introduced into England, the starting-price bookmakers would have to pay the mutuel prices, and there would be the chance of any amount of sharp practice in this respect. A horse might be entirely neglected on the course and returns could be quite false.

It is often said that the stakes for jumping meetings in England are ridiculously small compared with what is given in France, which is fact. But this could be made so different if bookmakers in England were charged so much a day for the privilege of betting, as was the case in the palmy days of racing in the United States. The fee charged then was one hundred dollars, or twenty pounds, a day, with a guarantee that there should be at least five races on the card. Very much the same thing should be done in the principal enclosure in England. Put it at four pounds a race and reckon out what would be collected, and how much better the prizes would be, and how the entrance money to the big enclosure could be reduced. In the smaller rings this daily licensing fee could be perhaps divided by half, and in the silver "tanks" merely a nominal charge should be made, and, as at one time in America, the minimum sum to be invested could be one shilling and the maximum five shillings. This worked very well when in vogue "over home." In that case, it was a dollar as the topmost bet, but that was swept away when eventually any amount could be put on. This spoilt racing and the charge came up of the turf being commercialised. There could not be a five-hundred-dollar bet made without it being tick-tacked across, and they were as "wise" outside as were the big men inside. That kind of thing should be immediately suppressed. The tick-tackers are an infernal nuisance and it would be only fair to sweep them off if, as has been suggested, the big men contributed towards the day's fund. It would only be for the big fellows to have as much of the business as could come their way, and smaller ones paying a much less fee to be restricted to lesser clients and rather petty business.

I do not wish to be too dogmatic about all this, but my views as a spectator for the last fifteen years might suggest some new legislation, especially as the whole topic is approached from the view-point of experiences in four countries.

Mr. Bottomley gives his strong views on many matters, and it is a pity that such a man should not have some voice in race-course management. It would be interesting if he would give his ideas as to how bookmakers should be controlled. I know he has opinions of his own on the question. Perhaps a special committee should be nominated to control bookmakers and collect their licence fees. It might, too, be a question whether all the big men betting in Tattersall's ring should not be compelled to obtain a guarantee from the clubs they respectively belong to.

Mention of Mr. Bottomley makes me wish to record the sympathy and kindness he has shown me for years. I wish I could have another day like that enjoyed when his horse Le Blizon won a big sprint race at Maisons Laffitte some years back. I followed the tip of his fancying the horse, and the result put me on easy street for some months. There is another incident in connection with this horse which has not been recorded in these pages. It was when Jimmy Hare—the father—decided, because I would ride him, to run Le Blizon in the Eclipse Stakes. I think it was I suggested that he should take a chance with the horse, who, as the majority will remember, could not go very well over six furlongs. As in other cases, I assured Jimmy that his horse would not be knocked about and, although he didn't win, he was tickled to death at the show Le Blizon made.

I hung in behind all the way round at Sandown, getting the advantage of the wind-break of others in front of me, and was going great guns up to a furlong and a half from home, for he had run his race for over a mile, stretching out well within himself. It was only that final rise to the winning post of less than a furlong which beat him.

There are many other non-stayers who could perhaps do just as well if riders would only study that question of getting every advantage of "wind-break," just as a cyclist does from his pace maker; the screen is invaluable. This does not necessarily mean that a jockey should allow his horse to be "pocketed," but on occasions there is really nothing much against this, if a boy is alert enough to get out of it. It is difficult, sometimes, to discover a horse's best distance—so much depends on how he is ridden. There have been so many hundreds of cases where sprinters have developed into good two-mile hurdlers, and on round courses, with careful handling, many animals which are assumed to be quite incapable of staying a mile would do so if absolute patience were shown by their riders.

Failures with regard to a horse getting a distance he is capable of are attributable to various causes, chief of which is lack of knowledge of pace; and here I might perhaps be excused for putting in an extract from a speech made by Lord Durham at the Gimcrack Dinner in December 1898.

> "Another favourite instruction was 'Get off well and pull your horse at the back of someone else's heels.' No doubt this style of riding had caused numerous falsely won races. It was for that reason that he welcomed the visit of Sloan to this country. Sloan had taught English jockeys that they ought not to pull their horses about in races and waste their energies. He hoped English jockeys would pardon him for saying that he considered that excessively few of them had any tolerable idea of what pace meant, and they seemed to ignore the very elementary rule that the horse which could cover the allotted distance in the shortest time would win the race. He considered that Sloan's reason of success over our jockeys was that he was such a good judge of pace. He submitted that Sloan had been of immense advantage to them, simply by teaching their jockeys that they had not been acting wisely in pulling their horses about as they had."

XXXIX

Practical Jockeyship

"Fees" of Old-Time Jockeys — The Apprentice Question — Some Never Rise in Class — Well Balanced at Start — Lucien Lyne's Class

I HAVE JUST READ in an English newspaper how "Skeets" Martin had cleverly won a race. There is an idea about that Martin is much older than he really is. I have seen it stated somewhere that he is bordering on fifty. As a matter of fact "Skeets" is a year younger than myself. If memory serves me correctly, he was born in 1875. When in America we knew him as "Harry" Martin. I can remember hearing about him long before I was twenty. I believe he entered a racing stable when he was about fifteen. It was in California that he first made his appearance as a winner; Mr. David Gideon, who has been mentioned in this book, was the first to give him his chance and to take him east to New York. At that time Skeets weighed about 7-2, and it is astonishing how he has kept his weight down. He is something like myself: our great asset has been that we have not put on flesh. One year before he came to England, he had twelve hundred and fifty-seven mounts and two hundred and sixty-nine winners. In that same season he had two hundred and forty-two seconds and one hundred and eighty-one thirds. Remember, too, that he was only twenty-two years of age at that time.

The performances of other jockeys, both before my own time and during my career, have always been of tremendous interest to me. I have alluded to several. For instance, it was a matter of history to me that nearly a century before I came on the scene public subscriptions to successful jockeys had been raised, one rider having received nearly one thousand pounds from his admirers for having won the St. Leger. There seems to have been no difficulty at that time about a jockey receiving presents from others outside the owner of the winning horse he had ridden! What would have been thought to-day of a jockey having to stand bare-headed and thank his owner for a present of twenty pounds because he had won the Two Thousand Guineas and One Thousand Guineas in one week? This was what the celebrated John Day received from the Duke of Grafton. Lord William Beresford was my authority for this. However, twenty pounds was rather a fine present in those days, I suppose, for a successful jockey, if he were a married man, received in addition to his usual wages a present of a side of bacon, a bag of potatoes, half a cheese or a barrel of home-brewed ale. Jockeys then were little more than grooms. What a difference it is from potatoes to gold watches, half a cheese to scarf-pins, or a side of bacon to gold cigarette-cases with jewelled initials. We used to read in America that the great George Fordham was the first to ride successfully on American horses. He had been engaged by Mr. Richard Ten Broeck, and, from what one can hear, did extraordinary things on many moderate horses belonging to that sportsman.

Good jockeys came in plenty long before my period of riding: such men as Harry Griffin and Snapper Garrison, also the coloured rider Willie Sims who was five years older than me. Fred Taral was eight years my senior. Then there were McLaughlin and Hayward. It appears that about fifty years ago, when Mr. Ten Broeck first went over to England, Gilpatrick, who had a reputation in America, was not a success in England and was much criticised; nevertheless, he was riding in America for many years after that. At the same time there were others, the Lairds, the Purdys, and Gil Crane, who rode longer than any other jockey in my country, and I believe more years on the track than even John Osborne. It was Crane who rode in that historic race on the Long Island Union Course, of five four-mile heats, and won on Black Maria.

* * *

Is the present system of training jockeys a correct one? There seems a good deal lacking in it. To begin with, there should be far more events for apprentice jockeys only, and these affairs should not be so poor in interest as many are to-day. If a boys' race happens to be the last on the card, many go home, refusing to look at it from either a spectacular or investing point of view. By this, kids are apt to get discouraged. In France, many a good lad was brought along by the flat races confined to apprentices which used to be run on the old Colombes course. There jockeys such as Alec Carter and George Parfrement learned race riding: full-fledged flat-race jockeys could not ride there. Any race-course in England which could occasionally put at least one or two events in the programme for apprentice riders should be specially subsidised by the Jockey Club for the schooling they are giving. Jockeys can be made, although, of course, some are more adept at picking it up than others. Richard Wooton must be a great teacher, judging by the number of clever boys he has turned out. However skilled a lad may become by his work at home, he must have practice on a course to bring him on.

The whole apprentice system is absolutely and entirely wrong, according to the views I have held for many years past. Apprentices should not be allowed to ride in regular jockeys' races until they have graduated and become qualified—in the opinion of others—to be trusted with the care of a horse in a serious race. Some of them never would for years, while others, after a year or more experience, would be promoted from the ranks. This apprentice question is one of the most important in racing, and, writing as I do in the early spring of 1915, I can say that there was never a better opportunity for the Jockey Club to make experiments by the passing of rules which could be only temporary, or "try-out," if thought fit. It is one of the firmest convictions of my life, and I would put it in my dying Will and Testament—if anyone would heed me—that the curses of racing nowadays are: first, the 5 lb.

allowance; and the next, the fact that ordinary apprentices are allowed to spoil many races by riding with tried and proved jockeys. When alluding to the Starting Gate, there will be more to say on this score.

With the greatest respect for the English Jockey Club, it might be suggested that the whole system of apprentices' privileges should be revised. Apprentices should only be allowed to ride in races put in the card for them. There might be a special committee of, say, three to notice how they behave and what form they show in a race. Every part of the exhibition should be noted: whether they keep their line, how much use they make of a horse, and what they do with their whip. Good marks should be given, just as in a school, and a subsequent bad example wipe out the previous records if made. Careful watching by competent judges would "discover" good boys. The knowledge that they were being watched need not necessarily lead to nervousness nor stage fright. Their honesty would be tried and proved, and altogether they would want to get to the top of their class to obtain advancement. Let them keep to their class until they have proved their ability to go with their assumed betters and certainly more experienced rivals. Some boys might attain the distinction when fourteen or fifteen years old; others—even on a fair trial— might remain until over twenty-one to secure the lifting up into jockey class: this would all depend on their performance.

The committee appointed should be from the Jockey Club or gentlemen of good social class, so that no favouritism was shown. While on this topic, I would favour stipendiary stewards, but only if men of a certain class would accept the position; it would be impossible with any of those about whom a doubt could exist. The deterioration of the American Turf came about to a great extent by the appointment of what were called "Control Judges" and "Paddock Judges," for included among them were many who could not be expected to wield authority over, nor obtain the requisite respect from, those they were chosen to control.

Another point I have heard discussed is whether if paid stewards were appointed, they should be placed at various stages down the course to watch the incidents of a race, or whether it would be better for a presumed trio to be in a crow's-nest above the judges' box. With all modesty, I would suggest that the latter would be infinitely the better course, but again with a reservation that the whole idea of salaried stewards would be absurd unless the right men could be drawn into it.

Alluding again to the apprentice question, with the exception of the starting gate, the present apprentice arrangement has been the worst enemy possible to racing. If the idea mentioned above were carried out, and apprentices up to a certain stage of proficiency kept to their own class, there would be a pride of spirit to encourage them to learn riding and not play monkey tricks in the saddle. The best way possible is for them to observe other riders in their own races, and take lessons from their elders or the promoted who were expected to give good exhibitions. During the last few years, judging from the performances of many fully licensed jockeys, I have no hesitation in saying that many should be put back to the apprentice class. This is not said in any way because I do not happen to be in the saddle myself, but because for absolute incompetency, many would take a medal. They seem to lose all idea of equilibrium, and altogether may have lost their nerve and any knowledge of pace ever possessed, and genrally are no good at all. Ask anyone in England, from the Stewards of the Jockey Club downwards, whether race riding has deteriorated, and they will all agree that it has. Yet it is possible for riding to be revolutionised within the next generation or so. I would repeat, and this very emphatically, that, like aviation in this year of 1915, race riding may be only in its infancy and what Harry Griffin, Lester Reiff, Johnny Reiff, and perhaps myself have done is only the beginning of what may be discovered by those coming after us.

But the first thing to do is to battle with the apprentice question and remove that horrible 5 lb. allowance and let them learn properly. One of the effects of this present allowance business may be that a trainer has perhaps only two more rides left for a jockey before he cannot claim it. Those two mounts which may be winning ones are very valuable to him, and he may get a big premium for the services of his boy. Of course, a topic of discussion which may be raised is how far a boy should have to stick to his indentures of apprenticeship, and whether, when he is promoted to a proper jockey, his trainer should derive the income from his mounts. I leave this to the judgment of others, but there would be an obvious objection if a trainer ceased to have the benefit from that boy's services. To begin with, there might be the question of a contract where another would withdraw patronage if a certain boy were not available; and then again, a trainer might retard an apprentice's progress so that he should have the benefit of his services for the full term of years. As I have said, it would be better for others to answer this question.

It must be remembered that the gate, too, has been responsible for many faults, especially where apprentices have not learned exactly what methods are to be adopted. They say the gate has done wonderful things. Has it? Were not the starts just as good before with the old flag start? It was in many ways far more satisfactory, the children riding having spoilt the new.

The gate has been responsible for more inconsistency of form than anything else. Various records will show that, in the thousands of races I have ridden in with the gate, I have very frequently got first away. Looking back, the percentage is remarkable. I first became accustomed to it in California in 1904; in fact, I had controlled it and was off in front more times than ever before. There are so few who really know it. I should include in those with knowledge such riders as Lester Reiff, Maher, George Stern, Lucien Lyne, Frank Wootton, and Frank O'Neill. Now what percentage does this give of those riding within the last few years in England, France and Belgium? It has been spoilt altogether by apprentices when mixed in with horsemen. The youngsters do not know what action a horse is in when he "breaks" for the start. That is why so many of them are thrown right up in the saddle, and even lose their seats, not being in any way in unison with the horse.

Let it be said here, too, that it is not always the horse which gets away that can be looked upon as a winner. A well-balanced horse getting away last or nearly last has frequently the "bulge" on the others from the very beginning. Look for yourself in any race meetings you may go to, and the horse which slips into his stride when the tapes go up will certainly have to be reckoned with before the finish. Referring, too, to inconsistency owing to inability at the gate, it must be remembered that a horse never gets away quite twice alike. It is not always the boy's fault when it is said of him that he has ridden a bad race; it is often because he is ignorant of the first principles of how to get away.

I don't suppose any of us can look for any alteration in the rules of racing, and it is certainly not for me to criticise them, but some day the question of the betterment of racing will have to start on the questions of apprentices and the gate; and alterations made in this respect for these two blots on what is best for the game. It is no use arguing whether the standing start or the walk-up would be better. Let other things be settled first. The gentlemen who rule the Turf are not jockeys, nor will jockeys ever be stewards, so perhaps what may be considered expert opinion—and in this, others' views are being reflected— might be worth more than passing notice. Time after time, the sporting papers in England voice the opinion that certain starts at Newmarket and elsewhere have been simply terrible, and that a race has been lost at the post, there being no possible opportunity of winning. Look at the reports and see how many times incompetent youngsters have caused this.

The unnecessary use of the whip is something boys have to learn about, but I think by the rules of many apprentice races there are, neither whip nor spur is permitted. With regard to the latter, I never used them for years before ceasing riding, looking upon them as a totally unnecessary cruelty on a horse, and they should be barred altogether from the race-course. It is a wonder that this topic has never been taken up by the Jockey Club. Nobody who understands racing has ever discussed it from the cruelty point of view, and it may seem strange that a criticism should come from one to whom racing is part of life. There is indeed a strong chance for anyone to take up the question of prohibiting spurs. Many a good horse has been ruined in temper or courage by a spur, and it was a wonder to see them in use so long. Neither do I believe they are at all necessary for cross-country races. As, however, I have not sufficient experience in that respect, perhaps it would be as well for others to give their views on this. Such a lot could be said on the spur question.

The whip can be of use if properly applied, but at the same time it can be a stopper to a horse. The one great advantage for any jockey who knows how to handle the whip is that an animal can frequently be kept straight, and anyone who knows anything about jockeyship will agree with me. Lucien Lyne, whom I have always looked upon as one of the best riders I have ever seen, has had to use spurs in Belgium out of deference to public opinion on a race-course, and all those critics and "knockers" he has been up against. If he brought a horse in a loser without a mark of the spur on him, it could so readily be alleged that he hadn't tried, whereas public opinion was so easily stilled if the horse was bleeding. They would say that he "took something out of that one at all events," and they would think they had had a good run for their money.

Lyne is a great fellow to take any tip, although he is so well up in his profession and so well off. I suppose we can all learn a little bit from others, and many pointers which I have been able to give him he has always been ready to take at once, and in that way kept himself in touch with what practical men or lookers-on can see of the game. I have always tried to make him take little notice of something which might dash past him in a race, and not go after him at once; and even if a second came with a rare "bat," so long as there was plenty of time to win a race, not to be led away in putting steam on to catch him. It has always been a main idea with me, and I know that many others share it, that a real race-horse knows his business just as well as a rider does, and even a moderate animal well encouraged by not being driven too hard is flattered by the attention, and, by the encouragement given, will put his own bit in to go after those in front of him. It is the first principle of riding, and race-horses thus left to themselves with a little hand riding will in the majority of cases do their level best and show the most astounding intelligence as to what is expected of them.

Just another reference to spurs. When first success began to come my way, they were put aside altogether. Some owners and trainers have come to me saying, "You must use spurs on this horse; he's a very sluggish animal and you won't get him along unless you do wear them." In these instances, I have made the invariable and polite answer: "I'm afraid you will have to get someone else if you insist upon the spur business, but why not let me try my best without them?"

Just another word, too, about the "crouch" seat or "riding short" which I have heard so much discussed. This is rather an important matter in connection with the "revolution" in race-riding of, say, twenty years ago. It is a great mistake to think that some of us rode short; in fact, it is a misconception altogether. In walking and cantering, my stirrups were frequently as long, in fact nearly always, as the old school of English race riders. When breaking into a canter it was often the same, but once a race had begun, and by the strength of legs the "crouch" assumed, there would be an immediate difference in the action of a horse and his speed. Since then others have quite shortened the stirrup—not with the best results. That is why the term "riding short" came in. Hands and brain have more to do with successful race riding than anything else.

XL
More Suggestions

Mr. Manning and My Weights – Cash and Santoi – Parading a Mistake

THE BEST STARTERS, apart from Mr. Rowe who has been previously mentioned, that I have ever come in contact with have been Mr. C.J. Fitzgerald in America and Mr. Arthur Coventry in England. The former was the best all-round official ever known in my country; he was the same to everyone—owners, trainers and jockeys—and had a tremendous experience before being put in a greater position in New York. He was Canadian born, but spent most of his life in the United States, going there when quite a boy. He started as a sporting journalist and spent some years at this. He knew as much or more than the next fellow on the Turf. He officiated at various meetings in Canada and America. He was so thorough in all his methods, having his own ideas and carrying out what he considered was best. He was one of the first to favour the starting gate, and in that he might be criticised, but it was more in the spirit of progressiveness that he took this up. One of his first ideas was that representations should be made to owners and trainers as to the necessity of schooling their horses to the starting gate. He was quite impartial in the way he ladled out punishment, and did not bother about praise, for that was not, to his ideas, ever necessary to his duties.

I have spoken of Mr. Coventry and one particular complaint which he made about me at Sandown Park. Goodness only knows whether I shall ever come under his orders again, so what is said may be taken as really meant. His ability in grasping a situation and throwing his eyes over a very big field is one of the most remarkable powers he has. A thorough horseman himself, he knows when the impossible cannot be tried and would rather risk a delay at the gate than leave an animal, whatever it might be or however unruly it might show itself before the start. While the greatest consideration is given to small boys, he can be severe to the older school, but none of the riders I have seen ever like to take a liberty with him; this comes from both respect and the desire to help him in difficult duties. The task of a starter is so little understood by the general public. "He's got 'em now, why didn't he let them go," they can say. People several furlongs away imagine they can see all which is taking place, but this is one of the greatest mistakes possible. However, this does not upset Mr. Coventry, who rides down placidly on his pony, does what he has to, and returns. There was no one madder than he when Nunsuch was left for the Cambridgeshire, which has been described in a previous chapter. He bent down and I am sure that he was cursing hard at the misfortune, but I suppose it was only human to be particularly wild that the King's colours had met with a disaster. I watched the starter and his furious regrets, and it took off my attention from what had happened to myself.

I have met Mr. Coventry in town on many occasions and he has always been most kind and considerate and with an utter lack of snobbishness; in fact, he was altogether different from many others who were not so well placed nor of such good family. He would stop and talk sometimes about racing, but more frequently of other matters. I wish that I could get under his orders again.

This reminds me that when I visited Ascot a few years back I ran across Mr. Manning, the Clerk of the Scales, and it was most charming of him to encourage me in the way he did. I was just outside the weighing enclosure and he came behind me saying: "Hurry up, Sloan, and get on your colours. I should like to weigh you out again."

Charlie Wood was standing near and he said to Mr. Manning: "I should like to see him going to the post, too."

Mr. Manning added: "That's right, and if you know anyone, Charlie, who can do him any good, don't you forget what I have said."

And Charlie promised he would do all he could.

Mr. Manning was always very fair, having no favourites when at his work, usually sharp and severe in his manner. When I first came over I could not get used to stones and pounds. He would ask me my weight and at first I would reply 102 lb. or whatever it was. He gave me a little time, but even later on it was inevitable for me to give the weight as I had always been accustomed to in America. "Will you give me your weight properly?" he would repeat, and then I had to do a bit of lightning calculating and divide by fourteen. Sometimes I was uneasy about whether I had said the right figures, and would have to borrow a card from someone to check what I had given in, but was usually right. When I met Mr. Manning away from the race-course he was always congenial and friendly, although, as I have said, he is very sharp and quick to the boys at the scale. But that is his official manner. By the way, Mr. Fitzgerald, of whom I have spoken, was Clerk of the Scales before he came to be a starter.

Speaking again of that visit to Ascot I saw a lot of my old patrons and those I had ridden for, but I was diffident about going up and speaking to them. Sir R. Waldie Griffith sent Bob Sherwood over to tell me to come and speak to him. He asked me where I had been hiding myself and why I hadn't come over to him; and I explained that I had been shy about doing so. He was extremely nice and tried to encourage me with hopes that I should "get back," in fact, he was so amiable to me—and this was backed up by Sherwood—that I feel quite certain, were I to get my ticket again, that he would put me up on something, even if I couldn't sit a horse. At all events, he would give me a try-out. The kindness I met with that afternoon at Ascot has been one of the gladdest experiences of recent years. It seemed funny to be walking about and not be looking for my horse.

I was reminded by that trip to Ascot of the one and only time my brother Cash rode in England before taking up an engagement in Russia. He had come over from

America, it being his first trip abroad. I was anxious that he should get a chance, if he could, where I was doing so well, and he came down to Maidenhead where I was staying with Mr. George Edwardes for the Ascot week. I mentioned my brother's name and Mr. Edwardes asked how he could ride. I told him that Cash had been in the first class in 1893 and 1894, and I had no doubt that he would do all right; at the same time, I didn't know that he had not been on a horse for some while. As a matter of fact, he plumped right into England and on to that mount at Ascot without getting any preliminary work at all. Mr. Edwardes then said he would give him a proper chance and he should be entrusted with Santoi, who was a real good thing. Cash was delighted of course, especially when I told him what class of horse he was to be on.

I could see as the hour of the race drew near, he was getting a bit nervous. But, going down to the post on such a course and before such a crowd, he was to be forgiven for having a touch of stage fright. The worst happened that was possible, and surely neither Cash nor anyone else ever rode a worse race. When we were about five furlongs from home my brother sang out to me: "He is hanging with me," of course referring to the horse. "Then let him drop in behind just for a while," I answered. But he couldn't do that and gave a shocking exhibition, as he himself would admit. Santoi came again with him, but I just beat him a head. I would have done anything for him to win, short of pulling my own horse, but he ought to have won easily. I said to him, "Sorry, Cash, I'd have given anything to see you win," and his amiable reply was, "Why the hell didn't you let me, then?"

Of course, Mr. George Edwardes and others were furious at the race being thrown away, but I defended my brother with, of course, just the reservation that he hadn't found his confidence. If Cash had won that day, I believe he would have stayed in England for good instead of going over to Russia. It was fortunate yet unlucky for him that he had a chance on such a good horse. If he had been on a moderate animal then not so much attention would have been drawn to him. A lot of boys, however, have not shaped so well when they first appeared in a new country as they did afterwards. That is why we should not be too severe in our judgment on them when everything is new to them.

* * *

As several officials have been mentioned in this chapter, and the starting gate discussed in the previous one, there might be just a word or two about the system of judging. Photographing the finishes has been tried in Belgium and the film records kept. I had a chance of seeing one privately on one occasion when it was proved beyond doubt that the judge's verdict was incorrect. Perhaps the system of the film will never come into general use, but other things could be devised where a judge would be in a better position to be absolutely correct. To begin with, every horse should have his number largely indicated on the saddle cloth. This would help both the public and the official. I also favour raising the height of the judges' boxes;

there would be much more opportunity of viewing those in front, especially on wide courses, such for instance as Newmarket. But what also should be done is to erect a screen on one side of the box which should make it impossible for the judge to follow the race with his eye until the horses were almost passing him; then he could take in the first, second, third and fourth. As it is now, a judge follows the leaders for a long way and may get one set of colours fixed in his mind and not get it out of it even by the time the verdict has to be given. His duty is to see the horses as they pass the post, and that is all. This would be a scheme to try, and see how it worked. I am quite sure that there will be many criticisms of this suggestion, chief of which may be that the judge has to look out for foul riding and give his evidence if necessary. My Editor reminds me that in the Ascot Gold Cup, when Eider and The White Knight ran a dead-heat and the former was disqualified, the judge's evidence went a great deal towards the decision of the stewards. A judge should never be called upon for anything like this, his duty being solely to decide how the horses have finished and nothing beyond it. Looking for other incidents must take thoughts off the real work an official has to do, and he should have no more to say about the running than a man down town. Those matters are for the stewards only. Of course, photographing a finish and making the camera the final decider would be all right in the case of head and head results, but doesn't it strike you that the public would be very impatient waiting a quarter of an hour or twenty minutes until they could learn what had really happened?

Another matter which should be altered—again only according to my humble judgment—is the parading on the course which is so customary before big events. Parading round the paddock and the preliminary canter should be quite sufficient. A good horse is apt to get his temper spoilt by being marched down slowly behind others. Frequently an owner can get permission for his horse to be exempted from that parade—why should this be allowed? If a horse is a bad actor, why should a rattle-brained brute be given such a chance? If he has not been properly broken or trained, there is no reason why he should be given a better show than those who know how to behave. If is unfair to a degree. There should be no excuse for, and no favouring, those who are not fit to do as others do. One can only suppose that there would be a howl from the public if the parade before such a race as the Derby was done away with, but, after all, the race is the thing, and those not able to go to the paddock would have every chance as the field cantered past the stands of seeing all the runners.

Old customs die very hard but, as previously remarked about riding being in its infancy, the whole system of conducting racing may be revolutionised in a generation or two.

A Hospital Garden Scene
1915

XLI

Finis

Trying My Luck — Friends' "Comforting"

IN FINISHING WITH SOME EXPLANATION to the public, and especially my friends—those whom I know and those whom I am not personally on terms of acquaintance with—I should like to refer to several things.

In the first place, it must not be stated that there was no idea of earning money both from the first edition and subsequent issues: that, naturally, is the legitimate object of anyone who has something to tell which he feels may be of interest. Real earnings in wartime, too, can be looked upon as "money from home." Several times lately I have been asked to give the story of a career full of ups and downs, but just as regularly I have declined to do so, for various reasons, some of which may have appeared rather absurd. I suppose among racing people, especially among jockeys, there should be the discretion of silence. But I have waited so many years in the hope that I should be reinstated.

The wish has come several times to explain away what has not been quite clear to those who sat in judgment on me. In this I do not refer exactly to the English Jockey Club and the ruling bodies in France and America, for there are many thousands who have nothing to do with the control of the turf who have had a great deal to say from time to time as to my alleged weaknesses. These I admit, but some of these weak points have not been those charged against me; in fact, many shortcomings which have been alluded to in these pages have not been known to my critics.

As I have stated, altogether too much to my detriment has been made out over the Ascot incident, and what I was supposed to have said and done with regard to Codoman's Cambridgeshire. My Editor is satisfied that certain unreasonable ideas ought to be altered by what has been explained, but there is more to unburden myself of, and perhaps the best way to do this will be to reproduce a letter I wrote to Mr. Luckman when he was sporting editor of *The Daily Express* and "The Scout" of that paper. He was doing his best at the time, in a series of articles, to show cause why the time had elapsed for any more punishment.

Here is a reproduction of that letter of mine to him.

18th *October* 1909.

DEAR FRIEND LUCKMAN:—There has been some discussion as to what you have written about me which I feel may be too much in my favour, for you have carefully not specified certain things which are in the minds of many as to what I have done wrong.

For instance: you have touched very lightly on the score of my making wagers. People have said to me: "Why have you incriminated yourself so much by admitting that you took up betting, and also not glossing over any incidents of the life you have led."

Those people never stop to think that after the death of Lord William Beresford and Mr. Whitney I never had as a serious adviser any good powerful friend who would take upon himself the task of putting his hand on my shoulder and counselling me what to do. Just think of the following instance for a moment, and you will better understand what I mean.

There was a man whom Ionsifriend; he told me, *after my having done him a very big service*, that he had too much respect for the French Société to speak for me, but added: "Poor little fellow, I am sincerely sorry for you, because I believe you to be the most honest and straightforward of all riders I have ever known."

A few years after this, when he was promoted to be a steward of the French Jockey Club, everybody in Paris thought: "Now Sloan is sure to get his licence in France." All my friends insisted on me going to see the new steward at 3 Rue Scribe. They said to me: "Don't be backward about it. Get a hustle on you; it is all for your own good. He'll see you, all right." I thought it over and over and was very reluctant to take the advice given, but they persisted, in fact argued me stiff about it. Finally it was no use holding back any longer, and practically I was kicked off — quite in a good-natured way — to take the chance with the magnate. Even when I was in the courtyard and going up the staircase I nearly turned back, for I considered that I knew him better than my friends did, and I made the mistake — a very serious one — of not going on my own judgment. I have regretted it ever since.

He saw me all right, but made me feel like a worm. The first thing he told me was that I should never have fought the "Société" (the French ruling body) and that he could not help me. "Why on earth did you ever do it?" he went on to ask me. I replied: "Because, Count, you, who should have advised me, and what you thought then say now, never uttered a syllable as to what I should have done. It would have only required that for me to have dropped the case straight away, and now you ask me why I was such a fool as to do this, that and the other. What you did do was to turn your back on me, saying you were sorry for me, although you knew all the time that I was as innocent of wrong-doing as He who built the world. No one attempted to advise me; in fact, I stood alone, a persecuted man without the slightest help from anyone except Maître Labori, and he told me that I should surely win but also that I should surely lose by winning. He was right."

There are many other little matters I could mention as to those who were real good friends to me in England and France — that is, cheery companions, but who were powerless to move one log along to get me my licence. Some of them, good-hearted sportsmen, may have in some way done me more harm than good, for when a fellow is up against it, those opposed to him are always looking for reasons why the punishment should be continued, and take a yellow-jaundiced view of everything which is done in private life. Surely there must be enough justice left to allow me to follow up my calling. Perhaps they all think I could not ride! I will not say anything about this.

Sincerely,
J.T. SLOAN

In the pages of the book I have told how failure after failure has followed my repeated attempts to obtain a licence. This year (1915) another trial was made. I

My Editor

addressed a humble letter to the Stewards of the Jockey Club, but after waiting for three months there is still no reply. The book would have been completed in any case, for I have told a plain, unvarnished tale, not attempting to whitewash myself, nor posing as the lily-white, for those who go racing know a good many conditions of life. But, as the French steward just quoted said, I was "straightforward" and honest as a jockey: I liked winning too much. Why, therefore, the apparently permanent condemned position? I might not be able to ride, but I have relatives and friends who would think of me in the present and in later years so thoroughly differently if I had the stigma removed from me. The chance of making a living, too, at something I could do better than anything else cannot be overlooked in the many hours of anxiety.

Friends comfort me by saying: "Oh! you'll be all right some day." But when will that some day arrive? Will it ever? One after the other of my friends have gone—my patrons and intimates. I suppose I must think I am getting towards middle age but—here the "personal" is inevitable again—I feel as fit as ever to do anything. Men have been successful when far older than I; in fact, there are one or two riding to-day. And what about the veteran John Osborne, who retired only two or three seasons back, and still rides gallops? My weight has not increased, my muscles are as strong, while my vision and nerve are unimpaired. There can be surely be no "but" on the score of age-limit.

But again—and finally: why this book? To explain myself, to put the sworn-to-be-true story of previously distorted incidents. My one and only Turf misdemeanour was betting—nothing else during my whole career. I admitted this to the Stewards in 1900. I have not retracted in these pages, but I have repented that I was ever such a fool. It cut me off at the age of twenty-five. Having "done" fifteen years I can only pray that some day, in a spirit of clemency, mercy will be shown to a transgressor—who would never transgress again, even to the extent of a fiver.

This is not canting or whining, nor a question of "The devil a saint would be," etc., but an appeal and full explanation to those who can reprieve me; and in addition a recital of certain incidents to relieve the monotony of "too much Tod Sloan." I speak sincerely when I say that I would gladly obliterate myself if only my official obliteration would be cancelled.